PHILOSOPHY AND THE ABSOLUTE

ARCHIVES INTERNATIONALES D'HISTOIRE DES IDEES

INTERNATIONAL ARCHIVES OF THE HISTORY OF IDEAS

109

ROBERT GRANT McRAE

PHILOSOPHY AND THE ABSOLUTE
The Modes of Hegel's Speculation

ROBERT GRANT McRAE

PHILOSOPHY AND THE ABSOLUTE

The Modes of Hegel's Speculation

1985 **MARTINUS NIJHOFF PUBLISHERS**
a member of the KLUWER ACADEMIC PUBLISHERS GROUP
DORDRECHT / BOSTON / LANCASTER

Distributors

for the United States and Canada: Kluwer Academic Publishers, 190 Old Derby
Street, Hingham, MA 02043, USA
for the UK and Ireland: Kluwer Academic Publishers, MTP Press Limited,
Falcon House, Queen Square, Lancaster LA1 1RN, UK
for all other countries: Kluwer Academic Publishers Group, Distribution Center,
P.O. Box 322, 3300 AH Dordrecht, The Netherlands

Library of Congress Cataloging in Publication Data

```
McRae, Robert Grant.
   Philosophy and the absolute.

   (International archives of the history of ideas ; 109)
   Bibliography: p.
   1. Hegel, Georg Wilhelm Friedrich, 1770-1831.
2. Absolute, The--History--19th century. 3. Knowledge,
Theory of--History--19th century.  I. Title.  II. Series.
Archives internationales d'histoire des idées ; 109.
B2949.A28M37  9185      110        85-8783
ISBN 90-247-3151-8
```

ISBN 90-247-3151-8 (this volume)
ISBN 90-247-2433-3 (series)

Book information

This book has been published with the help of a grant from the Canadian Federa-
tion for the Humanities, using funds provided by the Social Sciences and
Humanities Research Council of Canada.

Copyright

This book
is for
Lynn Massicotte

CONTENTS

VIII

ACKNOWLEDGEMENTS

I would like to thank Professor Pierre-Jean Labarrière (Centre Sèvres, Paris) for his sound advice and criticism. Professor Lionel Ponton (Laval) encouraged the project from its earliest days and made helpful suggestions. Professor Thomas Langan (Toronto) and Professor Thomas De Koninck (Laval) offered constructive remarks on the manuscript.

INTRODUCTION

I have purposely limited myself to a rather brief statement in this introduction, in order that the summing up be not misrepresented for the discursive development of the whole. There is something more than mildly dangerous in setting oneself a series of goals in an introduction only to find them happily attained in the conclusion, as if getting from the beginning to the end was simply a question of transition. Of course, the destination of a speculative presentation includes the process of development in such a way that the end is always implicitly the beginning: each configuration simply forms a determinate moment within the on-going manifestation of the "absolute".

It is around Hegel's concept of the absolute, how it is known and how it presents itself, which the bulk of our discussion turns. We may say tentatively that the absolute *speaks*. This speaking is the manifestation of the absolute itself, not a dissimulation or mere appearance, and consequently can be known and known most perfectly in language. In Hegel's system, this speaking or discourse has exhausted itself and is complete, but in what manner this "close" is achieved remains the question which disturbs and provokes our own speech in what is to come.

This problem has most frequently been posed in terms of whether or not Hegel asserted that his presentation of absolute knowing marks, in some sense or another, the "end of history". The locus for this discussion is generally the *Phänomenologie*, where the relation between the temporal or historical appearing of the absolute and the knowledge of this absolute at the level of science is most fully accounted for, particularly in the chapter concerning absolute knowing itself. In the first chapter of our own presentation, we have correspondingly turned to the *Phänomenologie* in order to understand the significance of absolute knowing *vis-à-vis* the project of the entire text.

Through the course of this chapter, two central issues immediately come to the fore: (i) that the appearance of the absolute for natural consciousness, as displayed in the path of phenomenal knowing, must be understood from the standpoint of the fully determinate manifestation of the absolute in the system of the *Enzyklopädie*, i.e., that absolute knowing is nothing but the presentation of the system itself, and that both texts have their origin in the modes of absolute self-presentation; and (ii) as a consequence of the first remark, an absolute knowing as philosophic presentation exists for consciousness in the "thick immediacy" of a particular language, so that we must ask whether or not the thoughts expressed within the exoteric forms of representation can have any kind of "absolute" finality at all.

These two themes are again taken up from different points of view in the two chapters which follow, with the hope that the meaning of the Hegelian project will begin to reveal its shade and texture through an essentially discursive rendering. Having examined in the first chapter the *Phänomenologie* as an appearance of the system, wherein the modes of representation also appear, in the second chapter we turn to the system itself in order to understand the relation of spiritual representation in-and-for-itself to the needs of an absolute self-presentation. This discussion is limited largely to the *Philosophie des Geistes* from the *Enzyklopädie* and focuses particularly on the implicit tension between the regional representations arising out of intersubjectivity and a philosophic discourse in which the absolute is somehow present at hand.

The third chapter is a wide-ranging discussion, tied to no extended textual analysis, in which possible solutions are proffered for the problems adduced in the first two chapters. The attempted resolution occurs through the percept that the absolute is necessarily manifest through modes of existence, modes that include its appearing in "regional" representations, without this undermining its determinate truth for a particular natural consciousness. It is in this light that we can begin to gather the importance of the three syllogisms, which close off the system, for that presenting which exists as absolute knowing. But what is it about absolute discourse which destines it to be present in modes at this time, and is this determinate presence in any way final?

As for the citations from Hegel's works, all references are to the German critical edition under the editorship of Lasson, Hoffmeister, Nicolin and Pöggeler as listed in the Bibliography. The page number of the English translation is to be found in parentheses after its German counterpart, and these translations, too, are listed in the Bibliography. Some of the translations have been slightly altered by myself in the pursuit of clarity.

I. ABSOLUTE KNOWING AND PRESENTATION

1.1 *The idea of presentation*

There is reason to believe that Hegel would consider our concern with presentation a form of contemporary "misology", — the retreat of thought from the substantial contradictions of its own making to a mere interest in the vagaries of the immediate. But this concern, endemic to much current philosophic thought, represents a mediation of the present with the past in a truly speculative sense, for it is with the self-consciousness of the current standpoint that antecedent configurations progressively reveal their absolute depth. Let it be added that the necessities of presentation are particularly integral to the realization of Hegelian science, and it is our position that the link between absolute knowing, and the system proper, cannot be understood aside from the act of presentation itself.

Presentation has this significance because it is both an externalization by a universal self *and* a recollection of its absolute content, thereby closing off the self-alienation of the absolute as spirit in time. Indeed the tension between absolute substance and its self-knowing that is indicative of this alienation remains a part of speculative presentation itself, making presentation a peculiarly spiritual phenomenon. Naturally we hope that some of these suggestions will cease to have their assertive quality and become self-evident in the analysis to follow.

Generally speaking, according to Hegel, the absolute is already close to us through its self-presentation under three aspects. Absolute substance has been externalized in its fortuitous happening as real history, coming on the scene through the onesided determination of a "regional" natural consciousness. Once this externalization of the substance in history is complete, there arises the possibility and the need to present the *entirety* of this content according to its concept, but first as this content appears for natural consciousness.

This second presentation enables natural consciousness to understand the absolute determination of its universal self, and ends with the instigation to present that determination as it exists in-and-for-itself.[1]

Although the absolute content of each presentation remains essentially the same, this content appears under different aspects according to the fullness of its self-conscious appropriation. This differentiation has two immediate consequences: the second and third presentations merely "look back" on the original appearance of the absolute in history; and more precisely, these two presentations (i.e., the *Phänomenologie* and the system of the *Enzyklopädie*) fully present an identical content, but from different standpoints. Through speculative science, the absolute idea is present at hand and absolutely present as presentation, – the in-and-for-itself self-knowing essential structure of the actual.

Consequently, our analysis of speculative science must go beyond textual exegesis to an understanding of Hegel's justification of the "word" as the true element in which the absolute is present to us and to itself. This involves the concomitant delineation of the manner in which the labour of presentation supersedes the existence of the particular individual as speculative scientist, to become a presentation of a universal self for contemporary natural consciousness. As long as this consciousness is characterized by its intuitive time-viewing, the presentation of the absolute as text raises the question of the relation between its timeless actuality and spirit in its temporal mode.[2]

The beginning of speculative science, then, is that thinking which witnesses and merges with the will of the absolute to be present to itself. This beginning is "the free act of thinking which places itself at the standpoint where it is for-itself, and where it generates its object and presents it to itself".[3] However the full self-presentation of the absolute in the form of speculative philosophy is both the result of scientific witness and its immediate presupposition, a presupposition which determines presentation as the specifically philosophic comprehension of the non-philosophic life of the absolute content in history. This means that we must examine the extent to which a strictly philosophic presentation can offer itself as an exoteric truth to an initially non-philosophic natural consciousness.

That speculative science is intended as an exoteric knowledge for contemporary natural consciousness is evident from its differentiation into its appearing for natural consciousness and its actuality in-and-for-itself. In speaking of the path of phenomenal knowing as an introduction or a first part of speculative science we are simply designating the chronological succession of texts as they arrive on the scene for consciousness: looked at from the absolute standpoint, the *Phänomenologie* is an appearance of the entire content of the system of the *Enzyklopädie*. The transition from the one to the other is guaranteed less through the necessity of their succession "for" consciousness than through their original identity in the act of presenting a common absolute content. In other words, the transition is guaranteed through the differentiation of the mode of presentation, a differentiation ultimately determined by the exigencies of the absolute idea itself.

It is because of the systematic structure that lies "beneath" the exoteric path of phenomenal knowing, and hence is only yet an appearing, that this path has its salutary role as a ladder to the scientific standpoint. In the Introduction to the *Phänomenologie* Hegel states that, "the experience of itself which consciousness goes through can, in accordance with its concept, comprehend nothing less than the entire system of consciousness, or the entire realm of the truth of spirit. For this reason, the moments of this truth are presented in their own proper determinateness, viz. as being not abstract moments, but as they are for consciousness, or as consciousness itself stands forth in its relation to them".[4] The presentation of phenomenal knowing is a "whole" in itself because it comprehends the full range of the determinations of the concept as they first appear in consciousness, but the mode of appearance itself is related to the question of presentation.

The works posterior to the *Phänomenologie* regard the latter as an appearing of speculative science and as the appearing of speculative science's absolute content. In the *Wissenschaft der Logik* (*Wiss. d. Logik*) Hegel says that "the concept of pure science and its deduction is therefore presupposed in the present work in so far as the *Phänomenologie des Geistes* (*Phän. G.*) is nothing other than the deduction of it", and again that "pure science presupposes liberation from the opposition of consciousness".[5] However, inspite of these statements as to the necessary presupposition of the *Phänomenologie*, the closed circle of the system itself seems to rule out an introduction to speculative science which is also somehow a part of that system. The only solution to this dilemma is the conception of the *Phänomenologie* as an appearing of science, − an appearing which leaves the dialectical integrity of the system intact while at the same time presenting its truth for consciousness.

In addition to this "necessary" first appearance of speculative science for consciousness as described in the *Logik*, we find in the *Enzyklopädie* the suggestion that the determinations of the system, too, have their presentation first as they exist for consciousness in the *Phänomenologie*. Hegel says, "In my *Phänomenologie des Geistes*, which on that account was at its publication described as the first part of the system of science, the course taken was to begin with the first, simplest appearance (Erscheinung) of spirit, with *immediate consciousness*, and to sketch the dialectic of this consciousness developing toward the standpoint of philosophical science, the necessity of this latter being shown through the process''. This appearing science, like the system itself, looks back on the fortuitous manifestation of the absolute in history and re-presents that content according to its concept.

Again we must emphasize that the difference between the two is that the *Phänomenologie* presents the determinations of the system as they first appear to natural consciousness. Hegel continues:''The development of the *shapes*, the specific object of philosophical science, thus is just as much a part of what at first only appears in the limited form of the development of consciousness; this development must, so to speak, go on behind the back of this consciousness, in so far as its content is retained as the *in-itself* of consciousness''.[6] This absolute content, and its development in shapes, only becomes explicitly for-itself in the self-conscious presentation of the system, where consciousness understands that content as its own.

Well, what evidence is there to suggest that the main determinations of the system appear first along the path of phenomenal knowing prior to their recollection in absolute knowing? The section of the *Enzyklopädie* devoted to phenomenology offers some interesting indications in this regard, particularly paragraph # 437.[7] Hegel says, ''Reason as the *Idea* (# 213) appears here in the determination of the opposition between the concept and reality in general, of which it is the unity, and has here the more precise form of the for-itself existing concept, of consciousness and the concept over against external objects present at hand''.[8] The significance of this remark is that Hegel seems to identify the conclusion of the *Logik* with its concrete determination in consciousness as ''Reason'', and the *Zusatz* attached to this paragraph merely confirms this impression.[9]

In the *Phänomenologie* this formal unity of concept and objectivity in reason then goes on to realize itself in the observation of nature and as spirit until it achieves in absolute knowing the philosophic comprehension of the totality of its determinations through looking back on its content, – a realization that follows the broad outlines of the system itself. This equally implies that the configurations prior to that of reason, i.e., those that make up consciousness and self-consciousness in the *Phänomenologie*, roughly correspond to the moments of objective logic and subjective logic in the system. The extensive chapter on reason itself presents ''for'' consciousness the observation of nature and of subjective spirit (the logical and psychological laws, physiognomy and phrenology).[10]

But it is essential to keep in mind that the determinations of the logic, the philosophy of nature, and the philosophy of spirit are presented as they first appear from the standpoint of natural consciousness, and thus contain much inferential, historical material. For example the science of subjective spirit appears first to the understanding under the crude aspect of phrenology, because true science is possible only once this consciousness has traversed all the configurations in their immediate appearing and recollected them at the level of absolute knowing. Similarly, the moments of the logic are not presented in the *Phänomenologie* as they exist in-and-for-themselves, but as they initially are manifest in the configurations of consciousness.

The corollary of this suggestion that the broad determinations of the system first appear as the path of phenomenal knowing presented for natural consciousness is that the *Phänomenologie* constitutes a thematic whole. In other words, the theories which assert that the *Phänomenologie* "should" have terminated after the chapter on Reason,[11] as does the phenomenology in the system, cannot account for the necessity that the *Phänomenologie* must repeat all the determinations of the system if it is equally to "look back" on the totality of those determinations as they first appear in history. And if the "ideal" determinations of consciousness, self-consciousness, and reason did not make up a part of subjective spirit in its timeless actuality, then the system would be unable to supersede either the standpoint of the *Phänomenologie* or that of natural consciousness.

The necessity that the *entire* system appear as phenomenal knowing, thereby giving that knowing a systematic unity, derives largely from the exigencies of the speculative presentation of the absolute idea.[12] The absolute is already present at hand for contemporary natural consciousness of its own volition, so that it is for speculative science to simply witness this presence "when at the close it lays hold of its own concept, i.e., only *looks back* on its knowledge".[13] Thus philosophic presentation itself demands that the path of phenomenal knowing merely look back on the whole, without truncating that path in order to provide a partial and consequently external "introduction" to speculative science. The *Phänomenologie* is justly more than such an introduction because it is an appearance of the system of absolute determinations: the absolute is close to us only through its self-presentation, and not through any arbitrary propaedeutic.[14]

The absolute appears in the *Phänomenologie* not merely as presentation but as a specifically philosophic presentation. The efficacious effect of philosophic presentation as the pure element of absolute presence in which that presence achieves perfect self-certainty is the result — and most importantly — the presupposition of the system of science. This raises the question as to whether philosophic recollection and presentation can sympathetically look back on non-philosophic life and repeat that life according to the concept without inadvertently altering its particular essence. And if the answer is no, then we must wonder whether the path of phenomenal knowing can truly act as a ladder from non-philosophic natural consciousness to the standpoint of philosophic science, or whether that path is not simply the philosophic comprehension of non-philosophic life, – and thus the esoteric possession of a few individuals.

These questions turn on the ability of Hegel to demonstrate that the truth of philosophic presentation is somehow already implicit in the determinations of spiritual life. And if this demonstration is to be convincing "for us", then it must be clearly evident that contemporary non-philosphic life *needs* this presentation at the present moment if it is to supersede the spiritual divisions of its own making. In summary, an investigation into the mode of presentation as the "final" moment of spirit's self-externalization takes us into the heart of the problems that plague natural consciousness at this stage of its educational history.

1.2 *Natural consciousness and science*

Science comes on the scene, or appears "for" natural consciousness, in the shape of the *Phänomenologie*, and in the Introduction to this work, Hegel sets out for us just how we are to conceive this appearing. He says that, "science, just because it comes on the scene, is itself an appearance (Erscheinung): in coming on the scene it is not yet science in its developed and unfolded truth".[15] Science "appears" because it comes on the scene as a text, as a concrete philosophic presentation, alongside other modes of knowledge. This "being alongside" means that speculative science at first has no direct claim on natural consciousness as its self-evident truth, but simply appears for consciousness as *another* possible standpoint.

However, if the speculative presentation of science is to exist as the truth of natural consciousness, then it must throw off this aspect of phenomenality. It does this by turning against all other "untrue" modes of knowing, for an assurance by science, alone, that it is true, would merely appeal to an inferior form of its being, i.e., to the way it appears, rather than to what it is in-and-for-itself. By this Hegel means that speculative science supersedes appearance by itself appearing for natural consciousness as a presentation (Darstellung) of *how* knowing makes its appearance:[16] this presentation, as the appearing of science in its strict sense, is the *Phänomenologie*.

The *Phänomenologie* is not yet speculative science in its developed truth because its absolute content appears "for" natural consciousness, and not as it is in-and-for-itself in the system. But this "appearing science" is a necessary prelude to the presentation of the system because natural consciousness is not fully self-conscious of its absolute determination, and must first know the other modes of knowledge that appear alongside speculative science as phenomenal and as necessarily superseded by the standpoint of speculative science. Hegel says that, "Now, because it has only phenomenal knowing for its object, this presentation (Darstellung) seems not to be science, free and self-moving in its own peculiar shape; yet from this standpoint it can be regarded as the path of the natural consciousness which presses forward to true knowledge".[17] Although the modes of knowing may have their own proper occuring in history, it is speculative science that *presents* natural consciousness as a path of phenomenal knowing in the *Phänomenologie*, and the structure of this presentation presupposes, and "reflects", the determinations of science in its systematic form.

This path of phenomenal knowing reveals the essentially hybrid quality of appearing science: it is a presentation of the other modes of knowing that appear alongside speculative science, thereby demonstrating their lack of truth, and yet this same path of phenomenal knowing presents the absolute content of the system as it appears for consciousness. This is possible because presentation reveals that these modes of knowing are in fact mediated by an absolute whole, and that the self-consciousness of this mediation, which is the result and presupposition of the presentation of appearing science, prepares natural consciousness for the presentation of its absolute determinations as they are in-and-for-themselves. By means of appearing science, natural consciousness will show itself to be only the concept of knowing, or in other words, not to be real knowing.[18]

This last remark is, of course, "for us" at the level of speculative science, because natural consciousness takes itself to be real knowledge within each configuration along the path of phenomenal knowing. The consequence is that, as the untruth of each mode is demonstrated, natural consciousness experiences the loss of its own self: the path becomes for it the pathway of doubt, and Hegel says that, even more so, it is the way of despair. Natural consciousness does not experience merely that doubt which is the resolve not to give oneself over to the thoughts of others upon mere authority. Rather the path is the conscious insight into the untruth of phenomenal knowing, not as a mere resolve which is decided and done with, but as a series of configurations (Gestaltungen) which constitute the detailed history of the education of consciousness to the standpoint of science.[19]

The loss of the self is the loss of that onesided subjectivity of consciousness which is ignorant of its absolute mediation, of its universal self. We shall see later that by "loss of self", Hegel means that this subjectivity disappears into speculative presentation as the immanent self of its content. Whether or not presentation truly supersedes this loss of self must remain one of our considerations for the efficacy of appearing science.

Despair results from an exhaustive scepticism directed against the whole range of phenomenal consciousness, its natural ideas, thoughts, and opinions of everyday life. Hegel does not provide us with a detailed picture of the content of natural consciousness, for it has no fixed human nature as we might normally think of it, i.e., the content of natural consciousness, its mode of knowing, is relative to its historical appearing. What is constant, however, is that it appropriates these modes in an immediate manner, without penetrating their essential phenomenality. It is only the scientific demonstration of this phenomenality which forces natural consciousness from one mode to the next in a necessary development, and which leaves this consciousness in an irreconcilable state of despair.

But the scientific demonstration or presentation is not itself in the grip of the experiencing process of consciousness, it is not in despair, and must be distinguished from the experience of consciousness presented as phenomenal knowing. Presentation has its origin in the philosophic appropriation of absolute determination, i.e., in a knowing subject which has superseded the appearing of absolute knowing in consciousness through the systematic presentation of absolute subjectivity. Phenomenal knowing, on the other hand, is the presented experience of natural consciousness, − natural, because it exists in an immediate unity with a determinate situation. And because this situation changes, and is "historical", we may say that natural consciousness experiences modes of phenomenal knowing and may, potentially, be educated through their proper presentation.

This education leads to the liberation of consciousness from its inorganic, natural determinations (which is why it experiences a loss of self), and culminates in the appropriation of objectivity as essentially rational. It must be remarked, however, that the education of consciousness is still only a potential, and thus we must think of natural consciousness as necessarily a transition-point. Furthermore, the presented path of phenomenal knowing appears particularly "for" this natural consciousness conceived as transition-point, an appearing determined by the exigencies of the self-knowing absolute idea. For the presentation of phenomenal knowing to be successful, we must assume that natural consciousness and the presented path of phenomenal knowing are themselves already *appearances* of the in-and-for-itself existing idea.

As has been emphasized, Hegel does not believe that the simple resolve by natural consciousness of scepticism is an adequate preparation for the study of this idea as it is presented at the level of science in the system. The knowing subject must first achieve consciousness of objectivity as its own, an insight which can only be the result of the necessary progression of the forms of unreal consciousness. It is this insight which both determines the nature of the presentation of phenomenal knowing and marks the completion of its series of configurations, so that "the presentation of the untrue consciousness in its untruth is not a merely *negative* procedure".[20] Consequently, speculative presentation is not that kind of scepticism which sees pure nothingness in its result, but comprehends its result as a determinate negation wherein a new form immediately arises, so that the progress through the complete series of forms comes about of itself.[21]

The insight which is the goal of phenomenal knowing means that knowledge no longer needs to go beyond itself, for its concept corresponds to its object. However, on the way, no satisfaction is found by natural consciousness in any one configuration of phenomenal knowing, and it is continually forced to go beyond itself until its concept comprehends its absolute determination. With the discovery of the inadequacy of each standpoint, consciousness suffers violence at its own hands and spoils its own limited satisfaction, and it may be that its anxiety over this violence will make consciousness retreat from the truth and strive to hold on to what it is in danger of losing. "But it can find no peace. If it wishes to remain in a state of unthinking inertia, then thought troubles its thoughtlessness, and its own unrest disturbs its inertia".[22] It would seem from this that natural consciousness is motivated by an implicit *need* to grasp its own essence, that such a potential is a part of its very structure, and that the retreat from this project creates anxiety and unrest in consciousness.

Such presuppositions are in order if the path of phenomenal knowing is to truly present the absolute satisfaction and realization of natural consciousness. If consciousness was not motivated by this implicit need, there would be no reason why natural consciousness would feel impelled to appropriate Hegel's phenomenological presentation as its truth. The salutary effect of this presentation rests upon the adequacy of its understanding of natural consciousness and the absolute character of its reponse.

The alternative to this appropriation of its universal essence is, in Hegel's opinion, that vanity of thought which languishes in the conceit over its own understanding, an understanding which dissolves every thought and always finds the same barren Ego instead of any content. It is interesting to note that this vanity, or "irony" as Hegel sometimes calls it, does not seem to experience the anxiety of the striving natural consciousness we described above. It appears to be the only possible alternative to the appropriation of the science of the absolute, for all other phenomenal knowing is eventually superseded by the presentation of the system. Perhaps it is because this kind of conceit throws over the project of self-knowing altogether; Hegel himself concludes that, "this is a satisfaction which we must leave to itself, for it flees from the universal, and seeks only to be for-itself".[23]

For that natural consciousness which does follow tha path of phenomenal knowing, we do not yet understand how speculative presentation is "for" consciousness as its true object. If the written text presents the essential structure of what is actual, then its apparent, alien objectivity must be superseded by the knowing subject. This is done through the comprehension and recollection (Erinnerung) of objectivity as the rational externalization (Entäußerung) of the universal self: a comprehension which, while it is a result of the path of phenomenal knowing, is an implicit assumption for that natural consciousness which "impulsively" first seeks this path.

We use the word "impulsively" somewhat circumspectly, because there are reasons why natural consciousness should follow the path of phenomenal knowing, and why it should do so now at this point in its educational history, although natural consciousness itself is perhaps ignorant of these reasons. The determination of the moment of presentation is related to the appearing of science as a philosophic response to a need manifest in spiritual life, a subject we must leave until later. But we will suggest that modern natural consciousness can potentially appropriate the presented path of phenomenal knowing as long as that path is seen to extend and fulfill the movement toward self-consciousness implicit in all of its educational history, and if the presentation of phenomenal knowing is on the level of natural consciousness, i.e., is itself in the grip of at least possible experiences.[24] In other words, Hegel's concept of knowledge as presented in the appearing science must show itself to be the same principle upon which every natural consciousness rests.

But let us understand how presentation exists as an object of knowledge for natural consciousness. Hegel says that, "Consciousness simultaneously *distinguishes* itself from something, and at the same time *relates* itself to it, or as is said, this something exists *for* consciousness; and the determinate aspect of this *relating*, or of the *being* of something for a consciousness, is *knowing*".[25] Whatever is related to knowing, its being-for-another, is also distinguished from knowing as a being-in-itself, and this being-in-itself is called truth. In the presentation of appearing science, knowledge is our object, something that exists for us, and the in-itself is the being of knowledge "for us" at the level of science. Such a distinction reflects the structure of all consciousness, and the investigation of phenomenal knowing repeats this distinction to the extent that it becomes a comparison of consciousness with itself, — in what consciousness determines from within itself as being-in-itself or the true, we have the standard which consciousness itself sets up by which to measure what it knows.[26]

There are two points to keep in mind in this description of knowing. First, the presented distinction between the experience of natural consciousness as phenomenal knowing and the being of this knowing "for us" at the level of speculative science imitates the distinction carried out by all knowing, at least according to this presentation. If its description of knowing is correct, then the presentation of phenomenal knowing, as a progression of configurations which achieves absolute knowing, will simply make explicit a movement already implicit in natural consciousness. Second, this determination of knowing necessarily implies a concomitant expansion of self-knowledge, since consciousness is both a consciousness of the object and a consciousness of itself, i.e., consciousness of what for it is the true, and consciousness of its knowledge of the truth. This consciousness is itself their comparison.

Appearing science is the attempt to recollect and present the modes of this comparison, which have had their first appearing in history, in a systematic manner, so that the final standpoint, the standpoint of science itself, will be shown to supersede and include the phenomenality of all other knowledge. However at the level of natural consciousness, this presentation appears for it as a series of experiences: "In as much as the new object issues from it, this *dialectical* movement which consciousness exercises on itself and which affects both its knowledge and its object, is precisely what is called *experience*".[27] The determination of each new object, proceeding from the previous transformation of the in-itself to an in-itself *for* consciousness, contains the nothingness of the first, i.e., it is what experience has made of it.

In other words, the determination of new objects for knowing does not mean that we merely move from one object to another. Hegel's idea is that our knowledge of the first object, or the being "for" consciousness of the first in-itself, itself becomes the second object. This means that the new object contains the experience of the last, and that consciousness is not simply the pure apprehension of what is in-and-for-itself, but plays a role in the determination of its own objects. Naturally this knowledge of how objects are determined is attained only at the level of speculative science, and it is through this knowledge that the presented succession of experience through which consciousness passes is raised into scientific progression. It is not known to the consciousness we are observing.[28]

Hegel says that this origination of the new object, which presents itself to consciousness without its understanding how this happens, proceeds, as it were, "behind the back of consciousness". However, although only we at the level of speculative science comprehend the formal aspect of the movement of phenomenal knowing, that is, its pure origination, the content does exist "for" natural consciousnes.[29] This content is the content of the absolute determinations presented in the system, but as it first appears for consciousness. Once consciousness grasps its own essence and is absolute knowing, then its absolute content will be presented as it is in-and-for-itself.[30] Presentation, as the true realization of this absolute knowing, supersedes consciousness, so that the subject loses its semblance of being burdened with something alien and becomes simply the immanent self of that presentation.

2. THE ELEMENT OF CONFIGURATION

2.1 *Labour and thinghood*

Presentation is "for" natural consciousness and is its true "other" because presentation is first and foremost an externalization of its implicit universal self. As the ideal mode of externalization, presentation first appears for consciousness in the *Phänomenologie* as the action of labour. Hegel suggests that through labour on a thing consciousness achieves the certainty of itself in objectivity, an objectivity which is independent of the wavering recognition of an other because it is the other. This simple mode of externalization, and the concomitant self-recognition that derives from it, introduces natural consciousness into an understanding of its potential being-for-self in objectivity. Already in labour, consciousness learns to behold itself in an "other" present at hand: "Opposed to an other, the 'I' is its own self, and at the same time it overarches this other which, for the 'I', is equally only the 'I' itself".[31]

However the self is first an object for consciousness not in the shape of philosophic presentation, but as another self-consciousness. Self-consciousness becomes certain of itself in truth only by superseding this other that *presents* itself to self-consciousness as an independent life, so that self-consciousness is "desire" (Begierde).[32] Through desire which appropriates the presentation of the other, self-certainty becomes explicit for self-consciousness in an objective manner, that is, self-consciousness in being an object is just as much "I" as "object".

The universal self appearing for natural consciousness in presentation only becomes a self-consciousness in-and-for-itself through its recognition by natural consciousness. The concept of this spiritual unity is manifest for the first time on the path of phenomenal knowing as the dialectic between the independence and dependence of self-consciousness, i.e., as lordship and bondage, in which the importance of recognition (the prototype of belief in presentation) becomes explicit. In being confronted by another self-consciousness, self-consciousness has already come out of itself, since, in superseding the other independent being in order to become certain of itself as the essential being, it proceeds to supersede its own self, for this other is itself.

Hegel describes the situation thus: "Each [self-consciousness] is indeed certain of its own self, but not of the other, and therefore its own self-certainty still has no truth; for it would have truth only if its own being-for-self has confronted it as an independent object, or, what is the same thing, if the object had *presented* itself as this pure self-certainty".[33] Of course the object presents itself as a pure, absolute self-certainty ultimately in the presentation of speculative science, and such a presentation has its salutary effect only when consciousness recognizes its true self displayed therein as not attached to any determinate existence, not to the individuality common to existence as such.

Consequently the two self-consciousness' enter a life-and-death struggle in which each seeks the death of the other and in so doing equally stakes its own life, for each seeks to raise its certainty of being-for-self to truth. However the death of one or both does away with the truth that was supposed to issue from the struggle. In this case, Hegel says that their act is an abstract negation, not the negation coming from consciousness, which supersedes in such a way as to preserve and maintain what is superseded, and thus survives its own supersession. This experience teaches self-consciousness that life is as essential to it as self-consciousness, so that instead of resulting in the two abstract extremes of death, the struggle devolves into an independent self-consciousness whose nature is to be for-itself and a dependent consciousness whose nature is to be for-another.

This struggle has caused the dissolution of the simple unity of immediate self-consciousness, the simple "I" that is absolute mediation and has as its essential moment lasting independence, but at the same time this struggle has brought self-consciousness out of itself so that it must find the truth of itself in an other. The master relates himself mediately to the thing through the slave, and the slave, *qua* self-consciousness in general, also relates himself negatively to the thing and takes away its independence. Yet the thing nonetheless preserves a certain independence *vis-à-vis* the slave, for he does not negate it to the point of annihilation, – he only labours on it.

The master's immediate relation to the thing, through this mediation by the slave, is therefore the sheer negation of the thing. The master "takes to himself only the dependent aspect of the thing and has the pure enjoyment of it. The aspect of its independence he leaves to the slave, who labours on it".[34] But it is this independence of the thing that provides the matrix for the externalization and recollection of the self in objectivity; in the sheer negation of the thing, the self remains closed in upon its individual particularity.

This relation to the thing determines the concomitant mode of recognition that was orginally desired by each self-consciousness. Because it is the master's will which negates the thing, or, in other words, because it is the master which is the essential action in this relation, the recognition operating between master and slave is equally onesided. The unessential consciousness of the slave is for the master the object which constitutes the truth of his certainty of himself. Obviously this object does not correspond to its concept, for the object in which the master seeks to behold his self-consciousness is not at all an independent consciousness but a dependent one. Thus he is not certain of being-for-self as the truth of himself.

The slave, on the other hand, has the master for its essential reality, so that the truth for it is the independent consciousness which is for-itself. However, as Hegel points out, "servitude is not yet aware that this truth is implicit in it".[35] The mere *beholding* of self-consciousness as its objective truth is not enough for the slave to appropriate that truth, − it must understand this objectivity as the externalization of its universal self through an act of presentation, i.e., through labour.

In order that this universal self be "for" consciousness, the slave must supersede his own particular existence, and this pure negativity toward existence necessitated by being-for-self is justly experienced when the slave's whole being has been seized with dread (Angst). This universal moment, this absolute negativity, is implicit in this consciousness at the same time that being-for-self is explicit for the slave as his object in the shape of the master. The slave is able to supersede his particular existence and appropriate this object not through an arbitrary decision, but through the prolonged *experience* of service and labour.

As with the simple beholding of the master as his truth, fear of the master, alone, is not enough to make the slave aware that he is a being-for-self. Consciousness of self is primarily achieved through the externalization and recollection of the self in objectivity, − or, as Hegel says, through labour the slave comes to itself.[36] In desire, as the pure negating of the object, the master has an immediate feeling of self, but it is a satisfaction that is fleeting because it lacks the side of objectivity and permanence. Labour, in contrast, holds desire in check and forms objectivity.

The negative relation to the object characteristic of being-for-self becomes the object's form, and something permanent, precisely because the object continues to have independence for the labourer. Through the formative activity of labour the slave is able to externalize and behold in objectivity, i.e., in a labour outside of consciousness, its own individuality. It is particularly within the mode of externalization that labouring consciousness comes to intuit this independent being of objectivity as its self.[37]

However, if the mode of externalization is to be efficacious for the achievement of a consciousness of self in objectivity, then that objectivity which is the product of formative labour must not in any way take on the aspect of an alienation (Entfremdung): the slave must be able to recognize himself in the product of his labour just as natural consciousness must be able to recognize itself in the presentation of its universal self. This necessity of recognition assumes that the independence of thinghood, as for example in language, is not such that it makes all spiritual formation impossible, but that the natural element of objectivity can be raised to its spiritual truth. Hegel affirms that "The form does not become something other than [the slave] through becoming *placed outside* of him; for it is precisely this form that is his pure being-for-self, which in this externality becomes his truth".[38]

Thus the slave finds that it is in his labour, wherein he seemed to have only an alien sense of being, that he rediscovers the characteristic sense of himself. While in the shape of the master being-for-self was only an object "for" consciousness, and in fear being-for-self was implicit in him, it is in labour that the slave becomes conscious of being-for-self as his own self. Of course service and fear are necessary antecedent moments if the externalization proper to labour is to present the self in objectivity: without service fear would not extend to the conscious actuality of existence; without labour fear remains inward and consciousness does not become for-itself; without fear labour is not negatively in-itself since determinate being still attaches to the self, and its formative activity cannot give it a consciousness of itself as essential being.

These conditions for the recognition of the self through labour can equally be extended to philosophic presentation. As long as presentation remains an objectivity which is only "for" natural consciousness, that consciousness cannot appropriate the presentation as its own. Natural consciousness must come to recognize the presentation of its universal self as an externalization of its own individuality, and it is just this awareness which the *Phänomenologie* sets out to create. The labour of presentation which makes up the system is implicitly its own labour, not an alien knowledge that is imposed on natural consciousness. This is what Hegel means when he says that the standpoint of speculative science is implicit in every consciousness.

For this recognition and appropriation of science *qua* object to occur, natural consciousness must also experience the antecedent moment of fear, through which it assumes an absolute negativity toward its particular existence. The being-for-self which is the result of this fear can thus potentially become the immanent self of presentation in objectivity. We see, then, that the path of phenomenal knowing, designated as a series of experiences for consciousness, will be salutary only if it includes in some form (i) the full presentation of the determinations of the universal self as the true object of consciousness, i.e., the content of the system; and (ii) the absolute negation of all particular or finite standpoints of consciousness.[39]

With the universal self as its object, and the experience of the "loss of self" resulting from the negation of its particular existences, natural consciousness at the level of absolute knowing comprehends the presentation of the system in-and-for-itself as its own proper externalization and truth. That death which was risked by the master and then forgotten becomes superseded in the labour of presentation as a determined attitude of negativity toward particular existence, whereby the sacrifice of individuality is preserved in its object. And only through such a complete sacrifice is science able to witness and raise to certainty an absolute that is already present at hand.

2.2 *The linguistic object*

The labour of self-presentation finds its ideal object in language. In the element of speech, the opaque resistance of the thing to the formative process of labour is all but overcome, and consciousness finds there the determinate being of its full expression. When we say that the resistance of thinghood is overcome it is not that objectivity *qua* language loses its independence, but that speech is the most adequate form in which the truth of natural consciousness is externalized.

Language, as with the product of labour in general, remains an externalization of the self at the same time that it is an object for that self. However language is superior to other products in the important respect that it cannot but express the self's determinations universally: the particular determinations of this particular self are translated through their expression into the universal determinations of a universal self. Consequently language *qua* object is the ideal element for the absolute to present itself as the truth of natural consciousness.

In the phenomenal knowing attributed to sense-certainty, Hegel points out that when we wish to distinguish a "meant" or particular Here and Now, we cannot help but say it as a universal. He asserts, "It is as a universal too that we *utter* what the sensuous *is*; what we say is: *this*, i.e., the *universal this,* or: *it is*; i.e., *Being in general*. Of course, we do not *envisage* the universal This or Being in general, but we *utter* the universal; or we do not strictly say what in this sense-certainty we *mean*".[40] Language translates our particular meaning into a universal determination, and Hegel believes that language is the more truthful because the universal is indeed the truth of sense-certainty.

This is the same process which occurs when we mean to designate this particular "I" but say that universal "I" common to everyone. The externalization of the self in language becomes not only an object in which I behold myself, but an object "for" natural consciousness as such. The universality and independence of this object at once establishes the presented self as an "other", and yet, because it is an externalization, it remains even so "my" object. If, on the other hand, language *qua* object in any way limits this recognition of the self in otherness, then the salutary effect of a presentation "for" natural consciousness is put in question.

This independence of language in its objectivity raises the possibility that a former externalization of the self may become an alien and unrecognizable commodity. Hegel explores this inner and outer dimension of language in the chapter on Reason: "Language and labour are outer expressions in which the individual no longer keeps and possesses himself within himself, but lets the inner get completely outside of him, leaving it to the mercy of something other than himself".[41] Both language and labour give the inner directly, and yet, once externalized, this inner can turn into something other than the meaning intended by the particular individual.

Furthermore, through these external influences, the expressions lose their character of being something constant in front of other individualities. Thus this breakdown between the individual and the recognition of himself in his object − i.e., this alienation − means that the individual has no real existence for others in ethical life. This is so because language *qua* object is the being-there of the pure self as self: in speech the for-itself existing individuality of self-consciousness as such comes into existence so that it is for others. In every other externality, the pure "I" is immersed in an actuality from which it can withdraw itself, and reflect back into itself from its action.

In language the self is absolutely present to itself and present to others, but present universally. Hegel says, "Language, however, contains [the "I"] in its purity, it alone expresses the "I", the "I" itself. This *existence* of the "I" is, as *existence*, an objectivity which has in it the true nature of the "I". The "I" is *this* "I" − but equally the *universal* "I"; its appearing is also immediately the externalization and vanishing of *this* "I", and as a result the "I" abides in its universality".[42] Hegel describes the "I" that utters itself as an infection which immediately passes into a unity with those for whom it is "there" and is a universal self-consciousness. This vanishing of the self's determinate existence is thus, itself, immediately its abiding; it is its own knowing of itself, and its knowing of itself as a passing over into another self that has been beheld and is universal.

Therefore if we posit a lapse in the self's recognition of its universal presentation in language, natural consciousness can attain neither full self-knowledge nor full being for others. It is, certainly, not altogether clear what happens when the presentation of the self in language undergoes changes in externality due to the influence of others, but there seems to be both a positive and negative aspect to this influence. As we have already emphasized, if the externalization of the self in language *qua* object is altered to the extent that the individual no longer beholds himself in objectivity, then that object becomes a *commodity* which is essentially alienated from the labour of the individual and plays no part in his rise to self-consciousness. If, on the other hand, the externalization of the self is altered so as to become the presentation of that self in its universality, then the particular self *continues* to abide as an immanent self for its absolute content, and the appropriation of the universal self as "its" object introduces this self into the life of spirit.

It is the peculiar role of language to act as the matrix for the recognition moving between the particular and universal self, and consequently it is above all a spiritual phenomenon, − indeed, Hegel describes language as the "being-there" of spirit.[43] While we attain a consciousness of self in objectivity through language, language is also this self-consciousness existing for others, i.e., self-consciousness immediately present at hand.

Being present at hand means that the self beholds itself just as it is beheld by others, so that the certainty of self attained through presentation becomes at once objectively true. It follows that language is the effective element of all presentation, because "it is the self that separates itself from itself, which as pure I = I becomes objective to itself, which in this objectivity equally preserves itself as *this* self, just as it coalesces immediately with other selves and is *their* self-consciousness".[44] The phenomenologist, who in presenting a path of phenomenal knowing looks back on his own educational history, is thus able through a specifically linguistic externalization to offer that consciousness of self which is his own object as the truth of natural consciousness as such.

In other words, an absolute which is already present at hand for this particular individual can attain universal consciousness of self through its presentation in language as the universal self of consciousness. This possibility immediately raises certain questions, the most important of which arises from the fact that our discussion of language has not taken into consideration its determinate existence as the "thick immediacy" of a particular people. To what extent does the determinate being of a particular linguistic group limit or qualify the "truths" expressed within that group? Does the self-presentation of the absolute for natural consciousness as such transcend national-linguistic boundaries, or is this presentation, rather, a regional response to the specific needs of a determinate people?

There are no direct answers to these questions in the *Phänomenologie*, but we can draw certain implications from the texts already presented. To begin with, it is clear that the individual has no objective existence until he has "plugged into" the linguistic universe of his own community. Only through the verbal limits established by that community does the individual achieve "rational" expression, – as well as self-knowledge and social integration. All expression which attempts to break through these limits with a desire to describe the original or specific, that which we might call the unutterable in terms of the standards of this community, Hegel sloughs off as the "untrue" and "irrational" (das Unvernünftige).[45]

The linguistic group, therefore, provides the horizons of signification for presentation, and that presentation is rational to the extent that it does not transgress the accepted definitions of names-meanings within the proper domains of application. While the path of phenomenal knowing presents the educational history of natural consciousness, it presents that history "for" contemporary natural consciousness using language that is by and large common to its experience. But do not the concepts expressed in that presentation somehow transcend the precise linguistic and national determinations of their externalization? This raises the more general question of the relationship between presentation and the spirit of a people.

2.3 *The spirit of a people*

What we might call the "permeation" of philosophic presentation by the particular *Volksgeist* receives at best an ambiguous treatment in the *Phänomenologie*. In the chapter on absolute knowing, as we shall see later, there seems to be the suggestion that philosophic recollection is related to its determinate spiritual realm. Certainly, philosophy reconsiders previous spiritual realms in its course, but it does so motivated by the concerns of its own epoch, i.e., it mediates the past with the present. In this case we must think of presentation as an essentially regional response to local needs, and the finality of its program is equally relative to these perceived needs.

However there are reasons for this ambiguity, some of them purely structural and pertaining to the necessities of presentation itself, and others which seem to be historical. First of all, Hegel states unequivocally that the actualization of self-consciousness, achieved through the externalizations of labour and language, is strictly a matter involving the life of a nation. In that section of the chapter on Reason that has to do with the actualization of self-consciousness, he says "It is in fact in the life of a people (Volk) that the concept of the actualization of self-conscious reason, – of intuiting in the independence of the *other* the complete *unity* with it, or having for my object the free *thinghood* of an other which confronts me and is the negative of my self, as *my* being-for-*myself* – that the concept has its complete reality".[46]

Reason appears as the relation between these selves in community, as the substance of their mutual recognition which both binds them together and distinguishes them as being-for-themselves. These selves are conscious of having the fluid universal substance of reason as their soul and essence, but equally that this universal is their action as individuals, the work that they have brought forth. In the beholding of the other as other, and of the universal product of their labour as an objective other, these individuals achieve a consciousness of their universal self, – universal in the sense that the collective product is a *national* object of regard.

Labour within the context of a people becomes something different than it is within its concept, which we discussed earlier. There we saw that labour as such meets the needs of a particular individual, but within a community of individuals it becomes equally a universal labour. Certainly, the particular activity and occupation of the individual refers to the needs which he has as a natural being, i.e., as an existing individuality, and yet these activities have actuality through the universal supporting medium of the entire people. The individual act is incontrovertibly entwined with the action of all.

Hegel says that the labour of the individual for his own needs is just as much a satisfaction of the needs of others as of his own, and the satisfaction of his own needs he obtains only through the labour of others. To the extent that the mode for the satisfaction of his particular need takes on this universal determination, the individual comes to behold the product of all their labours as his own object. Hegel continues: "As the individual in his *individual* labour already unconsciously brings forth a *universal* labour, so again he also brings forth the universal as his *conscious* object; the whole becomes, *as a whole*, his own work, for which he sacrifices himself and even in so doing receives back from it his own self".[47] The relationship of the labourer with the whole here described is entirely reciprocal, so that any dissolution of his particular being-for-self, any loss of self, is recompensed through the positive signification it has for his universal being-for-self.[48]

This is the same kind of relationship that holds between natural consciousness and philosophic presentation, if we conceive of that presentation as a
universal product of labour into which the particular individual disappears
only to become the immanent self of its content. The loss of self which consciousness experiences along the path of phenomenal knowing, this dissolution, redounds with an affirmation of its true universal self that satisfies its
needs for recognition. The universal product of a people, which equally exists
as an object "for" the particular individual, becomes in presentation the
complete externalization of the absolute as it exists present at hand.[49]

Immediately, however, the universal substance of reason finds its expression in language, i.e., as a universal language, in the customs and laws of a
people. Again, these laws represent not an alienation of the individual from
the whole, but the unity of being-for-another and being-for-self. Indeed this
unchangable essence which is language-as-law expresses the very individuality which seems opposed to it: the laws proclaim what each individual is and
does. Hegel says that, "the individual knows [the laws] not only as his *universal* objective thinghood, but equally knows himself in them, or them as indi-
vidualized in his own individuality and in each of his fellow citizens".[50]

Language-as-law is that transparent objectivity in which the individual
beholds his universal self and knows that self as himself in otherness.
Through the efficacy of this universal externalization of language, the individual has a certainty of himself in universal spirit, and finds nothing but
himself in actuality. This common identification with being-for-self in
linguistic objectivity, – presented in an immediate manner through laws and
customs, – brings about a free unity with others such that the individual intuits them as himself and himself as them. Thus Hegel draws the corollary
that in a free nation reason is in truth actualized, and cites the admonition
of the ancients that wisdom and virtue consists in living in accordance with
the customs of one's nation.

However the ethical life (Sittlichkeit) of a nation manifests reason merely
in its immediacy, i.e., the customs and laws are a determinate ethical
substance, which in a higher moment viz. in the consciousness of its essence,
sheds this limitation and in this cognition alone has its absolute truth. In
ethical life spirit is in the form of mere being, and the self is not aware of itself
as pure individuality existing for-itself. Once the self attains this self-consciousness the immediate unity with spirit is lost and we enter the realm of
spirit in its self-alienation as culture.[51]

The suggestion in the foregoing is that at a "higher moment" natural consciousness transcends the beholding of itself as a determinate national object.

Hegel says that consciousness sheds this limitation, and henceforth spirit presents itself not explicitly in the form of a people but as shapes of a world for consciousness. The shape which follows the self-alienation of spirit in culture is, conspicuously, a moral *Weltanschauung,*[52] and the self-presentation of spirit within the apparatus of particular nations becomes secondary to its division into a this world and a beyond. The true nature of the interrelation of the latter supersedes the concerns and needs of a specific people: "the goal and result of that development will arive on the scene as the actual self-consciousness of absolute spirit",[53] i.e., ultimately as the presentation of the determinations of the absolute in the system.

This result, certainly, includes the antecedent moments of spirit's presentation in the concrete process of labour and in the ethical life of a nation, but also supersedes them as limitations that are on-the-way to the timeless witness of the absolute in speculative science. The final unification of shapes along the path of phenomenal knowing, a unification which responds to the crisis in contemporary natural consciousness, is between a *Weltanschauung* and an absolute present at hand. And the relationship between this unification and the surrounding nation is decidedly ambiguous, although the implication is that we are speaking of modern Protestant Germany.[54]

The significance of this particular surrounding nation fades as we rise through the echelons of spirit's self-conscious shapes, such that the need to which philosophic presentation responds is related not to a determinate people, but to the history of absolute manifestation as a whole, and which finds its expression everywhere in the modern Occident. There are two essential reasons, however, for the apparent denigration of the national origin of this need and the concomitant philosophic response. The first relates to the structure of the presentation of the path of phenomenal knowing itself: contemporary natural consciousness is already a *Weltanschauung*, and has left the immediate relation to the nation far behind in its educational history. Consequently the shapes of spirit are designed from this point of view, i.e., at the level of contemporary consciousness, and the true significance of the nation will become evident to it only once it has transcended its particular worldview in the higher standpoint of science.

The second reason is that Hegel must have felt that the German nation of his own day, at least in the period in which the *Phänomenologie* was written, was in a state of transition and could not be wholly brought into a discussion of morality as the politics of France was brought into the description of culture. If this is so, is not the reconciliation between this sketch of a moral worldview and the consciousness of absolute religion wholly utopian in character, i.e., an "ought" which is divorced from the social matrix of its existing implicit accomplishment?[55] Perhaps the hope in the "beginning of a new world" which is apparent throughout the *Phänomenologie*, and especially in the Preface, arises just through this perceived lack in the current political arrangements, — arrangements which do not yet correspond to the highest levels of spirit's presentation in speculative science. However, we arrive once again at the fact that, even if the presentation of the path of phenomenal knowing does not merely look back on its content, but, on the contrary, points forward to the dim outlines of a new world which are just now becoming clear, this presentation arises nonetheless from the needs manifest in the surrounding nation and gives its response a decidedly determinate character.

Thus the act of philosophic presentation as "response" remains essentially tied to the mode of absolute manifestation known as the spirit of a people, the *Volksgeist*. This is the position held in the final system, and it is a position which is merely implicit in the *Phänomenologie* largely due to the demands of a presentation at the level of contemporary natural consciousness. The needs arising from the divided spiritual life of this consciousness become expicit in the chapter on absolute knowing, as does the salutary response in the form of philosophic presentation itself.

3. RESULT AND PRESUPPOSITION

3.1 *Absolute knowing*

The path of phenomenal knowing presented by the *Phänomenologie* results in absolute knowing, which is the reconciliation *in consciousness* of the distinction between the in-itself and for-itself established by the Introduction. The in-itself that was previously comprehended as the quality of alienation in objectivity is now exhaustively "for" consciousness. This does not mean that the in-itself or "otherness" of objectivity totally collapses, but that this objectivity is recognized as an externalization (Entäußerung) of the self. Hegel says, "This surmounting of the object of consciousness is not to be taken onesidedly to mean that the object showed itself as returning into the self, but is to be taken more specifically to mean not only that the object as such presented itself to the self as vanishing, but rather that it is the externalization of self-consciousness that posits the thinghood and that this externalization has not merely a negative but a positive meaning, a meaning which is not only for us or in-itself, but for self-consciousness itself".[56]

Self-consciousness posits itself as object, while at the same time superseding and recollecting this externalization and objectivity, so that it is in communion with itself in its "otherness" as such. This recollecting of the externalization is the movement of *consciousness*, which relates itself to the object in the totality of its determinations. But the totality of its determinations establishes the object as an implicitly spiritual being, and it becomes a spiritual being "for" consciousness when each of its individual determinations is grasped as a determination of the self, i.e., through the speculative presentation of the system.

Absolute knowing, as the result of the path of phenomenal knowing, is still a knowing of the moments of the concept proper in the form of shapes of consciousness. In other words the spiritual essentiality of the object presented by the system is only implicitly "for consciousness" in absolute knowing: the absolute content of consciousness is understood on the one side as the totality of the moments of the object and the relation of consciousness to it, which the phenomenologist brings together, and on the other side as a shape of consciousness as such.[57] Absolute knowing is still alienated from its content as it is in-and-for-itself in the system, an alienation that can only be superseded through the salutary act of speculative presentation.

The concept of the reconciliation of self-consciousness with the consciousness of its absolute content first comes before us in the particular shape of a self-consciousness, as self-assured spirit that abides within its concept and is called the "beautiful soul". It is a self-consciousness that knows this pure knowledge of pure inwardness as spirit, but in which consciousness is completely submerged and for whom all externality as such has vanished. This self-consciousness itself vanishes because it fails to put its trust in the absolute difference between thought and being and in the salutary act of presentation as its supersession.[58]

Just as action is the first implicit sundering of the simple unity of the concept, so too action is the return out of this dividedness. The reconciliation of the consciousness of absolute content in religious representation with self-consciousness is brought about by the action of the latter, − self-consciousness appropriates the absolute in-itself "for" itself, as an in-itself determined by the self. Hegel explains this double movement of appropriation in the following: "This concept fulfilled itself on the one side in the self-certain spirit that *acted*, and on the other, in religion: in religion it won for consciousness the absolute content *as content* or, in the form of representation, the form of otherness for consciousness; on the other hand, in the prior shape the form is that of the self itself, for it contains the self-certain spirit that *acts*; the self accomplishes the life of absolute spirit".[59] In the system, Hegel indicates that the ultimate realization of the life of absolute spirit is philosophic recollection and presentation, so that we must take into consideration that the act of appropriation on the part of this self-consciousness finds its proper fulfillment in philosophic presentation, making the transition from absolute knowing to the presentation of the system a necessary one.

Conversely, an absolute knowing that withdraws into itself and that does not thus act and is not actual is, according to this scheme, simply evil. Such a withdrawal into the self, sometimes described by Hegel as the "vanity of thought" or the attitude of "irony", appears evil because it constitutes the antithesis of the concept, – the knowing that does not act.[60] Again it follows that if philosophic presentation is the consumate act of self-knowing spirit, then that self which refuses to make the transition from absolute knowing to the presentation of the system of science is the most irredeemably evil of all.

However, this appearance of the opposition between the self and its essence means that the pure knowing of the essence has in principle renounced its simple unity, and that this self-sundering is also implicitly for consciousness. Through the explicit mediation of its determinate difference, each side renounces its onesidedness, so that the concept within itself in its individuality completes itself through the moment of universality which is essence, and the abstract universality through the universality which is the self. But we must emphasize once more that it is by means of *action* that spirit comes on the scene as a pure universality of knowing, as self-consciousness that is the simple unity of knowing. Hegel asserts, "It is only through action that spirit *is* in such a way that it is really *there*, that is, when it raises its existence into *thought* and thereby into an absolute *opposition*, and returns out of this opposition, in and through the opposition itself".[61]

Therefore, what in religion was content or a form for representating an other, is in absolute knowing the self's own act, for the concept requires the content to be the self's own act. This concept is the knowledge of the self's act within itself as all essentiallity and all existence, the knowledge of this subject as substance and of the substance as this knowledge of its act.[62] Of course this insight into the efficacy of action, which is the result of the path of phenomenal knowing, is itself dependent on the act of philosophic presentation which gathers together the separate moments of spiritual self-knowing and displays their necessity according to the concept. The instigation to action which appears for natural consciousness at the end of this path is thus found to be the presupposition for its potential absolute knowledge. The extent to which the path is determined by the necessities of philosophic presentation again raises the question whether this path is meant to be a ladder for non-philosophic natural consciousness to ascend to philosophic presentation, or whether it is simply a presentation of philosophy's comprehension of non-philosophic life.[63]

Absolute knowing is spirit that knows itself in the shape of spirit, − where truth is not only in-itself completely identical with certainty, but also has the shape of self-certainty, or is in its existence in the form of self-knowledge. In this way that which is essence, the concept, enters the element of existence by becoming the form of objectivity for consciousness.[64] But the very existence of the *Phänomenologie* demonstrates that it is necessary, according to Hegel, for natural consciousness to follow the presented path of phenomenal knowing if it is to become self-conscious of its absolute determinations, and if the appearing concept is to achieve self-certainty. The concept which has its fortuitous happening in history in the form of shapes of consciousness merely provides the absolute content for the recollection and presentation of speculative science, a presentation which displays that content not according to its chronological appearing, but according to the dialectical determinations of the concept itself.

This path of phenomenal knowing displays the manner by which natural consciousness appropriates and determines its absolute content, and is implicitly an absolute knowing. As an absolute knowing, natural consciousness continues to be this particular and no other "I", but no less immediately, a mediated or superseded universal "I". This is possible because it has a content which it differentiates from itself. Hegel says, "In it, as differentiated, the "I" is reflected into itself; it is only when the "I" communes with itself in its otherness that the content is *comprehended*".[65] In the *Phänomenologie* this content exists as the total universal self of the "I" through its presentation by speculative science as a phenomenal knowing for consciousness, so that the "I" *must* find itself reflected in the content of philosophic presentation. To the extent that philosophic presentation remains an alien "other", this reconciliation of the particular and universal "I" breaks down.

In other words, if the "I" of natural consciousness is to recognize itself in philosophic presentation, speculative science must first present the substance of its absolute content as it is "for" consciousness. Such a presentation is possible "now" because contemporary natural consciousness is at a point in its educational history when the substance of its absolute content has achieved full externalization in time. Hegel says that speculative science does not appear in time and in actuality before spirit has attained to this consciousness about itself, so that speculative science is essentially a looking back on a completed process in-itself, and a raising of that process to its existence for-itself in self-consciousness. "Now, in actuality, the substance that knows exists earlier than its form or its concept-determined "shape".[66] Once this substance is for-itself in the form of self-conscious subjectivity, then the self sets aside the time-form of its previous externalizations in history and presents those externalizations according to their timeless absolute determination. Time is the necessity of spirit that is not yet complete within itself, the necessity to enrich the share which self-consciousness has in consciousness, to set in motion the immediacy of the in-itself.[67]

This dependence of science on an "antecedent" spiritual substance derives from the thesis that "nothing is *known* that is not in *experience*".[68] In this statement Hegel is seeking to describe the manner in which knowledge arises in experience with an inherent self-certainty, so that in experience something is "felt" to be true, as if it is a truth so revealed that it must be believed. The result of such an insight can be seen in the very process by which he sets out to convince natural consciousness of its absolute determination, i.e., through a presented series of experiences that make up a path of phenomenal knowing. Furthermore, this knowing itself supersedes and includes the relations of feeling and belief characteristic of all experience, as we shall see later.

Until spirit has completed itself as world-spirit (Weltgeist), it cannot reach its consummation in speculative science as self-conscious spirit. Hegel tells us that the movement of carrying forward the form of its self-knowledge is the labour which spirit accomplishes as *actual history*, and begins with the religious community so far as it is at first the substance of absolute spirit. Here the struggle that the self has with its essence, with the alien content of its consciousness, ends only when consciousness has given up hope of overcoming that alienation in an external, i.e., alien manner, and turns to itself, – for the overcoming of that alienation is the return into self-consciousness. Hegel adds that, "not until then does it turn to its own present world and discover it as its property".[69]

Hegel then sets out, in the space of one long paragraph, to present a history of the major principles of modern philosophy from Descartes to Schelling, and including himself.[70] There are two aspects of this history that are nothing less than striking: first, as an example of spirit externalized in history, and as a description of the spiritual substance which makes up the absolute content of science, Hegel gives us a history of *philosophy*; second, Hegel uses the same tactic of presenting a brief history of modern philosophy, viz. the "presentations of thought to objectivity", as an introduction to the content of the system proper, and in the *Phänomenologie*, too, this history precedes a shadowy outline of the role of the system.

Are we then to assume that a history of philosophy, or a history of absolute spirit, provides the proper introduction to the system, and if so, what is the role of the *Phänomenologie*? To begin with, we may say that the *Phänome-*

nologie already contains the principles of this history, not as they appear in history, but as they are for consciousness in the presented path of phenomenal knowing. In addition, a comprehension of these principles as they are mediated by the concept demands a prior knowledge of the system of absolute determinations, so that such cultural histories are necessarily posterior to the presentation of the *Enzyklopädie*. The point of these brief histories used as introductions is to demonstrate the *need* of the system by consciousness as the fulfillment of its own essential educational history.

This need arises from the description of the positions of Fichte and Schelling which seem to have fixed themselves in irreconcilable opposition, revealing a state of division in contemporary spiritual life. Hegel continues by asserting that, "Spirit, however, has shown itself to us to be neither merely the withdrawal of self-consciousness into its pure inwardness, nor the submergence of self-consciousness into substance, and the non-being of its difference; but spirit is *this movement* of the self which empties itself of itself and sinks itself into its substance, and also, as subject, has gone out of that substance into itself, making the substance into an object and a content at the same time as it cancels this difference between objectivity and content".[71]

Science comprehends and mediates these immediate oppositions as they appear in the educational history of natural consciousness, and presents the need for the knowing subject at the level of absolute knowing to abandon the form of consciousness and proceed to the presentation of the absolute determinations as they are in-and-for-themselves in the system. Hegel says that with absolute knowing spirit has superseded the difference of consciousness from its object, a difference that was particular to the yet incompleted movement of spirit giving shape to itself.[72] Indeed the movement which we find expressed as a path of phenomenal knowing is movement at all because of this difference and the negativity of thought which perdures within it (thus leading us to successively more determinate figures of consciousness). When we are told that spirit has won the pure element of its existence, the concept, this means that the difference is abolished and the alienation of consciousness from its object-world is tacitly overcome: consciousness now beholds in the alternations of its spatial field a matrix for the peculiar rhythm of its own self-determination. Through this recognition, the content of absolute knowing is "liberated" to the concept and its movement is shown to be *free* development, since this content is in fact nothing less than the self-externalizing self. We must be careful, however, not to associate the being-free of this content with such notions as caprice, because freedom here carries with it the idea of self-sufficiency. On the one hand this content is said to be free because it is self-determining, but on the other hand this self-determining is rooted in a peculiar rhythm of self-externalization, with the corollary that the content of absolute knowing is made equally necessary. In other words, this content is determinate because it stands in a mediate relation to the self and to the negativity of thought, with the difference that whereas under the form of consciousness this negativity was external and a reflection away from the content, in absolute knowing this negativity is externalized and the content is its own process of superseding itself. Hegel says that negativity is also the self, and so to the extent that the knowing subject goes over to the content to become its immanent self, the content is concept.

It is only when spirit thus closes with itself, when the absolute content is exhaustively mediated with the self and made determinate, that spirit is *science*. As speculative science, the moments of spirit are no longer posited as specific shapes of consciousness but as specific concepts and as their organic self-grounded movement. Hegel says that, "Whereas in the phenomenology of spirit each moment is the difference of knowledge and truth, and is the movement in which that difference is cancelled, science on the other hand does not contain this difference and the cancelling of it. On the contrary, since the moment has the form of the concept, it unites the objective form of truth and of the knowing self in an immediate unity".[73] Consequently speculative science does not seek to demonstrate the dialectic of consciousness and self-consciousness that we find constituting the path of phenomenal knowing, but simply presents the moments of spirit freed from this appearing as the determinate movement of the self-knowing concept. Being freed from appearance means that the moment has been raised to the level of the concept, and this signifies that speculative science merely re-presents the determinations of absolute spirit which first appeared within the fortuitous happening of spirit in history and again within the presented path of phenomenal knowing. The appearance of moments here referred to is the latter, the mode of appearance characteristic of the *Phänomenologie*, so that speculative science present at hand as the system is related to appearing science by the modes necessary to absolute self-presentation and self-knowledge.

To state this more precisely, the *Enzyklopädie* and the *Phänomenologie* present the same absolute content under different modes, with the difference that in the *Phänomenologie* Hegel has presented the close of spirit with itself for the natural consciousness of his own day: the systematic self-mediation of the absolute is thus only apparent in the *Phänomenologie*, and is not made actual as it is within the pure element of speculative science. Hegel confirms this rough parallel and the systematic basis of both texts when he asserts that, "to each abstract moment of science corresponds a shape of appearing spirit as such".[74] In the *Phänomenologie* we find the pure concepts of science in the form of shapes of consciousness, which constitutes the side of their reality and as they initially appear to natural consciousness. However we must not look for an exact concordance of moments between the *Phänomenologie* and the *Enzyklopädie* beyond this broad systematic parallel, since the concept of speculative science is broken assunder and presented within the path of phenomenal knowing as the inner antithesis of consciousness and self-consciousness.

In continuing our discussion of absolute knowing, we are now faced with the necessity of confronting the concluding paragraphs in this last chapter of the *Phänomenologie*, paragraphs whose singular density and opacity would seem to militate against any definitive interpretive scheme. It must be remarked, in a preliminary way, that these paragraphs do *not* appear to offer simply the abbreviated sketch of a tripartite system of science similar to the *Enzyklopädie* which, we might assume, would include a logic, a philosophy a nature, and a philosophy of spirit. If we were to find such an outline in these last paragraphs, then that paragraph we have discussed above which compares phenomenology to speculative science must in fact be a veiled reference to the *Logik*.[75] But nowhere in this paragraph is there a reference to the science of logic in particular, and so we must conclude that this paragraph, describing as it does the presentation of spirit in the ether of its life, refers only to speculative science in general and a science which includes all three speculative modes. Rather than seeking to delineate the roles of other texts, we propose that these paragraphs concern themselves with the manner in which speculative science brings about its own indwelling in natural consciousness and is mediated with the on-going, free contingent happening of spirit.

Hegel follows his description of the way in which absolute content is raised to the level of the concept in speculative science with the statement that, "Science contains within itself this necessity of externalizing the form of the concept, and it contains the passage of the concept into *consciousness*".[76] As we shall see in the Preface to the *Phänomenologie*, Hegel affirms repeatedly that speculative science must offer itself as an exoteric path of self-knowledge for natural consciousness because it is only through the public appropriation of speculative science that it can be said that spirit closes with itself and is self-knowing spirit. Of course the passage of the concept into consciousness occurs by means of the *Phänomenologie* presented as a ladder to the scientific standpoint, and we may thus infer that speculative science necessitates this ladder if it is to posit the close of spirit. Furthermore, the immediate identity of self-knowing spirit as speculative science is no less the immediate difference of the standpoint of sense-consciousness, that moment with which the *Phänomenologie* begins; but we return to this standpoint as it exists "for us" or for the phenomenologist and as it is absolutely mediated. In our return to the beginning, we return to a beginning comprehended and concept and are now able to understand the manner in which speculative science is the presupposition, and not merely the result, of this appearing of the concept in consciousness. It follows that the implicit appearance of the concept in natural consciousness and in the *Phänomenologie* is already determined by the exigencies of the absolute idea explicated in the system: while the system appears for consciousness as the final result of its educational history, it is also implicitly the timeless ground of its pure essentiality.

This return to sense-consciousness by self-knowing spirit following the public appropriation of speculative science indicates a re-newed certainty of immediacy, with the difference that now this immediacy is no less absolutely mediated and comprehended and freed from the dialectic of consciousness and self-consciousness. The knowing subject simply goes over to this self-determining immediacy to become its immanent self, which is why Hegel describes such a "loss of self" as the supreme freedom and assurance of spirit's self-knowledge. Already in an earlier chapter of the *Phänomenologie* Hegel provides us with an idea of how we are to understand the indwelling of speculative science in natural consciousness and the concomitant return to the world of sense. He says that, "If [consciousness] knew that *reason* is equally the essence of things and of consciousness itself, and that it is only in consciousness that reason can be present in its own proper shape, it would go down into the depths of its own being, and seek reason there rather than in things. If it did find it there, it would be directed to the actual world outside again, in order to behold therein reason's sensuous expression, but at the same time to take it essentially as concept".[77] Following upon the public appropriation of speculative science, self-knowing spirit returns to the certainty of immediacy and, as Hegel says, beholds in the actual world reason's sensuous expression.

Consequently when Hegel says in the next paragraph that self-knowing spirit's externalization of the form of the concept in speculative science is still incomplete, that spirit has not thereby won its complete freedom, he is suggesting that spirit must equally be open and directed toward the contingent world of sense. Self-knowing spirit knows not only itself as the accomplished speculative system, it knows the negative of itself, the world of contingency, and thus must supersede the system and sacrifice itself to the process of its becoming spirit in the form of *free, contingent happening*.[78] We may say that spirit properly wins its complete freedom not through a purportedly final, presented system but through the mediation of this self-knowledge present at hand with spirit's own free contingent happening; speculative science is thus a watershed or a transition into a new era, the recollected truth of a previous age summoned up and offered to that spirit which is never at rest but always engaged in moving forward. In the Preface to the *Phänomenologie* Hegel describes well the manner in which speculative science is the foundation for and mediated with this new era. "But this new world is no more a complete actuality than is a new-born child; it is essential to bear this in mind. It comes on the scene for the first time in its immediacy or its concept. Just as little as a building is finished when its foundation has been laid, so little is the achieved concept of the whole the whole itself".[79]

Spirit knowing itself as speculative science must supersede and sacrifice itself to contingent happening, to the immediate becoming of its natural existence which ever reinstates the individual subject, and to the self-mediated becoming of its historical existence which is spirit emptied into time. In his description of spirit becoming through time, Hegel provides us with a view of spirit as always this externalization of itself, the mediation of its self with the wealth of its substance, and finally the withdrawal into itself and its self-transformation into a new world and a new existence.[80] The new existence of spirit is, of course, mediated with that transformation wrought by speculative presentation, and, to the extent that the recollection of earlier spirit is the inner being of this new existence, spirit's new existence starts afresh on a higher level. What we appear to have, then, within historical becoming, are successive realms of spirit each built on those preceding it and linked to the others through the timely close of philosophy, − a close which both recollects the past and anticipates the future. Hegel says that the goal of these successive realms is the revelation of the depth of spirit and this is a goal which is accomplished in the absolute concept and self-knowing spirit, or, in other words, within absolute knowing itself.[81] Here we are invited to see the *Phänomenologie* in a new light, as not only an introduction or ladder to speculative science, but also as one of those moments which preserves and comprehends the wealth of previous spiritual existence and transforms it into a new existence and a new world, as self-knowing spirit open toward and freely projected into contingent happening. With this placing of absolute knowing within the context of the on-going tumultuous occurrence of absolute spirit, we may suggest that speculative science has at last come down from the mountain to live among men, and that its indwelling in consciousness is at least imminent.

3.2 *A phenomenology of presentation*

The Preface, completed after the chapter on absolute knowing, reviews in a general way the central theme of Hegel's appearing science, – the relation of natural consciousness to scientific cognition.[82] Hegel is convinced that natural consciousness "needs" the system as the completion of its educational history, and through the appropriation of the system it can overcome the current divisions in its spiritual life. But these divisions result from the onesided determinations of the understanding, so that an appropriation of the system without presupposition is itself problematic. Natural consciousness as understanding gets fixated on the antithesis of truth and falsity and tends to either accept or reject a given philosophical system rather than comprehending the diversity of philosophical systems as the progressive unfolding of truth.[83] The elucidation of the necessity of this progress linking natural consciousness and the system is the aim of the presentation of the path of phenomenal knowing.

The aim of this path, as it sets out in the *Phänomenologie*, is to educate natural consciousness up to the level of absolute knowing, where it would know the system of philosophical sciences, the *Enzyklopädie*, as the presentation of its universal self. However, as the word "education" indicates, this result is nothing more than the self-conscious appropriation of the implicit content of its educational history. Hegel says, "For the thing itself (die Sache selbst) is not exhausted in its *aim*, but in its *realization*, nor is the *result* the *actual* whole, but rather the result together with its becoming".[84] The presentation of the system in its actuality simply raises to self-certain truth the content of phenomenal knowing as it first appears for natural consciousness.

Speculative science arrives on the scene for this consciousness in the form of a *Phänomenologie* for two essential reasons. As has already been pointed out, the path of phenomenal knowing is an appearing science because the absolute content of the system is presented at the level of contemporary natural consciousness, in order to raise that consciousness to universal selfhood. But the presentation of the *Phänomenologie* is potentially efficacious toward this end because it makes explicit the absolute determinations of all possible knowing by natural consciousness. Furthermore, science is the recollection of the "complete" externalizations of the universal self and appears at the end of a spiritual epoch: the educational history of natural consciousness is "ripe" for science.

Hegel explains the need for the system from the standpoints of both contemporary natural consciousness and spirit. He asserts that, "The inner necessity that knowing should be science lies in its nature, and only the systematic presentation (Darstellung) of philosophy itself is its satisfactory explanation. But the *external* necessity, so far as it is grasped in a general way, setting aside accidental matters of person and motivation, is the same as the *inner*, that is, in the shape in which time sets forth the existence of its moments".[85] To show that the elevation of philosophy to science is in time, Hegel concludes, would be the justification and accomplishing of the aim that philosophy be actual knowing.

Through systematic presentation natural consciousness grasps its implicit essence, and through this same presentation spirit, too, grasps its essence as concept. Indeed, a presentation of the moments of spirit according to their concept would be identical to their self-conscious appropriation, and hence science itself. Such a presentation of the moments of spirit "in time" is none other than the path of phenomenal knowing, which is an appearing science, – but this presentation demands the prior knowledge of the system of absolute determinations. Consequently, although science is implicitly "for" natural consciousness, and for this consciousness in the salutary form as its educational history (i.e., the *Phänomenologie*), science must first exist for spirit and for the phenomenologist as the presented system. The path of phenomenal knowing is a looking back by the universal self from the standpoint of science on its ideal spiritual development with the new comprehension of self-consciousness.[86]

This looking back intends to demonstrate the necessary truth of the system for natural consciousness, that natural consciousness needs the system if it is to grasp its essence. At present, there is division and strife in spiritual life between the consciousness of absolute content in-itself, and a self-consciousness for-itself that is locked in an insubstantial reflection of itself into itself. But Hegel points out that natural consciousness is aware of this conflict and of the need for a solution arising out of it. He says, "Spirit has not only lost its essential life; it is also conscious of this loss and of the finitude that is its own content".[87] The difficulty lies in the fact that, in renouncing its former wickedness, natural consciousness now demands not so much knowledge of what it is, as the lost sense or feeling of solid and substantial being, i.e., edification rather than insight.

This division is an absolute division, since its supersession leads to a new spiritual realm. But mere edification cannot bring about this transition, indeed it is a symptom of the problem. The unification (Vereinigung) that is still lacking is the simple unity of the concept,[88] the self-conscious mediation of spiritual moments according to the systematic whole. It is the whole which, from out of its temporal succession and spatial extension, has returned into itself, and is the resultant simple concept of the whole, i.e., the system.[89] This new self-conscious recollection, the "sunburst which in one flash illuminates the features of the new world",[90] is first presented for natural consciousness at the level of its understanding.

If science is to be intelligible to this consciousness, and not the esoteric possession of a few individuals, the distinctions of its presentation must be securely defined and stand arrayed in their fixed relations. Hegel says that, "Only what is completely determined is at once exoteric, comprehensible, and capable of being learned and appropriated by all. The intelligible form of science is the way open and equally accessible to everyone, and consciousness as it approaches science justly demands that it be able to attain to rational knowledge through the understanding; for the understanding is thought, the pure "I" as such; and what is intelligible is what is already familiar and common to science and the unscientific consciousness alike, enabling this immediate to enter into the domain of science".[91] As we see in this passage, the truth of the presented system for contemporary consciousness turns on whether the phenomenologist has properly discerned the structure of its knowing and its contemporary educational needs, a discernment that succeeds or fails with the ability of the *Phänomenologie* to first raise that natural consciousness to the comprehension of its essential determinations.

Of course natural consciousness must be able to recognize itself in the presentation of the system, and this, it seems, is the crucial question for a philosophic presentation which represents itself as an exoteric knowing. Hegel says that pure self-cognition in absolute otherness is the ground of science and knowledge in general,[92] for without it all presentation would be spurious. It is this recognition that is necessary if the knowing subject is to enter into and become the immanent self of the system of absolute determinations.

The presented system is the matrix of the self-knowledge of spirit, the essential structure of the actual. Science therefore requires natural consciousness to have been raised to this element of pure self-knowing, for the beginning of philosophy makes the presupposition or requirement that consciousness *dwell* in this element. On its side, the individual has the right to demand that science provide him with the ladder to this standpoint, should show him this standpoint within himself. Hegel says that this element of self-knowledge achieves its perfection and transparency through the movement of its becoming, and in the *Phänomenologie*, which is this ladder and this movement, consciousness becomes a thinking which has its being in spirit alone.[93]

The thinking which has its being in spirit alone knows the presented system as its self in otherness. But this is not the case in the beginning, for a natural consciousness which knows objects in their antithesis to itself is for science the antithesis of its own standpoint. And conversely, the element of science is for consciousness a remote beyond in which it no longer possesses itself.[94] The conflict for the natural consciousness which is to begin science is one between its inherent principle of self-consciousness and the apparent "loss of self" demanded by all scientific cognition, – a loss of self which natural consciousness does experience on the path of phenomenal knowing.

The solution lies in this notion of the "ladder", a ladder which will clearly demonstrate to consciousness that the presented system is in fact an extension of the principle of self-consciousness. Hegel declares that, "Science must therefore unite this element of self-certainty with itself, or rather show *that* and *how* this element belongs to it". The *Phänomenologie* sets out to do just this, seeking to elucidate for natural consciousness the manner in which the system is a presentation by the universal self, and is, consequently, the evidence of an absolute self-consciousness. But the failure of this justification of the system by the *Phänomenologie* as a presentation by the knowing subject would have grave effects for the exoteric intelligibility of science. Hegel concludes, "So long as science lacks this *actual* dimension, it is only the content as the *in-itself*, the aim that is as yet still something *inward*, not yet spirit, but only spiritual substance".[95]

Thus the potential self-recognition of natural consciousness in the system turns very much on the ability of the ladder or path of phenomenal knowing to offer itself immediately as the true realization of the essence of consciousness. And once it has done this, this same path must demonstrate that the true realization of the essence of the universal self is the presentation of the system, since it is only through the "act" of presentation as an absolute externalization that the content is "for" the immanent self. A lack of success in convincing natural consciousness at either of these transition-points would mean that the absolute content in-itself presented by the system had failed to become the content of a universal self for-itself, i.e., that natural consciousness had not recognized its essence therein, and that the system would become the inward, esoteric possession of a few individuals.

But Hegel argues that natural consciousness already has the standpoint of speculative science implicitly within it, and these transition-points simply depend on making this implicit an explicit, self-consciousness actuality. The particular individual is incomplete spirit, a concrete shape in whose whole existence one determinateness predominates, the others being at hand only in blurred outline.[96] However the other determinations are nonetheless "at hand", spirit is present to the individual as its substance. Hegel says, "This past existence is the already acquired property of universal spirit which constitutes the substance of the individual, and hence appears externally to him as his inorganic nature. In this respect formative education, regarded from the side of the individual, consists in his acquiring what thus lies at hand, devouring his inorganic nature, and taking possession of it for himself".[97]

Through the education of the presented path of phenomenal knowing natural consciousness becomes self-conscious of the full range of its absolute determination, its inorganic nature, and similarly spiritual substance too acquires self-consciousness and reflection into itself. In other words, science does not offer a special, esoteric knowledge of the absolute, but an exoteric knowledge for everyone that is already "present at hand". The standpoint of science is within each natural consciousness because the absolute is "in and for itself already close to us of its own will",[98] — the word *science* itself signifies a knowing that is self-certain of this absolute presence.

The self-certainty of the absolute content derives from and is dependent upon the self's recollection of its determinations through their systematic presentation. The educational history of natural consciousness has shown that it cannot overcome the divisions in its spiritual life without the response of philosophic presentation, and it is only by means of this presentation that a recollection of its inorganic nature can take place. This suggests, furthermore, that spiritual events which have their fortuitous happening in history already contain the inherent possibility of their re-presentation and recollection in textual configurations. Hegel claims that, "Science presents this educational movement in all its detail and necessity, presenting in its configuration (Gestaltung) what has already been reduced to a moment and property of spirit".[99] Without this presupposition as to the efficacy of the presentation of spirit as a series of configurations, the self-certainty of knowing spirit would be impossible.

The natural consciousness which traverses these moments of spirit at this point in its educational history appropriates a content whose immediacy has already been superseded, whose embodied shape has already been reduced to simple thought-determinations. This content is no longer existence in the form of being-in-itself, but is rather the *recollected* in-itself, ready for conversion into the form of being-for-itself. Hegel says that he is taking up this educational movement of spirit when the supersession of existence is no longer necessary, but what is lacking is the representation and acquaintance of its forms. The acquired spiritual property of contemporary natural consciousness still has the character of uncomprehended immediacy, such that existence has merely passed over into figurative representation. In the same way, the acquaintance of consciousness with these representations is merely a passing interest.[100]

What is presently needed is a genuine knowing of these spiritual forms which would be directed against this mere representation and acquaintance, a knowing which is the activity of the universal self and the interest of thinking. But how does this knowing first achieve the self-certainty of its universal self — a self-certainty which must be prior to the re-presentation of the configurations of phenomenal knowing according to the concept?

Speaking of the *Phänomenologie*, Hegel says, "a presentation (Darstellung) of this kind constitutes the *first* part of science, because the existence of spirit *qua* primary is nothing but the immediate or beginning, but not yet its return into itself. The *element of immediate existence* is therefore the determinateness which differentiates this part of science from the others".[101] Certainly, this presentation of existing spirit according to its proper forms "appears" as the first part of science for natural consciousness, a natural consciousness unable as yet to supersede the figurative representation of its educational history. However the phenomenologist presents this part from the standpoint of self-certain science, with the acquired knowledge of the determinations of the system, so that the path of phenomenal knowing is for him, rather, a looking back.[102]

This means that the knowing subject first recollects the externalizations of its universal self through the essentially esoteric philosophic presentation of the system for himself. This knowledge is then used in the exoteric presentation of the universal self for natural consciousness in the *Phänomenologie*. But what is missing in both of these presentations is the self-consciousness of presentation itself as the salutary element in which the absolute achieves both its "final" externalization and its "timeless" recollection.

Science knows the acts of the universal self, and is an act of this universal self, only through the act of presentation. Indeed the existential result of the path of phenomenal knowing is nothing other than the instigation of the act to *present*, an instigation which accounts for the appearance of speculative science in the first place. In other words, the return of the concept into itself must be presented according to Hegel, and it is only a speculative presentation which is the "existential" return of this essence into itself.[103]

If this is the case, then it is extremely important that we understand how philosophic presentation exhaustively supersedes the life of spirit in time and space, that is, how presentation is the true result of spirit's process. A study of the path of phenomenal knowing is, perhaps, not the best locus for such questions, since it already presupposes the salutary effect of presentation. Rather, we should turn to the various texts which show the system in its different stages of realization, in order to understand the problems involved in spirit's self-supersession as speculative philosophy. We might call this path of investigation a "phenomenology" of presentation.

Naturally the horizons of such an investigation are much wider than can be embraced within the limited scope of this study. We shall content ourselves with a summary examination of a part of the completed system — the philosophy of spirit — which we hope will clarify the manner in which Hegel's comprehension of spirit presupposes at every stage the technical necessities of its eventual textual presentation. The nature of the finality of the exoteric knowledge which science offers to natural consciousness depends to a large extent on the ability of its presentation to account for itself as the essential structure of the actual.[104]

Appendix

Appearing science	*System*
I-III consciousness	objective logic
IV self-consciousness	subjective logic
V reason	
— the certainty and truth of reason	the idea
— observation of nature	philosophy of nature
— observation of self-consciousness	subjective spirit
VI spirit	objective spirit
VII religion	absolute spirit
VIII absolute knowing	

NOTES

1 Heidegger concludes that we can know the absolute at all only because the absolute "lets itself" be presented. "In keeping with its absoluteness, the Absolute is with us of its own accord. In its will to be with us, the Absolute is being present. In itself, thus bringing itself forward, the Absolute is for itself. For the sake of the will of the *parousia* alone, the presentation of knowledge as a phenomenon is necessary". *Hegel's Concept of Experience*, ed. J. Gray (Harper & Row, New York, 1970) p. 48.

2 These are issues not foreign to biblical exegesis, and as we shall see, the relation of belief by a knowing subject to a text presented "for" it poses similar problems.

3 *Enz.* Einleitung # 17, p. 50 (22). Let is be noted here that the word "science" is the traditional English translation of the word *Wissenschaft*. Consequently no reference to natural science is intended. Hegel's use of the word carries with it the suggestion that speculative science, as certain knowledge, supersedes philosophy, or the mere love of knowledge.

4 *Ph. G.* Einl., p. 74 (56).

5 *Wiss. d. Logik* I, p. 30 (49).

6 *Enz.* Vorbegriff # 25 R., p. 59 (45).

7 The following interpretation seeks to reconcile O. Pöggeler's argument in "Qu'est-ce que la Phénoménologie de l'Esprit?" *Achives de Philosophie*, avril–juin (1966), p. 226f., that the *Phän.* is an appearing of the system and W. Marx's argument in *Hegel's Phenomenology of Spirit* trans. P. Heath (Harper & Row, New York, 1975), p. 87, that it is an appearing, of the absolute, through an understanding of the relation between absolute knowing and presentation.

8 *Enz.* # 437 R., p. 354 (III 75). Page numbers listed in parentheses citing the English translation of the section on subjective spirit from the *Enzyklopädie* refer to the Petry translation. Cf. Bibliography.

9 *Enz.* # 437 Zusatz (III 75). "What we have called in the previous paragraph universal self-consciousness, that is in its truth the concept of Reason, the concept as it exists not merely as the logical Idea, but as the Idea has developed into self-consciousness. For, as we know from logic, the Idea consists in the unity of subjectivity or the concept, and objectivity".

10 For a sketch of the correspondence of sections see the Appendix to this chapter.

11 Notably the theory of Th. Haering and his "disciples" Hoffmeister and Hyppolite. However Hyppolite admits that, "C'est comme une exigence interne qui pousse la raison individuelle à devenir un monde pour soi-même comme esprit, et l'esprit à se découvrir comme esprit pour soi dans la religion. La méthode de la *prise de conscience* qui a dominé tout le développement de la conscience s'étend à tous les phénomènes de l'esprit, et la *Phénoménologie de la conscience individuelle* devient nécessairement la *Phénoménologie de l'esprit en général*". *Genèse et Structure de la Phénoménologie de l'Esprit de Hegel* (Aubier, Ed. Montaigne, Paris, 1946), p. 58.

12 Because Hyppolite does not understand the importance of the initial presentation of the absolute content "for" consciousness, he claims, "Que Hegel ait pu présenter tout son

système sous la forme d'une *Phénoménologie de l'esprit* — traitant aussi bien du développe-ment de la conscience individuelle, que du savoir de la nature, du développement de l'esprit objectif aussi bien que de la religion — avant d'atteindre le savoir absolu, cela paraît bien indi-quer qu'il y a une certaine ambiguïté dans l'interprétation de l'hégélianisme". *Ibid.*, p. 59. Labarrière, on the other hand, correctly points out that, "Il ne faudra pas oublier cette signification essentielle du terme de "Système" ou de "Science", qui s'applique déjà au mouvement de la *Phénoménologie* comme telle, en essayant d'éclairer les relations qu'elle en-tretient avec les oeuvres postérieures: il n'y a en vérité qu'un seul déploiement de l'Esprit, même s'il se donne à connaître, ici et là, sous les modalités différentes". *Structures et mouve-ment dialectique dans la phénoménologie de l'Esprit de Hegel* (Aubier, Ed. Montaigne, Paris, 1968), p. 248.

13 *Enz.* # 573, p. 451 (302).

14 O. Pöggeler lays to rest once and for all the theories of Haering in his "Qu'est-ce que ..." *op. cit.*, p. 206ff., but introduces a new theory which emphasizes a shift in focus and plan (from that of a science of experience to a phenomenology of spirit) while Hegel was writing. Pöggeler centres on the chapter on Reason as the turning point in this shift: "Dans la science de l'expérience, un chapitre sur la réalisation de la raison a-t-il été prévu dès le début, cela demeure douteux. Cependant ce chapitre est au fond exigé par ce plan tel que Hegel l'ex-pose dans l'Introduction". *Op cit.*, p. 226. However W. Marx' remarkable "immanent analysis" of the Introduction and the Preface in his *Hegel's Phenomenology of Spirit, op. cit.*, has recently provided the most convincing account of the thematic unity of the *Phänomeno-logie.*

15 *Ph. G.* Einl., p. 66 (48).

16 *Ph. G.* Einl., p. 66 (49).

17 *Ph. G.* Einl., p. 66 (49). Let it be noted that it is the presentation of natural conscious-ness as phenomenal knowing that presses forward, and not natural consciousness in its for-tuitous happening in history.

18 *Ph. G.* Einl., p. 67 (49).

19 *Ph. G.* Einl., p. 67 (50).

20 *Ph. G.* Einl., p. 68 (50).

21 *Ph. G.* Einl., p. 68 (51).

22 *Ph. G.* Einl., p. 69 (51).

23 *Ph. G.* Einl., p. 70 (52).

24 W. Marx points out that, if the presentation of appearing science is to achieve its goal, then "the contemporary natural consciousness, which is not yet "scientific" in the sense of the system in prospect, must be convinced of the fact that science alone is capable of bringing the principle of self-consciousness — on which the unscientific consciousness is also already dependent — to fulfillment in a manner appropriate to the subject". *Op. cit.*, p. 22.

25 *Ph. G.* Einl., p. 70 (52).

26 *Ph. G.* Einl., p. 71 (53).

27 *Ph. G.* Einl., p. 73 (55).

28 *Ph. G.* Einl., p. 73 (55).

29 *Ph. G.* Einl., p. 74 (56).

30 Science appears "for" natural consciousness as its truth, because in-and-for-itself science is the presented system of the thought determinations of the "self". As W. Marx says, there is certainly no "boundary" between thinking and this presentation, because thinking itself is the "accomplishing" of the thought determinations, through their dialectical un-folding in the internally ordered system. *Op. cit.*, p. 11. But, although there is no boundary, there is certainly a "difference" which must be constantly superseded through the salutary *act* of presentation.

31 *Ph. G.* IV, p. 134 (104).

32 *Ph. G.* IV, p. 139 (109). My emphasis.

33 *Ph. G.* IV, p. 143 (113).
34 *Ph. G.* IV, p. 146 (116).
35 *Ph. G.* IV, p. 148 (117).
36 *Ph. G.* IV, p. 148 (118).
37 *Ph. G.* IV, p. 149 (118).
38 *Ph. G.* IV, p. 149 (118). Labour is clearly a mode of absolute self-externalization, and as such it is an antecedent form of philosophic presentation. However Lukacs goes on to suggest that labour remains the model for Hegel's concept of teleology as it is first set out in the *Logik*, with the consequence that there is an implicit tension within the entire system between the true ontological origins of the thought-determinations in labour and the purely logical development of the whole. Lukacs states that, "On the one hand [Hegel] discovers labour as the principle which expresses the genuine form of teleology, the positing and actual realization of the end by a conscious subject; on the other hand this genuine ontological category is structured into the homogeneous medium of a system dominated by logical principles, and according to this system we are still at a stage that has not yet produced life, man and society. For according to the logical principles of development of the identical subject – object, life can only take shape at the stage of the Idea, while the function of teleology here is precisely the logical and systematic one of effecting the transition from the stage of the notion to that of the Idea. In this way the logical hierarchy leads to the absurd situation of developing the categories of labour before life has come into being in the logico-ontological sequence". *Hegel's False and His Genuine Ontology* trans. D. Fernbach (Merlin Press, London, 1978), p. 53. Of course this tension dissolves if, on the contrary, we maintain that philosophic presentation is the absolute presupposition for all forms of labour and therefore fully supersedes the latter.
39 The absolute negativity arising out of being-toward-death makes it necessary for consciousness to traverse the *entire* system of the shapes of phenomenal knowing.
40 *Ph. G.* I, p. 82 (60).
41 *Ph. G.* V, p. 229 (187). Unfortunately Hegel does not elaborate on what it means to leave the products of language and labour to the mercy of something other, but the loss of labour and speech in a commodity which is "other" suggests a reprise of the discussion of alienation in the *Realphilosophie I*.
42 *Ph. G.* VI, p. 362 (308).
43 *Ph. G.* VI, p. 458 (395).
44 *Ph. G.* VI, p. 458 (395).
45 *Ph. G.* I, 88 (66).
46 *Ph. G.* V, p. 256 (212).
47 *Ph. G.* V, p. 257 (213).
48 This "ideal" description of labour within the context of a nation contains no mention of the alienation of the labourer from nature and from his society that is so striking in the *Realphilosophie I*. There Hegel admits that the connection between a particular kind of labour and the infinite mass of needs in the society is impossible to foresee, leaving the worker in a blind dependence which often renders superfluous and useless the labour of an entire class of men. This is far from the happy reciprocity described in the *Phänomenologie*. However some of these themes return in muted form in the final system.
49 In the *Realphilosophie I* Hegel describes this "whole" which is produced by the community of labourers as money, – the material concept, existing, the form of unity for, or the possibility of, all the needed things. The implication is that if the labourers beheld the movement of capital as their universal object, they would attain a self-consciousness of their position. In the *Phänomenologie* this universal substance is simply "reason", thus superseding its determination as capital, and opening up the possibility that a philosophic presentation, not an economics, may become the true object of the labourer.
50 *Ph. G.* V, p. 258 (213).
51 *Ph. G.* V, p. 258 (214).

52 *Ph. G.* VI, p. 316 (265).

53 *Ph. G.* VI, p. 316 (265).

54 Marcuse justly remarks, "The state alone can provide emancipation, though it cannot provide *perfect* truth and *perfect* freedom. These last are to be found only in the proper realm of mind, in morality, religion, and philosophy. We have already encountered this sphere as the realization of truth and freedom in Hegel's first Philosophy of Mind [*Realphilosophie I*]. There, however, they were founded on an adequate state order and remained in an intrinsic connection with it. This connection is all but lost in the *Phenomenology of Mind*. The state ceases now to have an all-embracing significance. Freedom and reason are made activities of the pure mind and do not require a definite social and political order as a pre-condition, but are compatible with the already existing state". *Reason and Revolution* (Beacon Press, Boston, 1960), p. 91f.

55 This is Lukacs' assessment: "The chapter of Morality (Spirit certain of itself) represents, then, Hegel's utopian vision of a Napoleonic Germany. It is noteworthy how lacking in content this chapter is compared to the preceding ones. Essentially it rehearses in systematic form the Jena critique of the moral theories of Kant, Fichte, and Jacobi ... In his earlier analysis of their position he had appealed to the ethical nature of society as an antidote to the abstract dogmas of subjective idealism in its various forms. Thus he had convincingly refuted Jacobi by pointing to the harmony between individual morality and the ethics of society that had obtained in Greece. However this avenue no longer remained open to him in the context of the *Phänomenologie*, since he would have to demonstrate this harmony in the case of a society where no such harmony existed as yet". *The Young Hegel*, trans. R. Livingstone (MIT Press, Cambridge, 1975), p. 503.

56 *Ph. G.* VIII, p. 549 (479). This statement is in direct contradiction to Lukacs' view that "Hegel's attempt to reintegrate 'externalized' reality takes the form of the abolition of the objective world. The greater one's understanding of the world, in Hegel's view, the more pronounced this tendency becomes". *The Young Hegel, op. cit.*, p. 513. Objectivity must retain a certain "alien" independence if the self is to behold itself in a presentation which is other. Lukacs is really following the classical Marxian interpretation in this regard: "But it is equally clear that a *self-consciousness*, that is, its externalization, can only establish *thinghood*, that is, only an abstract thing, a thing of abstraction and no *actual* thing. It is further clear that thinghood thus completely lacks *independence, essentiality*, over and against self-consciousness but is a mere artifice *established* by self-consciousness. And what is established, instead of confirming itself, is only a confirmation of the act of establishing which for a moment, but only a moment, fixes its energy as product and *apparently* gives it the role of an independent, actual nature". From the "Economic and Philosophic Manuscripts of 1844" in *Writings of the Young Marx on Philosophy and Society*, ed. L. Easton and K. Guddat (Anchor Books, New York, 1974), p. 324f.

57 *Ph. G.* VIII, p. 550 (480).

58 *Ph. G.* VI, p. 462 (399). "It lacks the power to externalize itself, the power to make itself into a thing, and to endure being. It lives in dread (Angst) of besmirching the splendour of its inner being by action and an existence; and in order to preserve the purity of its heart, it flees from contact with actuality, and persists in its self-willed powerlessness to renounce its self which is reduced to the extreme of ultimate abstraction, and to give itself a substantial existence, or to transform its thought into being and put its trust in the absolute difference".

59 *Ph. G.* VIII, p. 554 (484).

60 *Ph. G.* VIII, p. 554f. (484). To know the good is not necessarily to do the good. The self that "falls away" from presentation adds a new twist to this fallacy.

61 *Ph. G.* VIII, p. 555 (485).

62 *Ph. G.* VIII, p. 556 (485).

63 Fackenheim outlines one of the problems for the ladder theory: "A radical gap, after all, remains between the standpoint of absolute thought and even those standpoints of life

which are closest to it. Why ... should the standpoint of moral self-activity grasp the ladder to the scientific standpoint when, having done so, it finds its certainty of what is forever yet to be done point to a truth which is already done? Why ... should a faith humanly receptive to the Divine grasp this ladder when this requires no less a presumption than the rise in thought to divine Selfhood?" *The Religious Dimension in Hegel's Thought* (Beacon Press, Boston, 1967), p. 70. Hegel is convinced, inspite of these problems, that spiritual life feels a *need* for philosophic presentation at certain moments in its educational history.

64 *Ph. G.* VIII, p. 556 (485).

65 *Ph. G.* VIII, p. 557 (486).

66 *Ph. G.* VIII, p. 557 (486).

67 *Ph. G.* VIII, p. 558 (487). The comprehension of philosophic science as a "timeless" present is one of the most difficult concepts in the *Phänomenologie*. Lukacs suggests that this timelessness is socio-historically conditioned and is meant to coincide with the Germany of the Napoleonic and post-Napoleonic period. It follows that, "The enthusiasm of one of his closest disciples, Eduard Gans, for the July revolution, began the dissolution of Hegelianism". Indeed Gans' enthusiasm is significant as long as we concur with Lukacs that, "The chapter that concludes the historical development proper (which is followed by the mental recapitulation of the whole in "re-collection") is a description of how the French revolution and its Napoleonic sequel were transformed into spirit on German soil. It is this problem that gives rise to the ideal historic coincidence, unification and self-attainment of the Idea ..." *Hegel's False and His Genuine Ontology, op. cit.*, p. 15f. However the timelessness of presentation is no less related to the exigencies of philosophic response as such to a given epoch.

68 *Ph. G.* VIII, p. 558 (487).

69 *Ph. G.* VIII, p. 559 (488).

70 *Ph. G.* VIII, p. 559 (488). The paragraph beginning, "Die Bewegung ...".

71 *Ph. G.* VIII, p. 561 (490).

72 *Ph. G.* VIII, p. 561f. (490).

73 *Ph. G.* VIII, p. 562 (491).

74 *Ph. G.* VIII, p. 562 (491).

75 Werner Marx sees just such an outline of the tripartite system at the end of the *Phänomenologie*, but in a slightly modified form. We find here envisaged a logic, a philosophy of nature, and, instead of a philosophy of spirit, a conceived history. It remains, however, that Hegel refers to none of these texts *per se*, exept the "conceived history", in the paragraphs under discussion. *Op. cit.*, p. 60.

76 *Ph. G.* VIII, p. 563 (491).

77 *Ph. G.* V, p. 184 (146).

78 *Ph. G.* VIII, p. 563 (492). We are suggesting here that absolute knowing is no finished or completed thing, but carries with it the imperative to realize the concept within all reality, – the task of liberty itself. P. – J. Labarrière most perceptively describes this task, which is the essence of absolute knowing, in the following: "Qu'est-ce donc que la vie de liberté? L'assomption intégrale des conditions de l'homme – temps aussi bien que logique, extension autant que profondeur – dans l'acte qui les rassemble et leur donne sens. Ce qui implique deux choses: 1) un laisser advenir ce qui advient – c'est l'aspect d'histoire événementielle et contingente; 2) une parole risquée qui tente de rassembler ces éléments disjoints – c'est l'aspect de la saisie conceptuelle, toujours à remettre sur le métier". *Introduction à une lecture de la Phénoménologie de l'esprit* (Aubier, Ed. Montaigne, Paris, 1979), p. 270.

79 *Ph. G.* Vorrede, p. 16 (7).

80 *Ph. G.* VIII, p. 563f. (492).

81 *Ph. G.* VIII, p. 564 (492f.). Hyppolite wrongly identifies this absolute knowing, described by Hegel as comprehended history, with a philosophy of world history: "La suite de ces esprits qui se succèdent dans le temps est *l'histoire*; sous l'aspect de leur organisation conceptuelle elle est la science du savoir phénoménal (*la Phénoménologie*). L'unité de ces deux

aspects, que Hegel distingue donc de la *Phénoménologie* proprement dite, donne une philosophie de l'histoire: l'histoire conçue . . ." *Op. cit.*, p. 583. But what Hegel is describing here are the two sides, historical spirit and the science of phenomenology, which together make the phenomenology of spirit. Hegel is simply re-presenting the *Phänomenologie* not as it appears to natural consciousness this time but as it may be understood from the standpoint of the free contingent happening of absolute spirit.

82 Thus the Preface merely amplifies problems first discussed in the Introduction, pointing to the essential thematic unity of the work as a whole.

83 *Ph. G.* Vorr., p. 10 (2).

84 *Ph. G.* Vorr., p. 11 (2).

85 *Ph. G.* Vorr., p. 12 (3).

86 A variant of this position is held by S. Rosen, who emphasizes the presupposition of the Logic, rather than the entire system, to any presentation of phenomenal knowing. Rosen believes the standpoint of science was first achieved through a study of the history of philosophy, making the *Logik* the last step in a necessary historical process. In the *Phänomenologie*, Hegel "seems to have forgotten that only his individual presence, as one who has already taken the upward journey and has now descended to assist his lost fellow creatures, provides the necessary mediation between time and eternity. The ladder to the Absolute is not historical necessity, or even the negation of the negation, but the spirit of the philosopher". *G.W.F. Hegel* (Yale University Press, New Haven, 1974), p. 129.

87 *Ph. G.* Vorr., p. 13 (4).

88 *Ph. G.* VIII, p. 553 (483).

89 *Ph. G.* Vorr., p. 16 (7). But while science comprehends its educational history, comprehension does not supersede all action; presentation is itself an act of spirit, indeed, the "highest" act. Cf. A. Koyré in "Hegel à Iéna" from *Etudes d'histoire de la pensée philosophique* (Armand Colin, Paris, 1961), p. 141, n. 5.

90 *Ph. G.* Vorr., p. 16 (7).

91 *Ph. G.* Vorr., p. 17 (7).

92 *Ph. G.* Vorr., p. 24 (14).

93 *Ph. G.* Vorr., p. 24f. (14).

94 *Ph. G.* Vorr., p. 25 (15).

95 *Ph. G.* Vorr., p. 25f. (15).

96 *Ph. G.* Vorr., p. 26 (16).

97 *Ph. G.* Vorr., p. 27 (16). Self-knowledge, then, is not the result of a deduction of psychological faculties, but a phenomenology of self-externalizations. The self "is" what it "does".

98 *Ph. G.* Einl., p. 64 (47).

99 *Ph. G.* Vorr., p. 27 (17).

100 *Ph. G.* Vorr., p. 28 (17).

101 *Ph. G.* Vorr., p. 31 (20).

102 W. Marx has justly observed this paradoxical position of the *Phänomenologie*: "We said that the *Phänomenologie* is an "appearance" of the absolute, which reduces itself to this order to be able to meet the shapes of illusion, of untrue knowledge, on their own level, and to persuade them in so doing that the principle of true knowledge is already implicit in them. If the absolute spirit posits itself in this fashion through its own "decree", this implies that it has already attained itself through actual history, and now, in order to make itself perspicuous to the still fettered natural consciousness, has "released itself" to this appearance", *op. cit.*, p. 91.

103 *Ph. G.* Vorr., p. 53 (39).

104 Hegel himself seems to have pinned the success of this accounting on the decision of natural consciousness conceived as a "public": "We must hold to the conviction that it is the nature of truth to prevail when its time has come, and that it appears only when this time has come, and therefore never appears prematurely, nor finds a public not ripe to receive it; also

we must accept that the individual needs that this should be so in order to verify what is as yet a matter for himself alone, and to experience the conviction, which in the first place belongs only to a particular individual, as something universally held''. *Ph. G.* Vorr., p. 58 (44).

II. SPIRIT AND PRESENTATION

1. REPRESENTATION WITHIN THE SUBJECTIVE MODE

1.1 *The concept of presentation*

Precisely how we are to understand the deployment and movement of moments within the *Enzyklopädie* is a question which receives no clear answer from Hegel's writings themselves. Nowhere does he offer us a "method of presentation" delineated as such, and at the end of the system we are simply told that the concept of philosophy is the logical, but with the signification that it is universality certified in concrete content as in its actuality.[1] Of course the manner in which we conceive the logical as certified in concrete content and as a spiritual result can take on different nuances, depending on whether we view the logical as abstracted from concrete spiritual life or as the absolute *prius* of spirit in general. It is this nuance which leads us, correspondingly, to seek a mechanism of presentation valid for the deployment of moments within the system as a whole either within the speculative analysis of spiritual externalization and recollection or within the pure element of the logical concept.

Some recent research, in fact, has suggested that we are to find such a mechanism of presentation good for the entire system within Hegel's *Wissenschaft der Logik*, and particularly in that section devoted to the Doctrine of Essence. P. – J. Labarrière and G. Jarczyk suggest in the "Présentation" to their new translation of the Doctrine of Essence that such an original mechanism of absolute self-presentation is to be found in the movement of reflection, in which is expressed the ontological structure of everything that is, in its negative universality.[2] If this mechanism exists, then of course they are justified in describing the reflection-moment as a "fundamental referential structure" and a "fundamental rhythmic cell", since this mechanism would go a long way in explaining not only the deployment of moments within the *Logik*, but would greatly clarify the systematic structure peculiar to the *Enzyklopädie* as a whole. Our immediate task, then, is to try to understand the role of reflection within Hegel's *Wissenschaft der Logik*, and what implications this role may have for the nature of presentation within the system itself.

Limiting our discussion now to the greater *Logik*, why is it, then, that we are to find the original structure of presentation in the Doctrine of Essence, and more precisely in the first chapter describing positing reflection, external reflection, and determining reflection, rather than, for example, in the first chapter of the Subjective Logic describing the universal, particular and individual concept? The response to this question rests largely in the position of essence as the middle and mediating term in the logical syllogism of being-esence-concept, so that the movement of reflection which mediates externality with recollection and interiorization supersedes the simply external transition or "going-over" characteristic of being. In other words, essence determines the deployment of the first part of the *Logik* (Quality, Quantity, and Measure), in its role as the timeless past or background (Hintergrund) of being under its logical universality. Hegel says that, "Not until knowing *inwardizes, recollects* itself out of immediate being, does it through this mediation find essence. The German language has preserved essence in the past participle (gewesen) of the verb *to be* (sein); for essence is past — but timelessly past — being".[3]

The movement of reflection negates and mediates the immediate determinations and transitions of being, through the recollection that these determinations are in fact *posited*. Such a "recollection" is possible in the first instance because, as the negation of being, essence is being for-itself, i.e., simply negative self-relation, and must differentiate the determinations which are implicit in it. The process of differentiation and determining remains within this self-relation and is neither a becoming nor a transition, and although the determinations are in a sense self-subsistent, they are not "other" because they remain associated within the unity of being-for-itself. While essence is at first simple negativity, through the movement of reflection it is subsequently led to posit the determinateness that is implicit in it, in order to give itself determinate being.

Of course this entire process of positing and recollection hinges on the fact that the negativity of essence is reflection, whereby the determinations are reflected, posited by essence itself, and remain in essence as superseded.[4] It is by means of this movement of reflection that essence gives itself a determinate being that is equal to its being-in-itself, — the "posited" immediacy of the concept. However it is not our intention at this time to work through the dialectic of position and recollection by which essence attains actuality, but rather to understand the mechanism of reflection itself, through which essence "presents" those determinations that are already present at hand.

In the Doctrine of Essence we see that the discussion of reflection follows immediately on those sections with which this second book of the *Logik* begins, the "Essential and the Unessential" in Illusory Being. This is significant because Hegel identifies Illusory Being with the description of appearance attained by scepticism and Kantian idealism, and we may infer from this allusion that if we are to go beyond critical philosophy then we must understand the manner in which appearance becomes actual, i.e., we must understand the mechanism of reflection.[5] The study of this mechanism then leads directly on to the determinations of reflection, − identity, difference, and contradiction, − by which we comprehend the categories and their dialectical self-movement at work within all reality. Therefore it is through the explication of the mechanism of reflection that we are taken from the unknowable thing-in-itelf of Kant to the posited thing of Hegel, and contributes not a little to our understanding of how the actual is rational.

The movement of reflection is the negating of negation and is consequently self-relation, since the negation is present in such wise that it has its being in its negatedness, as illusory being. The becoming of essence, then, unlike that of being which is relation to other, is the movement of nothing to nothing and so back to itself. In essence it is rather the negating of nothing that constitutes being, and this pure absolute reflection that is this movement determines itself further as positing, external, and determining reflection.

However in the discussion of positing reflection we learn that the immediacy of illusory being itself is not the "starting point", since its immediacy *is* only as the return of the negative into itself, and is, therefore, a self-superseding immediacy or positedness. As Hegel says, "Accordingly, the return of essence is its self-repulsion. In other words, reflection-into-self is essentially the presupposing of that from which it is the return".[6] This presupposition of an immediacy from which reflection returns is in truth a positing because this immediacy only comes to be through being left behind and superseded. Presupposing reflection is positing reflection and *vice versa*, and it is *reflection* because the superseding is at the same time a coincidence with itself, − i.e., the positedness is an immediacy that is not distinct from the return-to-self and is itself only this movement of return.

The transition to external reflection comes about when we understand this positedness as immediately opposed to something, to an "other", whereby reflection is determinate. And as determinate, reflection has a presupposition, starts from the immediate as its other, and is external. But this time the immediacy which reflection presupposes is itself as superseded, so that it is related to itself as to its non-being. We may say that the immediacy which external reflection presupposes is not only positedness but self-relation as such, with the consequence that the determinations posited by external reflection in the immediate are to that extent external to the latter.

Of course external reflection is also a positing of the immediate and the supersession of this positing in so far as it presupposes the immediate. And the supersession of the immediate is equally a positing because the immediate from which external reflection seemed to start as something alien *is* only in this supersession. Hegel concludes that, "In this way, the immediate is not only *in itself* — that means, for us, or in external reflection — *identical* with reflection, but this identicalness is *posited*".[7] Thus the externality of reflection is superseded and its positing is the union of itself with the immediate, so that this union is now the immediacy of essence, — essence in and for itself.

When the self-relation of reflection is freely for-itself it is determining reflection, that is, the unity of positing and external reflection. Positing reflection starts from nothing, it has no presupposition, and positedness as such is not yet a determination of reflection since it is only determinateness as negation in general. But external reflection starts from immediate being and is in unity with this positing, with the result that this kind of reflection is a presupposing which posits the determinateness as determinateness of itself. Hegel states the matter concisely when he says that positedness as such is negation, — but as presupposed, it is reflected into itself and so a determination of reflection.[8] In contrast with the sphere of being where negation as quality is simply affirmative, the determination of reflection persists not through being but through its equality with itself.

Determining reflection accordingly effects a reconciliation of the two aspects of positing and reflection-into-self, through which determining reflection is reflection that has come forth from itself. Or, as Hegel says, "In so far, as it is the positedness that is at the same time reflection-into-self, the determinateness of reflection is *the relation to its otherness within itself*".[9] Thus the process of presentation is "closed" through reflection taking its otherness back into itself and superseding its positedness within an infinite self-relation. But this does not mean that the independence of the other is totally dissolved, for within this relation-to-self the posited determination abides by having brought into subjection its transitoriness and mere positedness. If essence, as infinite return-to-self, is to be a movement through *distinct* moments and absolute self-mediation, then the discrete character of its self-externalizations must persist through the supersession and recollection of the return.

Having briefly sketched out the mechanism of reflection as we find it described in the Doctrine of Essence, let us now return to our original question, – as to whether we can see in reflection a "referential structure" basic to the mode of presentation in the *Logik* as a whole. Certainly there is some indication that it is only in essence that we comprehend determinate being as posited being or positedness, and that there is a general correlation between the determinations within the sphere of being and the movement of reflection. However the suggestion that reflection equally structures the deployment of Subjective Logic is somewhat more problematic. While the immediacy of being is shown in essence to be mediated by the movement of reflection, is it not also true that "the new immediacy which has become characteristic of the concept, particularly in the transition to Objectivity, equally supersedes and puts by this mediation within a higher, more inclusive configuration? Indeed Hegel remarks that, "*objectivity* is the immediacy to which the Concept determines itself by the supersession of its abstraction and mediation".[10]

If in this return to an immediacy that has become the mediation of essence is superseded, then we must assume, too, that the mechanism of reflection is also somehow superseded. But this in itself need not diminish the claim that reflection is a referential structure: The immediacy of being is equally superseded by the mediation of essence and yet this immediacy abides within essence in the form of existence, actuality, and substantiality, not to mention "posited immediacy" generally. The new immediacy of Objectivity within the Subjective Logic is no less "posited" and hence presupposes the return – to – self explicated by the mechanism of reflection, through which all externality is recollected as self-externalization. Reflection explains the manner by which essence mediates being and concept, and while the logical progressions from being to essence and essence to concept are important transition-points, it is nonetheless reflection which holds the whole together within the *single* mediating process. In terms of the binary structure of the *Logik*, we might say that the reconciliation of the subject – object brought about by the mechanism of reflection, and existing as an immediacy that has become, is under an objective determination, so that it simply remains for this reconciliation to be realized within the realm of subjectivity, – indicating a shift in focus rather than a change in the process.

In any case the transition from an immediacy to an immediacy "become" can only be understood by means of some kind of mediation, and it is only in essence, and especially in the movement of reflection, that we understand the dynamics of this mediation in its logical universality. But if we accept that reflection is a referential structure for the greater *Logik*, then, certainly, we must extend this claim to take in the entire system,[11] and with this broadening of the discussion new problems arise in the attempt to isolate a universal mode of presentation. First and foremost there is the total absence of any description of positing, external, and determining reflection within the smaller Logic of the *Enzyklopädie*, which is a strange fate for a referential structure.[12] Hegel now explains the determinations of being not through the deployment or "positing" characteristic of the movement of reflection, but through the one concept which is "the underlying principle (das Substantielle) of all":[13] this would seem to suggest that the structural parallels within the determinations of being and essence are less the result of a mechanism of reflection than the *immanent* movement of the concept.[14]

While the Logic of the system states that essence includes the categories of metaphysic and the sciences in general, it does not provide us a mechanism or fundamental structure by which these categories are posited: instead, it asserts that they are the products of reflective understanding.[15] Thus in place of an explanation of the dynamic of externalization and recollection in its logical universality, we are referred to a moment of consciousness within subjective spirit, a moment anterior to, and superseded by, reason. Certainly there is at least implicit in this reference the suggestion that the manner by which the *categories of science* are posited is best studied within the realm of spirit, and, in particular, within the sciences of phenomenology and psychology. Indeed, the movement of reflection is given the greatest attention within the system as it is manifest in consciousness, which is described by Hegel as constituting the stage of reflection for spirit.[16]

Again, when reflection *is* dealt with more extensively within the Logic of the system, such as in the "Precise Concept and Division of Logic", it comes into poor comparison with the movement of the dialectic. Hegel says that, "Reflection is at first the going out beyond the isolated determinateness and a reference to it, whereby this determinateness is posited in relation and, at the same time, left its isolated worth. Dialectic, on the other hand, is the immanent going out, where the onesidedness and limitation of the determinations of understanding are presented as they are, that is, as their own negation. Everything finite is this, the supersession of itself".[17] In terms of the scheme outlined in the larger *Logik*, the reflection described by Hegel above seems to be more exactly "external" reflection, for the aspect of positive presentation (Darstellung) associated with "determining" reflection is here aligned totally with the dialectic, and in contrast with reflection in general. It should also be remarked that within this passage from the system we find a new distinction between the *positing* of reflective understanding and the *presenting* of dialectical reason, which may indicate that the positing of reflection as we have discussed it was no longer considered to be the model or referential structure for presentation by the later Hegel of the *Enzyklopädie*.

All in all, there is some evidence to suggest that the mechanism of reflection is important, even essential, to our understanding of the mode of presentation in the *Logik*, but that, in addition, this importance seems to have diminished greatly within the system. Presentation in the latter is not related to any one referential structure, – rather, it achieves clarity and determinateness with each successive configuration as the immanent process of the whole, and which attains its highest definition in the presentation special to philosophy. If this is the case, i.e., that there is no *single* referential structure of presentation good for the entire system, then it would appear that an interpretive approach consisting of a "phenomenology" of all possible structures of presentation demands our attention. This does not mean that we cannot use the mechanism of reflection as a model for reference in examining the presentation characteristic, for instance, of spirit, but that we must be circumspect in claiming for it universal applicability.

However there is a second implication to be derived from our investigation of the mechanism of reflection within the *Enzyklopädie*. The Doctrine of Essence in the lesser Logic not only gives short shrift to the mechanism of reflection, in its place it refers us to the derivation of categories within reflective understanding. In fact it is within the chapter dealing with consciousness in the Philosophy of Spirit that we find the most extensive discussion of reflection, so that, apparently, if we are to understand the origination of the categories of science and their presentation then we must examine first and foremost the spiritual mode of self-presentation peculiar to labour. The mode of presentation that we find in labour is, of course, itself deficient and does not adequately explain the deployment of moments within the system since labour is included and superseded within the higher moments of language creation and philosophic presentation. Indeed, if there is no fundamental referential structure within the lesser Logic, and if reflection itself is regarded as a lower spiritual moment within the system, then it would seem that such a structure of presentation would better be identified with philosophic presentation itself, as that moment which closes absolute self-manifestation and is the presupposition for all prior, even logical, configurations. This identification brings with it two suggestions for further research, first that we interpret the presentation described by reflection in the greater *Logik* from the standpoint of the necessities special to philosophic presentation, and second that we examine the adequacy of language as that element within which the presented certification of the logical occurs. It is, of course, to the latter requirement that much of our attention in the rest of this chapter will turn, and we trust that such an *a priori* reading of the structures of spirit will offer new insights into Hegel's proposed philosophical supersession of non-philosophic life.

How, then, are we to understand the concept of presentation within the life of spirit? Hegel suggests that, in a sense, the act of *philosophic* presentation is the definitive encounter of absolute spirit with itself. By the word "encounter" we mean that spirit only attains self-knowledge through self-presentation in externality, − an externality which is then beheld by spirit as its own. But philosophic presentation is not only the "final" moment of absolute externalization and return to self, the moment which terminates absolute manifestation within the existential modes of nature and spirit. Philosophic presentation is equally the ultimate configuration in the educational history of spirit in and for itself, and is consequently the truth of the finite representations of subjective consciousness and the objective formations of intersubjectivity.

This philosophic supersession of non-philosophic life is possible at all because, quite simply, spirit is not liable to diverse forms of construction. In other words, spirit is not a localized universal which is the product of isolated and particular inter-subjective relations; for example, the formation processes indicative of labour and language are not irreducibly separate activities which lead to different regions of human expression and knowledge. Spirit is present to itself through different *modes* that form a necessary, logical advance in its self-knowledge and that culminates in a knowledge of itself as absolutely present at hand. And absolute self-manifestation is itself complete when spiritual self-knowledge is identical with this knowledge of the absolute that is already "close to us". Accordingly, it is the intention of the following brief summary of the major thought-determinations of the *Philosophie des Geistes* to demonstrate the manner in which philosophic presentation, as the highest mode of absolute self-manifestation, supersedes all modes of spiritual presentation and knowledge as such. To put it in a slightly different way, we are seeking to understand the sense in which all spiritual activity presupposes the needs of an absolute return to self in philosophic presentation, with the consequence that this presentation is absolutely self-verifying and self-certain.

How, then, are we to understand this concept of spirit? Hegel says that "for us" at the level of science, who comprehend spirit as a mode of the absolute, spirit has nature for its presupposition, of which it is the truth, and thus its absolute *prius*.[18] In this truth nature is vanished and spirit has itself resulted as the idea being for-itself, of which the concept is just as much object as subject.[19] The concept which was alienated in the external otherness of nature now has itself for its object, and is a self-knowing that moves in the direction of a presentation-to-self in which the idea is fully for-itself. This growing into identity is fulfilled in philosophic presentation, where the knowing subject has its true self in objectivity, and this subject goes over to the presentation in order to become its immanent self. But as long as the subject beholds itself in objectivity as a sensuous other, then the certainty of self in truth will always contain an element of belief.

As a return out of the otherness of nature, the concept of spirit is absolute negativity. According to Hegel this means that the concept in its development as spirit is essentially freedom, and can abstract itself from its existence, negate its individual immediacy, and maintain itself as the identity with being-for-itself in otherness.[20] These are the determinations necessary if the concept is to "go over" to a presentation. Of course all of this is possible if we think of the concept as an implicit, abstract universality existing for-itself, a universality which particularizes itself while remaining in identity with itself. As spirit, universality presents itself within the concrete mode of existence, with the corollary that the determinateness of spirit is the *manifestation* of universality. What Hegel is saying here is that universality, which is the essence or true self of the concept, does not have an externality which is differentiated from itself — it does not reveal something — but that the determinateness and the content of universality is this revealing itself.[21] Therefore philosophic presentation, which is the highest and most determinate mode of universal manifestation, is not the approximate or apparent rendering of the absolute by a knowing subject: it is the self-manifestation of the absolute itself, absolute actuality.[22]

But we must remember that the universality which develops and determines itself as the concept of spirit is first the "truth" of nature. As spirit is free, its revealing is to posit nature as its world, but because this spirit is also reflection, the positing equally presupposes the world as independent nature. Thus revealing in the concept of spirit is the creation of a world as its Being, in which it gives itself the affirmation and truth of its freedom.[23] The "world of spirit" is a world which is both implicit in the determinations of nature and free from the necessity of nature, because spirit is reflection and has itself as an "other" for its object.

This process by which the concept of spirit recollects an "other" as in truth an externalization of itself reaches its culmination in philosophic presentation, when the concept recollects and supersedes all spiritual manifestations and knows them as its universal self. The presentation of the system is consequently the final creation of a world in which the concept gives itself the affirmation and truth of its freedom, but because this creating within the mode of presentation also presupposes and supersedes the independence of nature, an aspect of the sensuous other continues to attach to the text. This explains the sense in which absolute knowing is a "going over" to the presentation, in order to become its immanent self, and a "belief" in the witness of spirit as the certainty of objective truth.

Naturally this knowledge that the truth of subjective consciousness is spirit, and that spirit is a self-presenting universal or absolute, is a knowledge which is "for us" already at the level of science. In terms of the scheme of the *Phänomenologie*, the concept of spirit presupposes that contemporary natural consciousness has traversed the path of phenomenal knowing and raised itself to the truth that spirit is implicit in the very structure of consciousness. Hegel argues that, "consciousness must have related itself to the object in accordance with the totality of the latter's determinations and have thus grasped it from the standpoint of each of them. This totality of its determinations establishes the object as an *implicitly* spiritual being, and it does truly become a spiritual being for consciousness when each of its individual determinations is grasped as a determination of the self, or through the spiritual relationship to them that was just mentioned".[24] But that the *Phänomenologie* can be such a "ladder" to the scientific standpoint implies that consciousness is understood by the phenomenologist as a moment within the system of absolute determinations, and that consciousness is already mediated by spirit.

Where, then, does the phenomenologist's insight that the absolute is spirit originate? In a Remark attached to the last paragraph of that part of the Introduction entitled "Begriff des Geistes", Hegel asserts that this definition of the absolute was the tendency of all education (Bildung) and philosophy, the point to which all religion and science moved, and is the impulse by which to comprehend world history. In other words, the concept of spirit as a self-presenting universal is implicit in the determinations of the educational history of natural consciousness as such, although this does not fully explain how the scientist has managed to make sense of these particular "tendencies". The answer lies in Hegel's admission that the word and representation of spirit is first found in the content of Christian religion, where God is cognized as spirit. As we shall see later, representations are concrete pictorial images which have not been raised to the conceptual determinations of pure thought, so that in Christian religion spirit is a *given* representation and only the essence in-itself.[25] It is thus the task of philosophy to lay hold of this essence in its proper element, the concept, with the result that the particular determinations of spirit are understood as absolutely mediated and essentially systematic.

Religion provides the key by which the whole of spiritual life is comprehended, but the development of the concept, and its mode of presentation,
is implicit in the very structure of knowing itself. Just as spirit is a series of
configurations which display relative moments of externalization (Entäußerung) and recollection (Erinnerung), so, too, the absolute presents itself
to itself in order to attain knowledge of itself and actuality: the concept is the
direct manifestation, indeed the mode of existence, of this universality. Spirit
in its self-developing ideality is cognitive spirit, and when spirit cognizes the
absolute ground of its determinations in the presented system, it can equally
be said that the absolute is fully manifest for-itself. This is the sense in which
we must always consider philosophic presentation in the *Philosophie des
Geistes*, – as both the culmination of spiritual cognition and the "final"
self-manifestation of absolute spirit. And it is a sense which is implicit in
Hegel's preliminary dissertation on the concept of spirit.

We must hasten to add that this development of spiritual cognition set out
in the system is not to be confused with the education and instruction of individual subjects as such, whereby the universal spirit is brought to exist
within them.[26] Is this not the role of the *Phänomenologie* as an appearing
science? Rather, the philosophic notion of spirit considers spirit to be self-
educating and self-instructing in its concept, and its externalizations as the
moments of bringing itself to itself and closing with itself, by which it is actual
spirit.[27] The work which lies before us is to perceive in these moments the
presupposition of a mechanism of presentation and self-verification which
reaches its full expansion in philosophic presentation.

1.2 *The universality of soul*

The philosophic science of the soul, anthropology, comprehends spirit as the
absolute *prius* of nature, and we may say that the soul, as a moment of spirit,
intuits the spiritual determinations implicit in nature, and is accordingly a
spiritual self-knowing. Anthropology is thus the science of spiritual self-
knowing under its natural mode, and is distinguished from the philosophy of
nature to the extent that in nature spirit is still self-alienated in an unreflective
other. The soul is the region of the self-knowing of spirit as nature, and as
a self-knowing, it is an implicit act of reflection which has the determinate
significance of a free judgment: spirit, in the shape of soul, presupposes itself
in its concretion and totality as a simple universality.[28]

Through this judgment, soul is the universal immaterialism of nature, the
substance and the absolute grounding of all the particularizing and indivi-

dualizing of spirit.[29] Furthermore, the structure of self-knowing, the beholding and recollection of the self in a presented externality, is already implicit in the structure of soul itself: the soul is first, as existing, natural soul, an immediate natural determinateness; as individual, the soul enters into relation with this its immediate being, and is in this determinateness abstractly for-itself, or feeling soul; lastly, its corporeity is mouled into it, and soul is actual.[30]

Since spirit is the absolute *prius* of nature, we may say that, when the feeling soul enters into relation with its natural determinateness as an external other, soul is actually entering into relation with the content of its implicitly spiritual self and raising that content to the form for-itself. This is not unlike the relation of the subject to presentation, where the subject beholds his absolute content in an external other, and goes over to it to become its immanent self. In both cases, actuality results as the supersession of this differentiation between absolute content and form, an actuality which is the self-presentation of the absolute in-*and*-for-itself. For the *feeling* soul, its absolute determinations are already present at hand in the immediate determinateness of *natural* soul.

It is for this reason, when speaking of sensation (Empfindung) as the highest moment of natural soul, that Hegel says "*Everything is in sensation*: and if you will, everything that emerges in spiritual consciousness and in reason has its *source* and *origin* (Ursprung) in sensation; for source and origin means nothing other than the first immediate manner in which something appears".[31] In the sensation of natural soul, the determinations of the absolute already appear, just as these same determinations appear later as objectivity for consciousness. The universal soul is a universal *substance* which has its actual truth as individuality, so that when it presents itself as individual, it is so as existing soul.[32]

In other words, subjectivity comes into consideration here only as an individualizing of the natural determinations.[33] Therefore spirit as soul is not a universal intersubjectivity arising out of constructive social interaction, but is the absolute returning out of nature and beholding itself therein; soul is not subject to *diverse* forms of construction. It is the absolute in the process of particularizing itself, and as this process, the absolute supersedes its discrete moments as stages within a *single* logical development.

The absolute is immediately present at hand in sensation: sensation is the "finding" of the content-determinateness of the soul's sleeping nature.[34] Sensation is the form of the dull stirring of spirit in its unconscious and unintelligent individuality, in which every determination is still immediate because its content is not developed as an object posited over against a subject. The content of sensation is therefore limited and transient, belonging as it does to the soul's natural immediate being, to what is thus qualitative and finite.[35] At the level of sensation, the natural content and the form of the self are still confounded, although their higher determinations are already implicit. The sentient soul finds within itself the naturally immediate as ideally in it and made its own, and conversely, what is originally of being-for-self (which as further developed is the "I" of consciousness and free spirit) is determined as belonging to natural corporeity and so is sensed.[36]

In sensation, then, the modes of recollection and externalization can been seen in shadowy outline, though still as part of the natural immediacy of existing soul. Hegel suggests that, properly speaking, the mode of sensation in natural soul should designate only the side of passivity and finding, the immediacy of determinations in feeling, because the being-for-self mentioned above is not merely a formal moment of sensation. The soul as implicitly a *reflected* totality of sensation is feeling soul: the feeling individual is the simple ideality or subjectivity of sensation.[37] It follows that the transition from natural soul to feeling soul is marked by a distancing of the self from its natural content which enables that self to appropriate this content as its own.

This distancing, this movement of negation, is what makes the soul a reflected totality and implicitly self-knowing spirit, and with this scission we have formally left the immediate externality of nature behind. Hegel says, "The soul as feeling is no longer a mere natural, but an inward individuality; this individuality which in the substantial totality was first only a formal *being-for-self* is to be made independent and free".[38] And what determines the soul as independent and free is its ideality, or the negation of a real which is preserved and superseded. In this its ideality the soul is the existing concept in the form of an indeterminate mine of determinate sensations and the posited totality of its particular world. But what is most interesting in this relation between being-for-self and the mass of determinations which we may call the soul's inorganic nature, is that it is only when the "I" itself *recollects* a representation that the "I" brings these determinations out of this inner into existence for consciousness.[39] Similarly, it is only a presentation of phenomenal knowing which brings the inorganic nature of contemporary natural consciousness before consciousness, so that it may behold there the absolute determinations implicit in its educational history.

But what precisely is the mechanism by which the soul "mediates" the mass of feeling and thereby liberates itself from the immediate demands of the wholly particular sensation? Hegel asserts, "This self-formation of the particular or corporeal feeling-determinations into the *being* of the soul appears as a *repetition* (Wiederholung) of them, and the generation of habit as *practice* (Ubung)".[40] This "being" of the soul which is created by habit as practice is a reflexive universality, whereby the external many of sensation is reduced to its unity, and *is* this abstract unity as *posited*. Although there is no question of "presenting" the determinations of sensation to the self in order to be consciously mastered, there is nonetheless an intimation of the salutary effect of a *repetition* of the onesided determinations of the particular if the self is to take possession of its inorganic nature: a "practice" which receives its full realization in presentation itself. In the rather long Remark which follows paragraph # 410, Hegel points out that habit as it is developed and practiced in the spiritual realm is recollection (Erinnerung) and memory (Gedächtnis),[41] which tends to confirm this depiction of the practice of habit as an anthropological precursor to the practice of speculative presentation. Through both of these practices, the absolute appearing in sensation is appropriated by the self.

The antecedent moments of natural soul and feeling soul are superseded by actual soul, where the formation process of habit makes corporeity its own and the soul is an individual subject for-itself. The soul is for-itself because the determinate mass of sensation is appropriated as the posited externality of corporeity and made a predicate of the soul, so that the subject is only in relation with itself. This externality, which is formed by habit, thus represents not itself but the soul, of which it is the sign.[42] Again, it is not yet a sign that is presented to *consciousness*, for it has the significance at the level of the soul of indicating the identity of the inner and the outer, with the latter subject to the former. However it is clear that Hegel considers the formation of corporeity into a sign as an important moment within the self-presentation of absolute spirit. The soul has in corporeity its free *Gestalt*, in which it feels itself and makes itself felt, and which as the soul's work of art has human expression.[43] While this externalization and recollection of subjective spirit as a corporeal sign is still within the mode of human feeling, we see in actual soul the mechanism of presentation which will be developed later on.

For the soul existing for-itself, this mechanism appears as a distinguishing of its immediate being from itself, and a positing of the latter over against itself as a corporeity unable to withstand the soul's formation process. We must remember, though, that this immediate being, which is distinguished and appropriated, is originally the determinateness of sensation, in which the absolute is first present at hand as nature. This means that, with the supersession of this distinction, the soul is no longer immediate spirit, and furthermore, that this appropriation is equally a self-appropriation by absolute spirit. Hegel says, "The actual soul, in the habit of sensation and its concrete self feeling, is in-itself and for-itself existing *ideality* of its determinateness, and in its externality *recollects* itself and is in infinite self-relation".[44] This being-for-self of free universality is the awakening of the soul to an "I", which as thinking and subject, has the natural totality of its determinations as an object, as a world external to it. And to the extent that this "I" is related to this object, and in it is immediately reflected into itself, this "I" is consciousness.

1.3 *Individual consciousness and its truth*

Hegel describes consciousness as the reflected or appearing stage of spirit, where the immediate identity of natural soul is raised to a purely ideal self-identity. But that the "I" can become conscious of itself through this absolute negativity toward its independent object means that it is in-itself the identity with this being-other and, indeed, is itself the object.[45] The self-consciousness of this identity, attained through the consciousness of self in externalization, implies a self-appropriation of consciousness as spirit and a transition to a higher configuration of the presentation. The difficulty with this transition from consciousness to spirit in the system lies in the fact that it was the *Phänomenologie* itself, as a path of phenomenal knowing, which was supposed to have brought about this self-appropriation within the educational history of natural consciousness. How, then, are we to view this shorter phenomenology which is already a part of the system, and thus can have no such aspirations as an introduction?

First we must emphasize again that the presentation of the determinations of the system for consciousness in the *Phänomenologie* presupposes the comprehension of consciousness as a moment of subjective spirit, described in the system, if the *Phänomenologie* is to raise consciousness to its self-consciousness as spirit. In other words, the knowledge of the absolute determinations of the system makes possible the salutary effect of an introductory *Phänomenology*. But it is only in the shorter phenomenology of the system that we fully understand the pure structure of consciousness in terms of the self-presentation of the absolute, i.e., as a necessary moment leading from soul to spirit. We are not dealing here with an historical development of the structures of subjectivity, but with the structures which are implicit in every subject: contemporary natural consciousness is always implicitly spirit, and is explicitly so through the appropriation of the system.

That Hegel still considers this explicit recognition of spirit to have contemporary import for the educational history of natural consciousness is revealed in the Remark to paragraph # 415 of the section concerning consciousness in the system, where he says that, "The Kantian philosophy may be most determinately considered as having perceived spirit as consciousness, and as containing only the determinations of a phenomenology, not a philosophy, of spirit".[46] And even through Kantian thought touches upon the idea of spirit, this idea is reduced to an appearance, to subjective maxim. It is only through speculative science that contemporary natural consciousness fully apprehends itself as spirit. The manner in which the *transition* from the appearance of the idea in subjective cognition to its actuality within the absolute presentation of the system comes about will be taken up again in a discussion of the three syllogisms in the next chapter.

At this stage within the development of subjective spirit, the identity of spirit with itself is subjective reflection-within-itself. In fact consciousness is just this relationship generally, which involves the contradiction between the independence of the two sides and the identity in which this independence is superseded.[47] As we saw in the previous chapter, it is only when consciousness recollects its externalization as itself that it is raised to the concept of spirit. And yet it would seem that such an exhaustive recollection must take place largely through the appropriation of an "external" and "appearing" speculative presentation designed *for* consciousness by science. At the level of consciousness itself, the "I" for-itself is still only a formal identity, and so the dialectical movement of the concept is seen to be not the activity of this "I", but is in-itself and for consciousness the alteration of the object.

At the end of the *Phänomenologie* we understand this experience of the alteration of objectivity as that which primarily constitutes the time experience for natural consciousness. There Hegel says that spirit in time "is the *outer*, intuited pure self which is not grasped by the self, the merely intuited concept; when this latter grasps itself it sets aside its time-form, comprehends this intuiting, and is a comprehended and comprehending intuiting".[49] Consciousness in a sense suffers time through the *partial* beholding (as through a glass darkly) of the alteration of objectivity, without fully recognizing its own determinations within objectivity. In the shorter phenomenology Hegel goes on to say that it is the *logical*, progressive determination of objects that is the identical in subject and object,[50] hence we can assume that once this logical determination is fully grasped by the self – and this means that this logic must first be fully *presented* – then the time experience is superseded. Yet even the *Logik* itself seems to be at least partially in the grip of a time-experience, at least until "determining reflection" in the chapter on Essence. In other words, time is not completely superseded at the end of the *Phänomenologie* since it is in the Doctrine of Being of the *Logik* that we find the time-experience of consciousness externalized or posited, and thus it is only with the chapter on Essence (the timeless "past" of Being), which describes the mechanism of presentation, that time is fully superseded.

The presupposition here is that consciousness is somehow impelled to grasp its essence as spirit, that the transition from consciousness to spirit is somehow guaranteed through absolute self-presentation. And in fact Hegel says that the goal of spirit as consciousness is to make its appearance identical with its essence, to raise the certainty of itself to truth.[51] What impells consciousness to do so is the truth "for us" that consciousness is simply a moment within the presentation of absolute spirit to itself, and if it is so impelled, it is impelled largely by the on-going logical determination of the concept. Of course this necessity is self-evident in the system alone.

At present, the object is only abstractly determined for consciousness as its own, and in the object, consciousness is as an abstract "I" reflected in itself, so that its existence still has a content which is not yet its own. This content will become its own through a mode of externalization in which consciousness can recognize its full, absolute determination: there is a very real sense in which the deficiency in the appropriation of its essence by consciousness is at bottom a deficiency in presentation, as the development of consciousness gradually makes clear. This development follows the triadic form used in the discussion of the soul, and is broken down under the headings of consciousness as such, self-consciousness, and reason. As the highest moment of consciousness as such, the understanding appropriates the object as an appearance, while the object's reflection-in-itself is taken to be a for-itself existing inner and universal. But the object of the understanding is always, at least implicitly, consciousness itself in its determinateness, and if the understanding is to supersede the onesidedness of its determinations in spiritual life and pass on to reason, it must first come to know that object as a presentation of itself.

What makes this knowledge of the object as itself possible in the first place, is Hegel's contention that self-consciousness is in fact the ground of consciousness, for all consciousness of an other object is also self-consciousness. More precisely, it can be said that I know the object as mine because it is my representation (Vorstellung), and thus in the object I know myself.[52] The facility of this representation, and the success of the concomitant recognition of the self in it, is the basic assumption for the mechanism of presentation as it is developed right up to the complexities of philosophic presentation itself. The abstract self-consciousness which we are discussing here is the first negation of consciousness, and thus it is still burdened with an external object and in a sense is still consciousness.

However Hegel says that consciousness, and negation generally, is implicitly superseded in the "I" = "I" of self-consciousness, and as the certainty of itself over against the object, it is the *impulse* to posit what it is in-itself. Through this positing, self-consciousness gives the abstract knowledge of itself content and objectivity, and, conversely, it frees itself from its sensuousness, and supersedes the given objectivity through positing it as identical with itself.[53] What we see in this process of positing and superseding is an anticipation of the externalization and recollection of self characteristic of free spirit.

But what remains essentially unquestioned in this sketch of the structure of abstract self-consciousness is the origin of this "impulse" to externalize the self in objectivity. Perhaps it is best explained through the description of this process as a microcosm of the spiritual relation of the absolute to its own on-going externalization; abstract self-consciousness is simply one mode of this relation, and at that a deficient one, because it has not grasped itself in externality as a universal. Therefore abstract self-consciousness is not aware of its absolute determination largely due to the fact that it does not yet have the "tools" for such a self-presentation. While the development of these tools will inevitably bring us into the realm of intersubjectivity, the mode of the externalization propitious to a consciousness of self continues to be determined by the needs of absolute self-presentation. To the degree that the object is originally natural sensation, and nature has spirit for its *prius*, the present mode of self-consciousness is equally and always the self-consciousness of the absolute, although in a finite form.

Since, in the previous chapter, we have already discussed at some length the development of the tool and labour from out of the *need* for a recognition of the self in objectivity, and the pursuant life and death struggle, we will take up the dialectic of consciousness at the highest moment of self-consciousness, universal self-consciousness.[54] But let it be noted in passing that through the supersession (Aufhebung) of the immediate "otherness" of an external self-consciousness, into which the self is reflected and seeks its self-recognition, this self supersedes as well the first immediate presentation of self-consciousness in corporeity. Hegel says, "this immediacy is at the same time the corporeity of self-consciousness, in which as in its sign and tool it has its own *self-feeling*, and its being *for others*, and its mediated relation to them".[55] In the slave this immediate expression of self-consciousness in corporeity is suppressed, but expression finds a wider range and more "rational" mode through the externalization of self in labour where the slave works off his individualist self-will, supersedes the inner immediacy of desire, and in this externalization and fear of the lord makes the beginning of wisdom.[56]

Universal self-consciousness displays both the differentiation of the self from its universal content and the implicit supersession of this difference characteristic of reason. Hegel says that universal self-consciousness is the affirmative knowledge of itself in another self, where each self as free individuality has absolute independence: however, by virtue of the negation of its immediacy, each self does not differentiate itself from the other. Self-consciousness is thus universal and objective because it is not the consciousness of a particular or immediate self, but of a presented self which is common to everyone and is the universal and absolute essence of all "selves" as such.

Through this appropriation of its essence, the self is the concept which knows itself in its objectivity as a subjectivity identical with itself and thereby universal, and is the form of the consciousness of substance which is essentially spiritual.[57] It is *spiritual* because subjectivity necessarily differentiates itself from its presented objective essence, while at the same time it must have the ability to "go over" to its essence and become its immanent self. At the level of self-consciousness, the reciprocal recognition of the universal in each self signifies that the differentiation between independent individuals no longer exists, since consciousness and self-consciousness are now explicitly one. The truth issuing from the former differentiation is the in-and-for-itself existing universality and objectivity of self-consciousness, reason.

Reason, then, is the growing into identity of subjective cognition, the for-itself existing concept, and reality in the form of an opposed, external objectivity present at hand.[58] The realization of this identity as reason, the final moment of consciousness, means that the subject comprehends this objectivity as the externalization of its universal self. And yet it is a comprehension which is still in principle, because the determinate modes of externalization must be appropriated according to their absolute necesssity. Subjectivity has superseded its immediate presentation in corporeity through labour on an external thing, but the full range of objectivity has still to account for its absolute determination, and until the idea of reason is certified in concrete content as in its actuality, this idea is not universal. At the moment, that reason which knows itself as the pure "I" that permeates and comprehends objectivity is only implicitly spirit. Reason itself is simply that self-consciousness which is certain that its determinations, as the determinations of the essence of things, are no less objective than are its own thoughts.[59]

Thus the shorter phenomenology of the system, like the larger *Phänomenologie*, ends with the subjective certainty that objectivity presents the determinations of the universal self. But it is a certainty which can be raised to truth only through a *presentation* which displays that objectivity according to its absolute determination. As in the concluding paragraphs and Preface of the *Phänomenologie*, the transition from phenomenology to psychology in the system indicates a shift from the subjective consciousness of the idea in objectivity to the necessities involved in its self-presentation, especially that of language.[60] Psychology, as the science of spirit in its subjective manifestation, comprehends the manner in which the idea knows itself best through linguistic expression, and remedies the deficiencies in our understanding of self-externalization at the level of abstract self-consciousness.

1.4 *Spirit and representation*

Hegel says that spirit has determined *itself* as the truth of soul and consciousness. But it is this truth only because spirit is equally the absolute *prius* of soul and consciousness, as it is of nature in general. Therefore the moment of spirit within the development of subjective spirit is that moment when spirit is self-conscious of its implicit determinations, i.e., it is not limited by having its content for an object. Rather, it is the knowledge of the substantial which is no longer an objective "other", because it is now aware of itself as the other. Consequently, it can be said that spirit begins only with its own being and relates itself to its own determinations.[61] In spirit, the absolute is, at least implicitly, fully present at hand; however it is present only implicitly because, as finite, spirit has determinateness in its knowing and is still subjective or concept.[62] In other words, this knowing does not yet lay hold of the in-and-for-itself being of its reason, and cannot do so before the presentation of the determinations of this being by the system.

Thus the development of spirit is marked by the steps in its appropriation of the being of its reason, and by the steps in the supersession of its immediacy and subjectivity, whereby spirit lays hold of itself and frees itself to itself. As the concrete unity of the "I" with its other, this appropriation of reason has a double aspect: spirit's productions are the determinations of reason, which, in the content, exist in-themselves; to the extent that these productions derive from spirit's freedom, this rational content is also spirit's own. And if we look at spirit in its determinate beginning, we see that it has a double determinateness, – what Hegel calls the *Seienden* and the *Seinigen*, that is, spirit finds within itself something as existing, and posits this something as its own.

Hegel begins his discussion of theoretical spirit by stating that, "intelligence finds itself determined".[63] This is its seeming, from which in its immediacy it goes forth and as knowing posits what is found as its own. Thus the activity of intelligence consists in "finding" reason and in becoming reason for-itself − the activity of cognition − where formal knowing as certainty raises itself to determinate and conceptual knowing. It is in intuition (Anschauung), as the first moment of theoretical spirit, that intelligence finds itself so determined and has the material of its knowing, its abstract immediacy, as feeling.[64] Implicit in feeling is the abstract identical direction of spirit, attention, which Hegel describes as active recollection and the moment of "owness" that is the formal self-determination of intelligence. Over against this inwardness there is also a second moment of intuition which posits the feeling-determinateness as an *existence*, as the abstract being-other of itself, and projects this existence into space and time as the forms for intuition.[65] In sum, intuition properly speaking is that intelligence which is the concrete unity of these two moments, where it is immediately self-recollected in this outer-existing material, and in the recollection of itself is sunk in the out-of-selfness.[66]

But it is the second moment of theoretical spirit, representation (Vorstellung), that is without doubt the most interesting in this development of subjective spirit, and is the most important in our understanding of presentation as a mode of absolute externalization.[67] Within the general scheme of things, representation, as the recollected intuition, is the middle moment between the immediate finding-itself-determined of intelligence and intelligence in its freedom as thought. It is the property of that intelligence which is still onesided subjectivity, a property which is conditioned by immediacy and not in itself a being. And it is precisely this position of representation "between" intuition and thought that permits intelligence to make immediacy an inner, to posit itself in order to intuit itself, and to supersede the subjectivity of inwardness and externalize this inwardness so as to be implicitly in its own externality.

However it is equally because representation begins with the found material of intuition that it is burdened with the difference between intuition and thought, so that its concrete productions are as yet syntheses which are not raised to the immanence of the concept until the stage of thought.[68] It would seem, then, that as long as language is a part of the concrete production of representation, it will never be able to perfectly reflect the movement of the concept in a transparent manner, but must derive its "present" meaning from the on-going determinations and *interest* of thought itself.

In order to better understand this relation of representation to intuition and thought, we will examine more closely its individual moments. Hegel states that intelligence, as it first recollects the intuition, places the content of feeling in its inwardness, in its *own* space and its *own* time. In this way the intuition becomes an image which is freed from its original immediacy, and is appropriated by the universality of the "I", where it no longer has the full determinateness of intuition and so is arbitrary or accidental.[69] Isolated from external place and time, the image is given its time and space by intelligence as attention. It follows that intelligence is not merely a consciousness in which the image simply exists, but as a subject, it is the potentiality of its determinations, a night-like mine in which an infinite world of images is preserved.[70]

If it is to exist, this abstract, preserved image needs an already existing intuition. Thus recollection in the strict sense is this relation of an image to an intuition, whereby the immediate, individual intuition is subsumed under the formally universal, under a representation of the same content. What this means is that the image which was previously only a property in the mine of intelligence, is now truly a possession of the latter through the determination of externality, and is properly distinguished from both the outer intuition and the indeterminate "mine". Through this synthesis of the inner image with the recollected existence, which is characteristic of representation, the inner now has the determination of being able to be represented before intelligence and to have its existence in it.[71]

The second moment of representation, reproductive imagination, is that intelligence which is active in this "possession" of images, and brings forth these images out of the proper inwardness of the "I", — an "I" which is now manifest as the power over them. It has this power to the extent that the reproduced content, belonging as it does to the self-identical unity of intelligence, has a *universal* representation, an implicit concept or idea, as the relation which associates the images.[72] And of course it is because this concept is *latent* that a speculative, philosophic presentation can supersede the representations of non-philosophic life, raising the concept in-itself to its explicit determination within the system.

In this free combining of images by the imagination, intelligence is essentially self-intuiting by means of the appropriation of its inner content in existing images, so that in this unity intelligence has returned implicitly to identical self-relation and to immediacy. This process is essentially one in which the concrete self-intuition of intelligence is so determined as to exist, or, in other words, intelligence makes itself be, and makes itself be a thing (Sache). As such, this intelligence is self-externalizing within the mode of sign-making imagination.[73] It is clear, then, that Hegel regards the making of language by the reproductive imagination to be a mode of externalization, just as the making of the thing in labour is another mode within the same process. In fact Hegel goes so far as to assure us that it "should not seem surprising that intelligence makes itself exist, makes itself a thing, for its import is itself, as is its given determination".[74] This objective thing or intuition does not represent itself but represents something other, for the intuition-as-sign receives an independent representation of intelligence as its soul and meaning: the sign is a pyramid into which an alien soul has been conveyed and preserved.[75]

Therefore the vocal and the written sign, which is simply a sign of the vocal sign, are properly self-externalizations of intelligence to the extent that they engage its active *attention*.

But this combination of representation as an inner, with intuition as an outer, is itself outer or external, and it is only in the *recollection* of this externality that we enter the third moment of representation, memory. Through memory, intelligence makes this combination which is the sign, its own, and in recollection raises the individual combination to a universal or abiding combination, in which the name and meaning are for intelligence objectively united. The name is thus the thing in so far as in the realm of representation it is present at hand, just as the absolute is fully present at hand as an object for consciousness through its self-determination in language generally. Hegel says that, "The name, as the existence of the content of intelligence, is the externality of intelligence to itself, and the recollection of names is equally an externalization within which it posits itself".[76] In this recollection of names, which is itself a mode of self-externalization, the concrete image denoted by the name is superseded, for the name alone is the simple representation of intelligence. It is in names, not concrete images, that we think.

This highest recollection of representations in memory is at the same time the highest externalization of intelligence, where intelligence is the "being" of representations and the universal space of names.[77] But these existences-as-names need an other, the signification of representing intelligence, in order to be a thing and true objectivity. Thus it is in memory that intelligence is for-itself the existence of this posited identity between external objectivity and meaning, – an identity which, as active, is reason in-itself.[78] It follows that memory is the transition into thought when its objectivity is no longer differentiated from the subjective, and its inwardness is in-itself existing. In linguistic representation the opaque resistance of the "thing" is overcome and thought is fully present to itself, or, to express it in the terminology used above, thought is that self-recollection in an "other" which is equally its self-externalization.

However, we have yet to understand the manner in which this double movement of thought provides the basis for the *universality* of its externalization in language. Intelligence at the level of thought (Denken), which is the third and last moment of theoretical spirit, has in the name *its* universal as immediate or existing, i.e., intelligence for-itself cognizes itself, and in this process is in-itself universal. Its product, thought, is a thing, so that according to Hegel, what is thought, is, and what is, only is in so far as it is thought.[79] Of course at this point in the development of spirit, this universality and its being is the simple subjectivity of intelligence, and its thought is not in-and-for-itself determinate because the recollected representations still have a given content.[80]

In the realm of practical spirit the will nominally produces the "objective" satisfaction of its theoretical concept. Hegel declares that spirit as will is the fulfilled being-for-self which forms the side of existence of the reality of spirit's idea, but at this stage the being-fulfilled is only an abstract determinateness or "own-ness", and is not yet identified with developed reason. Rather, it is the determination of the will existing in-itself to bring the freedom of formal will into existence, and the concept of formal will, freedom, essentially is only as thought, with the result that, in order to make itself objective spirit, the way of will is to raise itself to thinking will.[81] Naturally the "thought" Hegel has in mind is that thought which is implicitly through the supersession of its two antecedent moments of intuition and representation, a thought which is actual by means of some form of linguistic presentation.

If the moment of thought dialectically precedes practical spirit, then this universal thinking is seen to be the proper theoretical basis for the ordering of objective reality, for a rational praxis: "True freedom in ethical life (Sittlichkeit) is this, that the will is not subjective or selfish, but has for its aim a universal content; but such content is only thought and through thought".[82] However there remains an ambiguity with regard to thought as a moment prior to practical spirit, because the thrust of Hegel's teaching on will is that will *completes* itself as thinking, which is its aim and universal content.

Consequently, practical spirit, as a formal will *vis-à-vis* an already existing reality, contains what Hegel calls a double "ought". First it is an ought in terms of the opposition between the determinateness posited from out of itself, and the well-tread immediate determinate-being in the guise of its being-there and condition. But more importantly for the above considerations, this first self-determination is itself immediate and is not at once raised into the universality of thinking, so that thinking implicitly constitutes an "ought" for self-determination in point of form, and can constitute it in point of content.[83] We may extend this analysis by suggesting that if will completes itself as a fully *thinking* will, where the content is the self's own act,[84] and spirit's self-externalization is simultaneously its self-recollection, then will completes itself most truly in philosophic presentation. It seems, then, that will realizes the implicit concept rather than being explicitly "directed" by theory, and completes itself in a theory which merely *looks back* on its determination in-itself.

For thinking will, this universal which is its aim and satisfaction is first denoted as happiness, the final moment of practical spirit.[85] However this happiness is still a represented, abstract universality of content which only "ought" to be. Instead, the truth of the self's particular determinateness and volition is the universal determinateness of will in general, i.e., its self-determination or freedom. Thus particular volition *becomes* the pure subjectivity of will in having this infinite determinateness, freedom itself, as its content and aim. And in this truth of its self-determination, where the concept and object are identical, the will is actual, free will.[86] We may say that, while happiness remains the somewhat illusory or "impractical" goal of volition, it is freedom which is the truth of all volition and its absolute determination.

What Hegel calls "thinking will", as the unity of theoretical and practical spirit, is in this way free spirit and the last moment of the psychology of spirit. It is a will which has successfully superseded the limits and contingency of practical content and has its universal determination, freedom, as its object and aim only in so far as it is self-thinking and is aware of this as its concept. In other words, will is free spirit because it is equally free intelligence.[87] This, then, is the realization of the abstract universal represented by happiness: to know yourself as free. But it is a knowledge and not merely a "feeling", and as such demands the acquisition of the tools of representation as an antecedent moment if this knowledge of the universal is to be actual.

The will which has achieved a knowledge of itself through self-externalization and recollection, and has its essence as its aim, is rational will or the idea in-itself, which is still only the concept of absolute spirit.[88] Therefore the idea merely *appears* in this finite will which is simply the being-there of reason: Yet this appearance of the idea is equally its advance and return to itself, since the activity of the will is to develop the idea and to posit its self-unfolding content as existence.[89] And as existing, the idea is actuality and objective spirit in which subjective will realizes its concept of freedom.

However we must emphasize that this concept is not simply an abstract universal or slogan which theoretical spirit has somewhat arbitrarily adduced in modern times, for the whole direction of Hegel's thinking on subjective spirit is to suggest that theoretical spirit merely "uncovers" the concept of freedom through a *reflection* on the will's impulses and acts, which presupposes the use of some kind of representation. Again it is not a question of directing the will according to privileged knowledge or an abstract theory, but of comprehending a determination which is already implicit in will. This interpretation is confirmed in the Remark to paragraph # 482 where Hegel says that,

"When individuals and nations have once laid hold of the absolute concept of for-itself existing freedom in its representation, there is nothing like it in its uncontrollable strength, just because it is the proper essence of spirit and in fact is itself its actuality".[90]

What gives the concept of freedom its virulence is its implicit absolute determination, a determination which is now made explicit by the presented system because, among other things, the system supersedes all previous, partial representations of freedom. Consequently, if the idea of freedom is the actuality of men, not something which they have but something which they are, then the explication of this idea in the *Philosophie des Geistes* is a knowledge of the actuality of men and thus can lay claim to perfect self-knowledge, the concept with which we began. The circle is not quite complete, however, for the concept of freedom is determined to develop itself in objectivity, into legal, ethical, religious, and ultimately philosophic actuality.

As speculative science, the concept of freedom is absolutely satisfied and exhausted in the presentation of the system, wherein it fully knows itself and is fully for-itself. But it is no less essential that the concept realize its content in the objective institutions of the state. For example, there is no ground on which to distinguish between the good and evil impulses of practical spirit within a strictly subjective rendering, since the ordering of the good and rational propensities resolves itself in the presentation (Darstellung) of the relations brought about by spirit itself as self-developing, objective spirit, — a development in which the content of self-determination loses its contingency and willfullness. Significantly, Hegel points out that, "The discussion of the true worth of impulses, inclinations, and passions is thus essentially the *theory* of the legal, moral, and ethical *duties*".[91]

The transition from subjective to objective spirit must be understood as an externalization of universal determinations implicit in subjectivity, so that they now have a universal *existence*.[92] Philosophic presentation itself supersedes this objectivity of spirit to the extent that it, too, lays claim to a universality objectively existing "for" knowing spirit as such. We might go so far as to suggest that institutions, which exist within the mode of language-as-law, are themselves a form of representation in which absolute spirit recollects itself in objective existence. This is an interpretation which would reduce the significance of institutions understood as the product of a pragmatic, formative intersubjectivity, and force us to understand their necessity according to the needs of absolute self-externalization. In other words, objective spirit is a necessary, antecedent moment to the self-appropriation of the absolute in philosophic presentation.[93]

2. REPRESENTATION AND INTERSUBJECTIVITY

2.1 *Law as "objective" representation*

Absolute self-presentation within the objective mode of spirit supersedes the particular externalizations of individual consciousness, in the sense that this objectivity is the true universal self of individual consciousness as such. Of course the antecedent configurations of subjective externalization, such as labour and language, implicitly presupposed their objective validation within the ethical life of the nation: there are no "private languages" according to Hegel. But there is a difference between the objective validation of an absolute manifestation "for" subjectivity, and the creation of an objective structure through the formation-process of intersubjectivity.

What we are suggesting in this respect is that there is a hidden tension between Hegel's interpretation of objective spirit as an intersubjectivity which supersedes the particular externalizations of individual consciousness on the one hand, and his parallel interpretation of objective spirit as the necessary self-manifestation of absolute spirit within the objective mode on the other. Do the objective structures created by intersubjectivity lead to "regional" social universals within diverse and separate domains, or can all of its formation-processes be tied into one mode of presentation according to the *single* logical development of the concept?

In order to understand this tension we must first come to understand the manner in which free spirit realizes its concept in objectivity. Hegel tells us at the beginning that the rationality of objective spirit, as the on-going realization of intelligent will, is inherently finite and retains the aspect of external appearance .[94] This is because free will is confronted with a set of circumstances and random data which is simply "given", much in the same way that sensibility was confronted with the data of sensation. "The free will has at first this immediate difference within itself, that freedom is its inner determination and aim, and is in relation to an external and already subsisting objectivity, which splits up into the anthropological objectivity of private needs, the external things of nature which exist for consciousness, and the ties of relation between individual wills which are conscious of their own diversity and particularity".[95]

The will realizes itself in overcoming this *difference* between its inner idea and its external objectivity. The inner aspect is the pure concept of freedom, and the individual achieves actual freedom in appropriating this objectivity as its own, so that the will "mit sich selbst zusammengeschlossen".[96] Appropriation consists in making an external "world" of the will's actions, and its freedom receives the form of necessity as an existing, objective event. The substantial nexus of this necessity is the social context of the will's actions, a system of the principles of liberty, the phenomenal nexus of which is authority and obedience. In other words, we might say that freedom is externalized through these acts of appropriation, and achieves *permanence* of presence by means of an objective organization of principles and power relations, i.e., through law.

The concomitant development of will in objective spirit and intelligence in theoretical spirit through appropriation is striking: just as appropriation by intelligence is empty without the structure and "permanence" of language, so appropriation by will is void without its systematization in law. Law in this sense represents merely a different manifestation of language, and its form and binding power remains characteristically linguistic. This universal, absolute aspect of law is emphasized by Hegel in his assertion that, "This 'reality', in general, where free will has existence in the *law* (das Recht) — the term being taken not merely as the limited juristic law, but as the comprehensive existence of all the determinations of freedom".[97]

But what is the nature of this appropriation regulated by law? Hegel's unequivocal answer is that the person, which is immediately only the inward sense of freedom, and as such is abstract and empty, realizes his freedom in the appropriation of an external "thing". This is first possible because the thing in its natural state is devoid of will and rights in front of the appropriating subject, and hence becomes a possession (Besitz). By "possession" is meant that I import my personal will into the thing, so that "through this determination, possession is property (Eigentum), which as a possession is a *means*, but as existence of the personality is an *end*".[98]

It is important to distinguish in this statement that property simply as possession is transitory, while the important function of property is rather the expression of the personality. Property, as a concretzation or reification of the personality, is a necessary externalization in which I recognize myself. This theme of the externalization of self on the road to self-consciousness we saw previously in our discussion of labour and language, and it is in this light that Hegel says, "In his property the person is brought into union with himself".[99] The implication, of course, is that human qualities are depersonalized and made into a quantitative thing, and if property serves as the matrix of recognition by others, then human personal relations, too, become quantitative of "thingly". As for the notion that property provides the means and horizons for the recognition of the self by others, Hegel says that "For them my will has its *determinate recognizable existence* in the thing by the immediate bodily act of taking possession, or by the formation of the thing or, it may be, by mere designation of it".[100] Property, in terms of its role in self-recognition by others, takes on here a clearly epistemological aspect: The concept of ownership described by Hegel is not merely the given economic reality of a particular society, — it is an integral part of the will's appropriation of the external world, and as such, a determinate realization of the idea.[101]

Nonetheless the role of property in self-recognition cannot be separated from its social reality, in that its very existence as "property" implies the recognition of this status by others. Property already indicates a form of contract which establishes the limits of holdings, and a background system of laws, however primitive. Indeed the contract itself, as an expression of the choice of property, replaces property as the true expression of the realization of individual will, and raises this expression from its form as concrete "thing" to that language. The emphasis on the latter represents a shift from the material externalization of personality to its exhaustive expression in language, in which word *is* deed and thing: "The utterance in the stipulation is complete and exhaustive. The inwardness of the will which surrenders and the will which accepts the property is in the realm of representation, and in that realm the *word* is *deed* and *thing* (# 462)".[102] The paragraph (# 462) referred to by Hegel is that section in subjective spirit in which he asserts that the name *is* the thing within the realm of representation, and, indeed, there is a striking parallel here between the absorption of the material, natural world into the structural presence of language as memory *and* as law.[103]

Property is at first the immediate appropriation of the external world by individual will, but this appropriation soon takes the form of contract and eventually of law. Within this development contract represents the intermediate stage in the on-going transformation of the mode of appropriation, from its existence within the concrete material world to its expression within that rhythm of presence created by language. The translation of sensation into names by *subjektive Geist* structures that sensation and creates distinct moments or units of experience — names — which can then be linked in a discursive development. The rational organization of reality by the *objektive Geist* follows a similar pattern, through the structuring or "leveling off" of the qualitative features of property by the language of contract. Hegel says that, "In this way there is put into the thing or performance a distinction between its immediate specific *quality* and its substantial being or *value*, so that value is changed from a qualitative to a quantitative determination. One piece of property is thus made comparable with another, and may be made equivalent to a thing which is (in quality) wholly heterogeneous. It is thus treated in general as an abstract, universal thing".[104]

The qualitative, contingent character of both sensation and property is here re-presented in the "quantitative" linguistic structure of language and contract. Of course the question arises as to whether this translation of the qualitative in terms of the quantitative is exhaustive, and if not, what has been left behind and why? We may tentatively respond by suggesting that as the natural world "enters" absolute discourse, the particular is consistently superseded within "broader" configurations of the whole, the whole being the optimum, the horizon, of possible self-knowledge.

The translation of the personalized thing (i.e., the thing as my property) into the commodity of contract still lacks a systematic form good for all such contracts. Consequently, as Hegel points out, "Das Recht, als Dasein der Freiheit im *Äußerlichen*, fällt in eine *Mehrheit* von *Beziehungen* auf dies Äußerliche und auf die andern Personen". [105] The law of contract, as the being-there of freedom in externality, is in this reflected moment merely a series of titles, each with a show of right *vis-à-vis* the intrinsic universal right.

This difference between the paricular claims to right and intrinsic right represents a distinction which has emerged between subjective will and the universal aspect of law. But it is a distinction within the *instrumentality* of subjective will, and is not an absolute conflict between the individual and law as such, for law only has its actuality through the appropriating will. "The 'reality' of right, which the personal will in the first instance gives itself in immediate wise, is manifest through the mediation of the subjective will, giving existence to right in-itself, or separating itself from this right and opposing its moment to it". [106] However, subjective will gets its truth and reality only to the extent that it realizes itself as reasonable will, i.e., if it wills the intrinsic right. Within the immediate conflict of wills, apparent right and intrinsic right are reconciled through a third party representing the disinterested judgment, and it is this particular will of the judge which gives authority to intrinsic right. Of course there is the assumption here that because the judgment is disinterested it will also be rational. Obedience to authority is, consequently, the realization of the reasonable will, and as such the subjective will is morality (Moralität). [107]

This is certainly a startling proposition. Morality is defined as the realization of the reasonable will, which is the subjective willing of the intrinsic right embodied in law. But this willing of intrinsic right has its origin in the desire to regulate and systematize contract negotiations and the exchange of property. The conclusion follows that morality is in truth the acceptance and necessity of a rational rhythm in subjective appropriation. It cannot be otherwise once freedom is understood as the expansion of the will through appropriation, and the development of the personality as its extension in property.

We begin to understand at this point the sense in which freedom is realized within Hegel's lawful society. He says that, "law itself and all its determinations are based on free personality alone – on self-determination, which is the very contrary of determination by nature".[108] The law is the means toward the development of the free personality, of self-determination: but we have seen that the free will is an appropriating will, and the law which "is based on free personality" is necessarily that law which institutionalizes property ownership.

Thus Hegel defines freedom in that section of objective spirit dealing with law as the freedom to own property, and morality as the rational rhythm of its appropriation. This is not the whole story, however, since with the willing of intrinsic right in morality, the will is disengaged from a particular object and becomes "a will reflected into itself, so that the will-determination in general, as existing in it as *its own* is differentiated from the existence of freedom in an external thing".[109] In this way the determination of the will is partly inwardized as the reason of the will, the basis of law and ethical life, and partly externalized as existent volition in actual deeds. This relation of the reflected will to its actions constitutes subjective or moral freedom, and the possibility of choice based on inward universal principles and the "ought".

It is clear in this transition from *Das Recht* to *Die Moralität* that property plays a crucial role in the interiorization of intrinsic right and in the creation of a morally free subject which has its personality for its object. Property is that first immediate reification of the personality as a sign, much as the human body was regarded as the first sign in our study of subjective spirit.[110] In this sense property is a primitive language which provides the means for the externalization of personality and its recognition by others. However this externalization is only adequate to the extent that the thing offers no resistence, that it has no rights of its own. A passage from the *Philosophie des Rechts* clarifies this point: "A person has as his substantive end the right of putting his will into any and every thing and thereby making it his, because it has no such end in itself and derives its determination and soul from his will. This is the absolute right of appropriation which man has over all 'things'".[111]

The free will is an appropriating will: if appropriation is delimited by a "resistence" of the thing, so much is our absolute freedom constrained. For the will to realize its concept (freedom), it must be able to mould its external world. This forming activity of the will is at first immediate in relation to property, i.e., as the attitude of simple possession. Property is the immediate existence of my liberty, the immediate "show" of my personality. It follows that the quality or quantity of property does not play a role in the immediate recognition of this expression of my personality by others.[112] Property does not express any determination other than the immediate existence of this person and his concomitant rights, but this first expression of right already brings the person into legal contact with others, and raises a question as to the duty of recognition by these others. This relation between possession, right, and duty is such that, "my right to a thing is not merely possession, but as possession by a *person* it is *property* or legal possession, and it is a *duty* to possess things as *property*, i.e., to be as a person – what, in the relation of appearance, the relation to another person, develops into the duty of someone *else* to respect *my* right".[113] This immediate relation of right and duty in recognition is found in the concrete form of contract, and contract introduces an aspect of universality to this recognition in two ways: As language, it translates the qualitative value of property into a quantitative commodity of exchange. Secondly, the "positive" nature of contract provides a public format for this recognition.[114]

The transition to the sphere of *Die Moralität* occurs when this immediate relation of right and duty breaks down, and this development has its origin in the "positive" character of contract. The multiplicity of contracts brings to *public* attention their conflicting claims to legal right, and the necessity to accept a universal intrinsic right as arbitrator of the proper duties. The subjective will, with its subjective rights and duties, now stands in a moral relation to its existent volition and external actions. In as much as subjective will gives existence to essential right, and "realizes the reasonable will", it is morality.[115]

But even as the subject wills the essential right, the will remains reflected into itself – it is the right of the subjective will. The sphere of *Die Moralität* is, therefore, the morality of the individual conscience, such that the relation between inward purpose and the actualization of that purpose remains contingent and imperfect. The external immediacy of this relation between right and duty that we saw in *Das Recht* is now concentrated on the affection of the subjective will as both essential will and existent volition. The "reality" of right is consequently dependent on the instrumentality of this subjective will, and the reasonable will is that will which dutifully recognizes the intrinsic right: but the whole development within the sphere of law has suggested that the recognition of rights has its origin in the recognition of another's property as an extension of his person. Therefore he wills the reasonable will who wills the systematic recognition of the lawful rights and duties of private property. Such rights and duties regulate the rhythm of appropriation by the free will, so that it is perhaps exaggerating only a little to suggest that morality as it is developed in *Das Recht,* as the willing of the reasonable will, is not based on transcendent values or moral principles, − rather morality is the *acceptance* of a determined rhythm of appropriation.

2.2 *The moral "ought"*

The moments of *Das Recht* and *Die Moralität* within objective spirit are linked through the inherent rationality of appropriation itself. Appropriation does not connote simply a "taking into possession", but is a moulding of the objective world by the will in terms of its concept (freedom). Thus appropriation is rational to the extent that it gives its concept the form of necessity within the organization of the principles of liberty, the phenomenal nexus of which is the awakening of the sentiment of obedience in consciousness.

The concept of freedom receives its immediate manifestation in the proclamation of the rights of property as the *existing* volition of the person. This abstract right (abstract because the entire discussion of right and morality takes place within a presupposed, existing society), has less to do with property than with the right of the person to be recognized as such. Contract raises this recognition to a certain objectivity through the speculative translation of language, so that recognition has its perfect manifestation in that universal law which is based on free personality alone.

In as much as the recognition of the person is predominant in *Das Recht,* property provides the existential matrix for the action of the will and for its recognition by others. It is only in property that the will at first *exists* for others, and recognition finds its immediate object in property prior to the individual. The relations of property in contract are the relations between objective commodities devoid of contingent qualitative characteristics, and it is the recognition of these colourless objects of exchange that provides the prototype recognition of the abstract political subject.

It is only because of the epistemological relation between property and the personality established at the beginning of *Das Recht* that the transition from the contractual person to the legal subject of *Die Moralität* is possible. Without this relation, commodities and rights would remain external to each other: a rationalized commodity exchange system and the recognition of individual rights are not necessarily coterminous.

The derivation of the abstract subject from the "universal" commodity permits, in *Das Moralität,* the distancing of this subject from its existent volition and its existence in an external thing. The reflectedness of the thing as commodity becomes the reflectedness of the will as morally free subject; but this "reflectedness" in both cases is only possible through the speculative function of language. We can only have "abstract" commodities through the language of contract, and it is only in language that one thing is made comparable to another. It is this translation of the particular "this" into the universal "this" that is the speculative aspect of language,[116] and makes possible the comparison of concrete persons as abstract subjects.

Consequently the morally free subject of *Die Moralität* is inconceivable without the former relation of property and personality. This role of property is rational and integral because it provides the matrix for the rise of the particular personality to the universal subject. However this rise to reflectedness creates a new multiplicity of relations between the subject and his actions, because the moral subject is ultimately an empty subjectivity, without any necessary relation to its objective world beyond the tentative "ought". Hegel says that, "This supreme pitch of the 'phenomenon' of will, even to this absolute vanity — a non-objectivity, certain only of its responsibility to itself, and a self-certainty in the nullity of the universal — is sublimated, and at the same time sinks to its immediate in-itself".[117]

The moral subject is superseded through the retention of the form of subjectivity and the appropriation of the determinate universal life of the nation as its content. In this way the standpoint of the ought is abandoned, and we have passed into the field of ethical life (Die Sittlichkeit). This exhaustive manifestation of objective spirit is evidenced for Hegel in that, "subjective *freedom* exists as the in-and-for-itself *universal* rational will, as the consciousness of its individual subjectivity in the knowledge and sentiment of itself, while in its application and immediate universal *actuality* is equally *custom*, — self-conscious *freedom* has become *nature*".[118]

2.3 *The ethical subject*

This final appropriation by the subject of the true universality of the nation comes about through three distinct moments. These are constituted by Hegel as (i) the family, in which the relations have natural immediacy; (ii) civil society (Die bürgerliche Gesellschaft) in which a formal universality is achieved through the "relative" relations of independent persons; and (iii) the state, in which the self-conscious relations are developed to organic actuality.

Beyond this distinction into moments, the ethical substance itself is the true community, in which the infinite form of sujectivity and the universal content of the nation are reconciled. Hegel asserts that, "The free, self-knowing substance, in which the absolute "ought" is no less an "is", has actuality as the spirit of a nation (hat als Geist eines *Volkes* Wirklichkeit). The abstract disruption of this spirit is its individualization *into persons*, while it is the inner power and necessity of their independence. But the person, as thinking intelligence, knows the substance as its own essence, ceases when so minded to be a mere accident of it; looks upon it as his absolute final aim . . .".[119]

While we may tentatively accept this initial vision of the true community as the nation, it remains for us to understand how it achieves actuality through its determinate moments. These moments are rather *social* events in which the subject undergoes transformations in his "relations of appropriation" toward property and other individuals. The question we must ask in terms of this development is whether these events exhibit an integral structure and logic which make their progress toward the true community a necessary one?

Just as the system of property ownership was the rational appropriation of the natural thing, so it is the family, for Hegel, that represents the rational organization and appropriation of the natural sexual bond. But the family establishes itself as a social unit not simply because of its satisfaction of natural impulse. Hegel says that, "The physical difference of sex thus appears at the same time as a difference of intellectual and ethical determination", so that the family is the necessary reconciliation of spiritual opposites as well, combining to form "a single person".[120] This "substantial" union is represented by the ethical community of physical and moral attachments, which goes on to include the "community of personal and private interests".[121]

The ethical event of family is distinguished in form by the physical relation of its members, a relation which Hegel feels is necessarily monogamic. The nature of these relations is characteristically immediate and is based on emotional ties rather than legal rights and duties, so that the individuals of the family do not exist as independent persons, but participate in a communal sharing of interests, education, and property. All of these become attributes of the family as the definitive social unit, regardless of their origin in one of its members. "By the community in which the various members constituting the family stand in reference to property, that property of the one person (representing the family) acquires an ethical interest, as does its acquisition, labour, and care for the future".[122]

This immediate appropriation of the communal life of the family by each of its members is broken only when the children grow to independent adulthood or when the marriage partners are separated. With this return to independent status, legal regulation enters the structure of personal relations.

Of course the assumptions at work in this description of the family are manifold: Hegel gives us no grounds to accept the fact that sexual differences are reflected in moral and intellectual types which then fit together as two halves forming one person; nor that family work and property is necessarily or factually regarded always as communal. While the family fulfills certain physical and educational needs, there is no reason shown why all of its members cannot participate as independent, *whole* persons with equal and separate intellectual and vocational interests. And while we may excuse Hegel for relying on an historical type from his own epoch, his description remains nonetheless without a certain historiographical rigour: the pure immediacy of the family's relations merely fulfills the necessary logical function of the first moment in a dialectical chain leading to the state as the true community.

Civil society (Die bürgerliche Gesellschaft) is the second, "reflected" moment of the dialectic constituting the ethical substance. The natural immediacy of family relations is here contrasted with an atomistic range of independent subjects each seeking their particular interests and loosely unified in a random series of relative relations and adjustments. Although the subject now achieves its infinite form, (in contradistinction to the family member), its horizons of appropriation include multiple superficial relations with others that lack the organic unity of the family. Hegel says that, "The developed totality of this connective system is the state as civil society or *state external*".[123]

The totality of civil society is a relative totality, in which each subject is bonded with another through the satisfaction of needs, but in which the subject lacks an organic relation to the whole. Indeed the whole exists only as an approximate system for the satisfaction of these needs, and not as an entity in itself. This lack of unity in civil society creates differences in the appropriation of physical necessities and property among subjects, and in their relation to the whole. Recognizing these differences, Hegel says, "In civil society the sole end is to satisfy want – and that, because it is man's want, in a uniform general way, so as to *secure* this satisfaction. But the machinery of social necessity leaves in many ways a fortuitousness about this satisfaction. ... The onward march of this necessity also sacrifies the very particularities by which it is brought about, and does not itself contain the affirmative aim of securing the satisfaction of individuals".[124]

Hegel speaks of these differences in the satisfaction of individual needs with a certain amount of resignation, adding that they result from such factors as the variability of wants themselves, the circumstances of locality, errors and deceptions, and especially from the "unequal capacity of individuals to take advantage of that general stock".[125] But this realistic resignation is paradoxically balanced by the rationalized justification of the social classes that result from these differences: "But the concrete division of the general stock, that is equally a common concern, into particular masses determined by the moments of the concept ... constitutes the *difference of estate*".[126]

While for the individual it is a matter of accident as to which social group he belongs, the standing of the social group itself is determined by the concept, i.e., by the dialectical logic of the development of the ethical substance. Hegel goes on to say that, "Where civil society, and with it the State, exists, there arise the several estates in their difference; for the universal substance, as vital, *exists* only so far as it organically *particularizes* itself".[127] As such, civil society has its integrity as an ethical event not in its particular manifestations (for which no structural totality is necessarily evident), but in the mode of particularity itself as the "reflected" moment of ethical substance.

The indeterminate quality of all "free" appropriation in civil society finds its legal definition in the shape of formal right,[128] which simply systematizes in positive law this external necessity of the satisfaction of natural need. The appropriation by the infinite subject of civil society is as yet the appropriation of an empty universality, for universality has reality for this subject only in the satisfaction of his particular needs.

The state, as the final "moment" in the dialectical development of ethical substance, represents the unification of the immediacy of family life and the particularity of civil society. Speaking of this moment as the unification (Vereinigung) of the appropriating subject with its universal principle in the form of the state, Hegel says, "This conscious universality, which in self-knowledge unfolds its determinations, is the absolute aim and content of the knowing subject, i.e., is reasonable will for-itself".[129] In other words, the state becomes the content of subjectivity through the subject "going over" to the state, as the objective realization of its implicit, reasonable will, in order to become the state's immanent self.

As such a unification, the state is self-conscious ethical substance, and therefore subject. Paralleling the mode of appropriation of *Der freie Geist*, the state is a self-making, having itself for its object, so that "The essence of the state is the in-and-for-itself universal, the reasonableness of will, but as self-knowing and self-actualizing, and as an actuality one individual".[130] The state has its integrity as an ethical event through its actuality as the ethical subject.

It is this aspect of subjectivity that gives the state its quality as a discrete "moment" within the logical syllogism that includes the family and civil society. While it includes the *natural* fulfilled by the family and civil society, the state goes beyond this in setting universal goals and horizons for the whole, thus adhering to the model of the spiritual configuration as both a revealing and a creating, – the revelation and subsumption of natural necessity and the creation of the horizons within which it can realize its concept. [131] We must emphasize, however, that the state has this integrity, this self-consciousness, because of its "reification" in the *language* of law, wherein it perceives itself and becomes conscious of itself. This process of the externalization of the subject in language, and its rise to self-consciousness, is a theme we have already encountered in our discussion of subjective spirit. The "written", positive constitution as it exists "for" consciousness, is that system of laws which is the substantial nexus of the will's concept (freedom): "The constitution is this articulation or organization of state-power. It comprises the determinations of the reasonable will, in so far as it is in the individuals only implicitly the universal will, coming to a consciousness and an understanding of itself and being *found*; also for that will being put in actuality, through the action of the government and its several branches, and there contained, but protected both against *their* fortuitous subjectivity and against that of the individuals". [132]

Spirit's "finding" of itself cannot be dissociated from the external constitution of the state's laws, nor can we understand these laws apart from the national spirit that informs them. It is clear from this relation that language in the form of the constitution plays an integral role in the rise of the state to subjectivity, since "the actual spirit only has a determinate consciousness of its principles, in so far as it has them existing before if". [133]

That the state should achieve its true integrity and permanence of presence as a spiritual configuration, that "this subjectivity should grow to be a *real* moment, an *actual* existence", means that the subjectivity of abstract and final decision should be existent in one person, – the monarch. [134] In paragraph # 542, which follows, Hegel outlines the logic which links the organic subjectivity of the state with its necessary realization as constitutional monarchy: "In government as an organic totality is (i) *subjectivity*, as the *infinite* unity of the development of the concept *with itself*, the all-sustaining, all-decreeing will of the state, its highest peak and all-pervasive unity, – the princely power. In the perfect form of the state, in which each and every moment of the concept has reached free existence, this subjectivity is not a so-called "moral person", or a decree issuing from a majority – forms in which the unity of the decreeing will has not an *actual* existence – , but an actual individual; – *monarchy*. The monarchical constitution is therefore the constitution of developed reason; all other constitutions belong to lower grades of the development and realization of reason". [135]

For Hegel, this question as to *whether* the organic subjectivity of the state necessarily finds its actuality in the person of the monarch, is somewhat beside the point: the constitutional forms of democracy, aristocracy, and monarchy are not a matter of choice, but have determinate roles within the history of the state.[136] However, for the will of the monarch to be the reasonable will, there must be a perfect coordination of the subjective appropriation of the monarch's "freedom" with its objective realization in the state as the self-conscious ethical moment. This situation makes two absolute demands on the monarch, — that he be the disinterested arbitrator, properly the universal subject, and that his self-consciousness equal the self-consciousness of the state as the final ethical configuration, i.e., that the king be also a philosopher. The determination of these spiritual functions in a single individual cannot but raise serious doubts about their reasonable realization, unless the royal will is reduced to an empty form for the universal content of the ethical substance. Such a reduction would make this will as abstract as the compromise decisions denigrated by Hegel in democracy and aristocracy.[137]

There is another problem in this glorification of the monarchical constitution, however, which may be due to Hegel's restoration context. The monarchy is the *actualized* subjectivity of the state, and yet in the syllogism that explicates this state, it is the first moment, followed by (ii) the moment of particularity in which goverment power is divided into various state businesses,[138] and (iii) the state in its immediate actuality as an individual, naturally-determined nation.[139] As the actual rise to subjectivity, one would think that the monarchy would represent the highest and most inclusive moment of the state, and that the dialectic of the foregoing syllogism would be reversed.

The answer to this problem lies in the issue of sovereignty: if the first moment of the state had been the immediate collectivity of the people as a nation, then this would imply that fundamental sovereignty rested with the people, and that the monarch was simply the collective voice raised to rational subjectivity. But Hegel wants to make it clear that sovereignty rests with the historical tradition of monarchy, that the state is first a principate and then a nation. In so doing, he maintains the political tradition of his own day, but renders senseless his dialectical explication of this tradition within the system. Perhaps more important, the transition from the random collectivity of civil society to the organic collectivity of the nation is disrupted, so that the government is seen solely in terms of its monarchical expression, and not as a necessary extension of the system of needs, the fortuitousness of which Hegel was not loath to lament.[140]

The three "moments" of ethical substance — family, civil society, and the state, — achieve their discrete quality through the differences in the structure of appropriation between the subject and its substantial content. Each mode of appropriation creates the horizons of a particular social configuration, a configuration which must be absolutely delimited if it is to take its place as a moment in the development of the logical whole. But does such a delimitation of the spiritual moment remain true to its objective content, while raising that content to its conceptual comprehension? The issue involved here is whether or not the "regional" formations of intersubjectivity such as family or a system of needs, can be understood as part of a single logical process which reveals a *pervasive* absolute within the mode of "objective" spirit. As we have tried to indicate in the preceding analysis, some intersubjective formations seem to have been forced into a logical scheme which does not fully take into account their social, ontological origins. At other times, the needs of the historical present transgress the accepted dialectical format, such that the transition from one moment to another becomes increasingly difficult to justify within the standard of reason Hegel has set himself.

The progress through one objective externalization to the next works best when we are dealing with moments which have their existence "for" consciousness in language. The contract *vis-à-vis* the relations of property, and the constitution *vis-à-vis* the relations of civil society, represent decisive turning points by which the subject immersed in objective spirit comes to know the objective whole as his self. This is because in language we can more easily comprehend a configuration as an absolute self-externalization; other moments, such as family or monarchy, seem to have a limited role within the overall presentation-to-self characteristic of spirit. The ambiguity of their position is not unrelated to the original presupposition of philosophic presentation as the "final" expression of absolute spirit.

3. ABSOLUTE SELF-PRESENTATION

3.1 *World-spirit*

The rise to subjectivity of the nation-state makes it the fundamental historical unit or moment upon which all historical development rests. As the actualization of spirit, the individual state is a *determinate* moment, i.e., it is delimited by natural particularities, geography and climate, and by the history of the rise to consciousness of its own particular principle. But this historical particular is only fully understood when it enters universal world-history (Weltgeschichte) and the dialectic of the several national minds (Völkergeister) [141]

The dialectic of the *Völkergeister* is "the path of liberation for the spiritual substance, the deed by which the absolute final aim of the world is realized in it, and the merely in-itself existing spirit achieves consciousness and self-consciousness". [142] This interacting of nation-states is at the same time a revealing of the implicit content of spiritual substance, and a creating of an outer universal and a world-spirit. However this world-spirit only exists "for us" because it is the determinate history of particular states: "As this development is in time and in real existence, as it is a history (Geschichte), its several moments and steps are the national minds; each of which, as individual and natural in its qualitative determination, is determined to occupy only one grade, and accomplish one task in the whole deed". [143]

The history of nations provides the *evidence* for the dialectical development of the *Weltgeist*. But how do we come to know this history, how does it achieve self-consciousness? Confronted with a random collection of historical data and events, what is the criterion with which we are going to elucidate the thread of spiritual dialectic? How does the *Endzweck* present itself?

The solution to this problem of interpretation is to treat the historical evidence, not as an historian, but as a philosopher. Hegel is not intent on "telling the story" of a certain epoch in full richness of detail, but in raising the contingency of that evidence to its concept, in showing how that evidence realizes a logic at work in history. Only the standpoint of the *philosopher* can show that history is founded on an essential and actual aim — that there is reason in history — and it is only on strictly philosophical grounds that the necessity of such assertions can be decided. [144] The argument forwarded by Hegel is that such presuppositions are unjustified only when arbitrarily adopted, and when they attempt to force events into agreement. The implication is that they are indeed justified when such presuppositions form a necessary part of a philosophical system and can be shown to be implicit in the historical evidence itself.

Furthermore, as Hegel clearly indicates, *all* historical recounting of the facts involves selection and interpretation. There is no such thing as the distinterested historian, so that we may as well base our interpretation on the most rational and self-conscious presuppositions possible. Now it has previously been shown that the nation-state is the fully developed form in which spirit realizes itself, and we may conclude that a history of these states must be the basis for our understanding of the movement of the *Weltgeist*.

This importance of the state, as the basic historical moment, is articulated in the following: "In the existence of a *nation* (Volk) the substantial aim is to be a state and preserve itself as such. A nation with no state formation (a mere nation) has, strictly speaking, no history (Geschichte) — like the nations which existed before the rise of states and others which still exist in a condition of savagery. What happens to a nation, and takes place within it, has its essential significance in relation to the state; whereas the mere particularities of individuals are at the greatest distance from the true object of history". [145]

While we may accept Hegel's assurances that the state is the realization of the folk community, it is not clear exactly how the state "has" a history, or how this history is different from that of other social forms. The answer to this difficulty is the crucial role that language plays in the determination of spiritual events: the state is a self-making and has a history only to the extent that it exists within the promoted presence of language, in laws and a constitution. The state only *is*, and knows itself, as language, − and it *is* "for us" in history largely as a linguistic event.

The manner in which the state enters into history is not at all adequately described in the *Enzyklopädie*, but we are given a hint of how this takes place in the second draft (1830) of the "Introduction to the Lectures on the Philosophy of World History" (known as *Reason in History*) in Hegel's own manuscript. Here he says, "But it is the state which first supplies a content which not only lends itself to the prose of history but actually helps to produce it. Instead of the merely subjective dictates of authority − which may suffice for the needs of the moment − a commonwealth in the process of coalescing and raising itself up to the position of a state requires formal commandments and laws, i.e., general and universally valid directives. It thereby creates a record of its own development, and an interest in intelligible, determinate, and − in their results − enduring deeds and events, on which Mnemosyne, for the benefit of the perennial aim which underlies the present form and constitution of the state, is impelled to confer a lasting memory". [146]

Within this conception of the state, history and historical writing merge to form one historical event. Individuals participate in this event only if they participate in the history of the state, so that their particularity then has universal significance. Consequently, our concern with historical figures derives not from their singular individuality, but from the way in which they *express* an age, a nation, a civilization. [147]

This interpretation of history has an inherent critical element, in that it isolates the spiritual moments whose dialectical interaction "make" history. What is not determined by these moments is external or contingent, as we see, for example, in the actions of a primitive community or a private individual *vis-à-vis* the state. Hegel asserts that, "The only truth for mind is the substantial, and not the trivialities of external existence and contingency". [148] The fault of the "impartial" historical writing of the past is that it has only told the story of these trivialities, largely because historical truth meant a correct reporting of externals, "without critical treatment save as regards this correctness — admitting, in this case, only qualitative and quantitative judgments, no judgments of necessity or concept".[149]

Our study of the determination of spiritual moments allows us to break through these externals and see the realization of the concept (freedom) in history, such that this final aim of spirit alone is the principle of movement. The realization of liberty in history through the growth of nation-states is accompanied by the attainment of self-consciousness, since the state is the fully self-conscious spiritual configuration. It follows that only at this moment in the historical dialectic will our historical interpretations achieve a critical, scientific stature, — meaning that they will recognize reason in history.

The particular state, as a self-conscious subject, realizes a particular stage of the universal spirit in giving spirit its being-there and its objective actuality, and spirit places its will in this state for a certain time. Against this absolute will, the other particular national minds have no rights, for this nation dominates the world. When this phase is fully actual, spirit goes on to use other states as the determinate moments of its dialectical development, so that the only absolute right in history is this liberation of spirit itself.[150]

Looked at from the standpoint of the *Weltgeist*, the rise and fall of states is representative of the discrete moments in the discursive realization of the Idea. Thus to comprehend the absolute we must study the unfolding of spirit in all its historical determinateness, for it is only in history that spirit is *for us*. Again in Hegel's draft (1830) of *Die Vernunft in der Geschichte* we find this comment: "This spirit [is] the substance of history; its nature is always one and the same; and it discloses this nature in the existence of the world. (*The world spirit is the absolute spirit*.) This, as I have said, must be the result of our study of history. But we must be sure to take history as it is; in other words, we must proceed historically and empirically".[151]

However, our historical study of spirit is intimately bound up with the existing realization of the concept of spirit (freedom) within the particular state. Hegel says, "For freedom in itself carries with it the infinite necessity of attaining consciousness — for freedom, by definition, is self-knowledge — and hence of realizing itself: for it is itself the end of its own operations, and the sole end of the spirit".[152] Our thinking of knowledge and freedom merges in the rise to subjectivity of the state, since the state is self-conscious substance: it follows that philosophical science is impossible under any other political structure.

To speak of the *Weltgeist* as if we somehow stood outside of its movement is erroneous in Hegel's view. Our thinking of the *Weltgeist* is at the same time its *Dasein*, its being-there , so that the moment of spirit as a particular state is also the moment of a "cultus" which includes a determinate family, civil society, art, religion, and philosophy. The ethical substance, potentially infinite, is actually a particular and limited substance, and its content is presented to it as something existing in time and tied to an external nature and external world. [153]

The historical, empirical consideration of the particular is not significant in itself, but it receives significance in as much as the particular is seen in relation to an end or aim, i.e., to a universal. Spirit is alienated and divided, but only so as to be able thus to find itself and return to itself. Only in this manner does spirit attain its freedom, for that is free which is not referred to or dependent on another. The myriad of differences perceived in the history of the *Weltgeist* is the expression of the Idea, for the Idea is the central point and the periphery, the "source of light" which in all its expansion remains present within itself. But this mysterious "permanence of presence" persists as the unthought determination of Hegel's Idea.

Although we cannot stand outside of history, we can apprehend the world spirit through an understanding of the essentiality of its moments. Within ethical life (Sittlichkeit), thinking spirit is able to supersede the finitude attaching to the temporal interests of the nation-state and contemplate its true essentiality. Hegel states that, "the thinking spirit in world history, while at the same time strips off those limitations of the particular national minds and their inherent worldliness, lays hold of its concrete universality and rises to the knowledge of absolute spirit as the eternal, actual truth, in which knowing reason is freely for-itself, and the necessity of nature and the necessity of history are only ancillary to its revelation and the vessel of its honour". [154]

This thoughtful overreaching of the finitude of the *Völkergeister* and the rise to the knowledge of *absolute Geist* happens in a very special way: Hegel describes this transition as the "moment " of negation through which the essential content of the starting-point is purged of its finitude so as to come forth free. What this means within the ethical life of objective spirit is that self-consciousness is purged of subjective opinion and its will freed from the selfishness of desire. The thoughtful overreaching of finite national spirits appears first as religion, and the growing awareness of the free universality of its concrete essence expresses itself as genuine religiosity and the Idea of God. [155]

Religion is the consciousness of the "absolute" truth, so that whatever is to be true in the world of free will must be a participant in that truth and subsumed under it. Hegel says, "It is evident and apparent from what has preceded that ethical life is the state retracted into its substantial inner, while the state is the organization and actualization of ethical life; but religion is the substantiality of the ethical life itself and of the state''.[156]

Consequently any allusions to the conflicting claims of religion and state are ill-founded, since religion is the substantial matrix of all ethical life, and the state is simply the rise of ethical life to subjectivity. Religion is the matrix of ethical life in that religion has the *genuine* content, i.e., the idea of God, as the pervading absolute and source of ethical determinations. The religious consciousness is a step back into the absolute horizons of this life, so that this self-consciousness, retiring upon itself out of its empirical actuality and bringing its truth to consciousness, has in its *faith* and in its *conscience*, only what it has consciously secured in its spiritual actuality.[157]

The concrete indwelling of the divine spirit in secular life is to be found in its ethical organizations, in the ethical life of marriage, in economic and industrial action, and in an obedience dedicated to the law of the state. The ethical principles actual in secular life must remain abstract and superficial so long as they do not have their last and supreme sanction in the religious conscience, in subsumption under the consciousness of absolute truth.[158] It is the same necessity of a sanction absolutely present which leads Plato to the thought that a genuine constitution and a sound political life have their deeper foundation on the Idea and of universal principles of righteousness.[159]

But the determinate presence of the Idea happens in thinking, and thought always contains the immediate self-subsistence of subjectivity no less than it contains universality. The realization of the universal is through the subjective appropriation of that universal, so that ''the genuine Idea of the intrinsically concrete spirit is just as essentially under the one of its determinations, subjective consciousness, as under the other, universality, and in the one as in the other it is the same substantial content''.[160] The thinking of *Der freie Geist* within the state is a constant stepping back from the empirical evidence of ethical life into the absolute ground of its determinations, a movement which is the *active* appropriation of the subject's true universality. This is far from advocating a mindless obedience to the sheer positivity of ethical organizations which we might carelessly infer from a superficial reading of the remarks concerning marriage, the economic system, and the law of state.

Such a reconciliation of political power with the absolute of religion and ultimately philosophy is possible, in Hegel's view, only through the principle of spirit, conceived as a self-consciousness and a self-making. The key to this reconciliation is the thinking of an appropriation which is the infinite form of subjectivity under one of its moments, and the universal content of the absolute under the other. Appropriation is neither wholly subject nor wholly universal, but a constant movement between these two poles, a movement which unfolds their true possibilities through a discursive realization. It goes without saying that this realization "exists" primarily as language.

3.2 *Absolute spirit*

Hegel opens the section on absolute spirit in the *Enzyklopädie* with the somewhat enigmatic statement, "Der *Begriff* der Geistes hat seine *Realität* im Geiste". [161] We may begin to understand Hegel's intent by suggesting that absolute spirit is the movement in which determinate spirit rises to grasp its concept, becoming fully self-conscious spirit. This appropriation of the absolute Idea is a "becoming", which distinguishes itself into the moments of art, religion, and philosophy.

For this identity of concept and reality to exist as a knowledge of the absolute Idea, the implicitly free intelligence must be in its actuality liberated to its concept. In other words, knowledge of the absolute Idea is only possible at that moment in history when the historical subject has appropriated the concept of freedom as his true universality, and this freedom is realized concomitantly as *Der freie Geist* and the constitutional state. Consequently Hegel looks upon subjective and objective spirit as the path on which this aspect of *Realität* rises to maturity, revealing the discursive content of the Idea and creating the form in which the Idea may recognize itself as its truth. [162]

The historical form in which free intelligence is explicitly for itself is the Protestant state, where the principles of religion and the ethical conscience become one and the same in the "Protestant conscience". Only here does *Der freie Geist* know itself in its reasonableness and truth, [163] and consequently we must assume that it is solely under these conditions that a knowledge of the absolute Idea is possible. Of course these are not merely the "logical" conditions set by Hegel for the would-be knower, but reflect the actual *historical* relation of the system to its epoch.

The absolute spirit exists as an idea for knowing at the end of spirit's discursive unfolding, within the context of the nation-state as the culmination of subjective and objective spirit. But absolute spirit, though it is this identity indicative of the formal idea, is an identity returning and ever returned into itself, and if it is the one and universal substance, it is so as spirit. That is to say, the absolute Idea comes to self-knowledge through its discursive manifestation, − it is manifest as spirit, "discerning itself into a self and a knowing, for which it is as substance". [164]

This aspect of manifestation adequately describes the finitude attaching to the knowledge of the absolute in its spiritual appearing as art, religion, and philosophy. These three moments reflect three kinds of appropriation of the absolute, with the mode of appropriation determining its realization as a particular spiritual event. Each discrete configuration, as a particular revealing of the idea and a determinate creating of the horizons within which it knows its truth, *presents* a moment of absolute spirit, while at the same time, because it is manifestation, points to its supersession by a more inclusive expression.

Amidst the various expressions of absolute knowing, the subjective form of this knowing remains constant. Hegel says that, "The subjective consciousness of the absolute spirit is essentially and intrinsically a process, the immediate and substantial unity of which is the *belief* (Glaube) in the witness of the spirit as the *certainty* of objective truth".[165] This consciousness is a process in that it knows the absolute in a series of moments, as a discursive unfolding, because knowing is finite and dialectical. But within the process of knowing, the attitude of belief is a constant creating, in the act of devotion (Andacht), of an implicit or explicit "cultus" wherein the absolute gains its concrete determination.

Indeed it is in the reification of the content of belief in a particular "cultus" that we come to recognize the moments of absolute spirit. Hegel suggests that it is the work of the philosophy of religion to comprehend the relation between the determinations of the absolute and their corresponding historical "cultus", including under this term the ethical life of the state, and its arts and sciences.[166] This evocation of the attitude of belief is a precision related to our earlier discussion of the appropriation of the absolute within the context of ethical life, and effectively denotes the nature of this appropriation not only in religion, but in art and philosophy as well.

Art is the moment of absolute spirit in its natural immediacy. The art-work remains in a merely external relation to both the artist and the *public*, since the concrete intuition and representation of implicit absolute spirit is a simple ideal. Hegel says that, "This ideal, as a concrete form born of the subjective spirit, and in which the natural immediacy is only a sign of the idea, is so transfigured by the informing spirit in order to express the idea, that the form shows it and it alone; − the form of beauty",[167]

Because the ideal rests in a sensuous externality, it is the unity of nature and spirit, i.e., it is immediate, the form of intuition, and not a strictly spiritual unity in which the natural would be put only as ideal, as superseded in spirit, and the spiritual content would be only in self-relation. It is evident from the preceding that this appropriation of the absolute as the ideal has its historical cultus in the Greek city-state, and Hegel does not fail to draw the political conclusions relative to this determination of the absolute.

He points out that the community does have an ethical life aware of the spirituality of its essence, and its self-consciousness and actuality are in it elevated to substantial liberty. "But in its aspect of immediacy, the subject's liberty is only a custom, without the infinite self-reflection and the subjective imwardness of *conscience*".[168] Furthermore, it would seem that the particularity of custom, in contradistinction to the inherent universality of conscience, permits the "freedom of the few", through not founding the abstract ground of that freedom.

The immediacy of liberty as custom finds its roots in the appropriation of the absolute as an immediate ideal. In the singularity of form characteristic of the art-work, absolute spirit cannot become explicit, so that the spirit of beautiful art is always a limited national mind (Volksgeist). When the attempt is made to determine the abundance in detail of this spirit, its implicit universality breaks up into an indeterminate polytheism.[169] This is explained by the unessential, merely formal relation of the art-work and its idea, so that the thought and the material may be of the most diverse kind and the work itself still be beautiful.

The art-work, as an absolute configuration, has within itself a tension which forces its resolution on a higher level. On the one hand the artist appropriates the absolute so as to leave no sign of his own subjective particularity and contingency *vis-à-vis* the content of indwelling spirit, and the enthusiasm of the artist is like a foreign power under which he is bound and passive. But on the other hand, the artistic production itself has the form of natural immediacy, since it comes from the genius of the particular subject and is a matter of technical understanding and mechanical externalities, so that the art-work is also a work of free will and the artist a master of the gods.[170]

We see in this tension that the content of the absolute and the subjective form of its appropriation stand in external relation to each other. The subject is unconscious of his implicit universality and the absolute is as yet an indeterminate "other", so that the historical manifestation of the absolute as a beautiful ideal must be a merely contingent, immediate sign. In Romantic art this tension is moving toward its ultimate resolution: the artist no longer attempts to show the absolute in a external form as the beautiful, but presents it as only condescending to appearance (Erscheinung), as the divine inner within an externality.[171]

This thinking of the absolute as a divine inner disengaged from sensuous immediacy has its truth in revealed religion. Revelation is the reflected moment in the manifestation of absolute spirit, in which the limited import of the Idea in art becomes an in-and-for-itself universality identical with infinite form. Immediate intuition (Anschauung), as a dependent sensuous knowing, passes into a self-mediating knowing, into an existence which is itself knowledge. "Thus the principle which is the determination of the content of the Idea is the free intelligence, and as absolute, spirit is for the spirit". [172]

The section of absolute spirit devoted to revealed religion is a bewildering array of syllogisms within syllogisms in the concentrated space of a few pages. This is not without a certain self-consciousness of intent however, since it is within the representational thinking of revealed religion that the moments of the absolute first achieve a certain dialectical clarity. This is because it lies in the concept of true religion to be revealed, and revealed by God as the absolute.

Hegel says that, "Knowledge, the principle by which substance is spirit, as infinite self-realizing form, is a *self-determining* – it is simply manifestation". [173] In religion, the absolute spirit no longer manifests its abstract moments, but manifests itself. Concomitantly, if we are to have a knowledge of this absolute, we must assert the possibility and necessity of knowing God fully and rationally.

The framing syllogism of absolute religion (# 565) is as follows: absolute spirit, in overcoming the immediacy an sensuousness of form and knowledge, is in point of *content* the in-and-for-itself existing spirit of nature and spirit. However in point of *form*, absolute spirit is for subjective knowing as representation (Vorstellung). This representation gives to the moments of its content an independence, and makes them presuppositions toward each other and appearances which succeed each other, so that these moments become a series of events according to finite reflective determinations. Finally, this form of finite representationalism is overcome and superseded in the faith in one spirit and in the devotion of the "cultus". [174]

The remainder of the discussion now centres on this second moment in religion, in which the form separates from the content and presents that content as a series of representational events. In this formal presence, the different moments of the concept part off into particular spheres or elements in each of which the absolute content is *presented*. The representational events of religion present this content as a succession of three interlocking syllogisms, and in the structure of this revelation we are able to perceive the first dim outlines of the system itself.

Under the moment of universality (Allgemeinheit), the sphere of pure thought and the abstract element of essence, absolute spirit is the presupposition, as the creator of heaven and earth. But in this eternal sphere we see the absolute only begetting himself as his son, while remaining in original identity with this differentiation. This determination of the son in its differentiation from the eternal essence is eternally superseded, and through this mediating of a self-superseding mediation, this first substance is essentially as concrete individuality and subjectivity — it is spirit.[175]

The logical development of these events is as yet obscure, lost in the opaque representationalism of religion. However the attempt to clarify this development through a one-to-one comparison of the syllogisms of revealed religion with the "three syllogisms" which close the system would be fraught with difficulties and unjustified. The basis for our objection is that the form or *mode* for the presentation of the moments of revealed religion is of an entirely different order to that which is adequate for the expression of the absolute system, i.e., to philosophic presentation. While the content of this latter is already implicit in revealed religion, the representational knowing of the understanding cannot fully display the speculative truth of absolute self-externalization. It remains for scientific philosophy to reconcile the infinite form of subjectivity with the content of absolute determination as it dimly appears in the Christian scheme of fall and redemption.

Inspite of these problems, of course, we can make certain comments about the syllogistic structure of Hegel's "philosophic" presentation of the representations of revealed religion. First it must be noted that, according to Hegel, the content of this religion is "for" consciousness through pictorial representations, especially as they exist in language, and not through any non-linguistic immediate knowledge of an absolute other. Furthermore, the depiction of the content of this religion within a syllogism made up of the moments of universality, particularity, and individuality is not a presentation derived from any religion of Hegel's day, but is a program imposed by philosophic presentation. It would seem, then, that philosophy does more than simply "look back" on its content: it actively raises the principles of that content to conceptual truth. The justification of this procedure must be tied to the presuppositions of presentation as a whole.[176]

In terms of the syllogism of universality described above (# 567), two issues must be kept in focus. Its moments describe the objective, existing scheme of redemption as it exists in the sphere of pure thought, — we might say, as it exists in the mind of God. There is a certain parallel here between this abstract element of essence and the ideal determinations of the first part of the system, the logic, which must be certified in concrete content as in their actuality. In addition, this syllogism describes the objective existence of the Idea of redemption as it is in-itself, as it lays immediately before consciousness, and ends with the reinstatement of the concrete subject as the implicit form of this content for-itself.

Turning now to the second syllogism of revelation, under the moment of particularity (Besonderheit) or judgment, this concrete, eternal essence is presupposed, and its movement is the creation of appearance. The eternal moment of mediation — of the only son — falls apart into the independent oppositions of, on the one hand, heaven and earth, elemental and concrete nature, and on the other hand, of spirit, standing in a relative relation with nature as finite spirit. This spirit, as the extreme of implicit negativity, rises in its independence to evil through its relation to an opposing nature, and in such opposition takes on its own naturalness. But equally amidst this naturalness, spirit as a thinking is directed toward the eternal, although only standing in an external relation to it. [177]

This syllogism of particularity is the syllogism of spiritual reflection in the idea, and denotes the difference and appropriation of a "natural" consciousness *vis-à-vis* its objective, ideal content. Its moments constitute the subjective advance of the idea, but because this subject stands in a negative and external relation to its truth, this advance remains within the realm of appearance. This judgment and self-certain independence is the burden of *finite* spirit, of the only Son, which, through its thinking, is directed toward the eternal.

The final syllogism of revelation is the moment of individuality (Einzelnheit) as such, — of subjectivity and the concept itself, in which the opposition of universality and particularity revert to their identical ground. The presupposition is the universal substance, actualized out of its abstraction into an individual self-consciousness. This immediate identity with the essence is the "son" of the eternal sphere, placed in temporality, so that in him evil is implicitly superseded. This immediate and sensuous existence of the absolutely concrete puts itself in judgment and expires in the pain of negativity, while the infinite subjectivity identical with itself remains as absolute return and the universal unity of universality and individual essentiality becoming for-itself, — becoming the Idea of spirit, eternal but living and present in the world. [178]

This objective totality (of the son become spirit), is the implicit presupposition for the finite immediacy of the individual subject. "For" the subject, this totality is at first an other, an object of contemplation, but the intuition of implicit truth in the witness of the spirit leads this subject to determine himself as nothing and evil in terms of his immediate nature. However, with this example of his truth, and mediated by a faith in the in-itself accomplished unity of the universal and individual essentiality, the subject is also the movement of renouncing his immediate natural determination and his own will. Through the pain of negativity the subject is reconciled with his example and notion and united with the essence knowing itself. This essence, through this mediation, effects itself as an *indwelling* in self-consciousness, and is the actual presence of the in-and-for-itself spirit as universal. [179]

In this last syllogism of revealed religion we behold the manner in which the scheme of redemption is "for" subjective consciousness as a spectacle of self-sufficient representational events. But this scheme is only *actual* through the appropriation of its truth in the belief of a concrete individual. Belief is understood as the "going over" of a subject to the absolute content in order to become its immanent self, i.e., the subject identifies with the agony and redemption of the Son, as his universal self, in order to supersede his own particular determinateness.

As with the presentation of the system, Hegel tells us that this universal self depicted in revealed religion first *appears* to natural consciousness as an "other", but through the intuition of its implicit truth and the witness of spirit, this consciousness goes over to its universal essence. In the terminology of speculative philosophy, we might say that the standpoint of the science of the absolute is implicit in natural consciousness, and in general, it can be added that, in the scheme of redemption analyzed above, the structure for the self-presentation of the absolute described by philosophy can be discerned in outline.

In terms of the development of the mode of presentation itself, the transition from the universal law of the constitution in ethical life to the linguistic representations of revealed religion marks a decisive change in the appropriation by consciousness of its true essence. In ethical life, the individual *obeys* the language of law as the representation of his universal, objective self, and this obedience is guided and sanctioned by the force of the state through a judiciary and through punishment. However, because there is this aspect of obedience and coercion attaching to law, we cannot avoid the conclusion that the laws and the constitution always remain external to the political subject, as if the appropriation of this objective representation, and his loyalty to the state, does not fully supersede the difference between the subjective and objective elements.

Indeed Hegel points out that the ultimate sanction for the representations of ethical life lie with our appropriation of absolute spirit in revealed religion. He says that, "The state rests on this relation to the ethical sentiment, and that on the religious. If religion is the consciousness of *absolute truth*, then what ought to pass as right and justice, as duty and law, i.e., as *true* in the world of free will, can be so esteemed only as it has a part of that truth, is *subsumed* under *it* and is a sequel *to it*".[180] Obedience to the language of religious representation understood as the self-presentation of law is dependent upon, and is superseded by, *belief* in the language of the absolute. Belief is a higher order of appropriation, in which the difference characteristic of mere law is overcome through a suppression of the particular self and a "going over" to the universal object of regard.

Philosophic presentation supersedes both of these modes of appropriation, and again, it is an appropriation which happens in language. This last form of presentation is singular because it reconciles the characteristics developed by representation in subjective and objective spirit, with the representation of revealed religion. In other words, speculative science presents absolute manifestation as an object of belief and as the outcome and product of inter-subjective relations, as the truth of intersubjectivity as such. But in order that it may do this, science lays a claim on consciousness by telling it that scientific presentation is a self-externalization of the absolute, which happens at a "special" time for consciousness.

3.3 *The close of philosophy*

The representation of religious events is a very special kind of representation. The various actions of God as the creator, as son, and as spirit are implicitly the actions of one absolute whose principle is to reveal itself. This means that all of the actions or events have one implicit ground, which eventually becomes self-conscious of itself as this ground, at a certain moment within the religious time-frame. The time-frame is determined by the ground itself as the time necessary for its self-realization. Beyond this moment, as a final judging of itself, time does not exist.

But these events are significant in another way, other than their having a common ground. Each act of God in his various manifestations, each religious event, has a certain independent integrity or discrete quality which allows it to form one moment within the discursive plan of redemption. While the son exists in an original identity with the creator, it is important that he retain a certain independence and integrity so that he may later die in the pain of negativity. However, what gives him this independence and pain, and is later superseded in his spiritual reconciliation with the father, is his human nature *vis-à-vis* his divine nature, i.e., his *natural* contingency.

We can gather from this example, then, that what determines these religious events as "events" is their finitude, their incompleteness, which equally points to their supersession in an inclusive totality. But if these religious events only *exist* to the extent that they are at least partially contingent, and consequently "historical", what are we to think of their repetition as moments in the circle of the concept? Does not this repetition, itself containing determinate moments, imply a degree of contingency? Is then the representationalism of religion truly superseded?

We must return to Hegel for clarification on this point. The three syllogisms setting out the religious events constitute the one syllogism of the absolute mediation of spirit with itself, "whose life is explained in the cycle of concrete figures of representation". [181] From this its separation into a temporal and external succession of moments, the unfolding of mediation appropriates itself in the result, as the closing-in of spirit with itself. This supersession of finite representationalism in the result contracts not only to the simplicity of belief and devotional feeling as indicated in the framing syllogism (# 565) of absolute religion, "but also to thinking, to this immanent simplicity in which the unfolding still has its extension, but known all the while as an indivisible coherence of the universal, simple, and eternal spirit in-itself. In this form of truth, truth is the object of philosophy". [182]

It is evident in this explication of the transition to philosophy, that the contraction of the series of religious events to belief, and ultimately to thought, does not essentially alter the content of these events as discrete *moments* of the absolute, since they continue to have their expansion in thought itself, presumably as a logic. Of course what is altered is the spiritual mode of the appropriation and manifestation of this absolute.

In this regard Hegel makes the claim that the science of philosophy is the unity (Einheit) of art and religion, and, we may infer, the spiritual form most suited to the realization of the absolute. The intuitive viewing of art, external in form, is but subjective production and splinters the substantial content into many independent shapes. The totality of religion, on the other hand, is the unfolding and mediation of this content through its separation into moments in representation. Philosophy not only keeps these moments together in a totality, but also unites them into a simple spiritual intuition, and in that unity raises them to self-conscious thinking. [183]

Hegel states that this philosophic knowing is the concept of art and religion, a knowing which cognizes the diverse content as necessary, and this necessary as free. We have seen in our discussion of the syllogisms of revealed religion the manner in which philosophy cognizes the necessity of the *content* of absolute representation. But philosophy also cognizes the necessity of both *forms* of representational thinking as (i) the immediate intuition and its "Poesie", the objective and *external* revelation presupposed by the repesentation; and (ii) the subjective retreat inwards, and the subjective movement and identification of *belief* with its presupposed object. [184]

This cognition by philosophy is "the *recognition* of this content and its form, the *liberation* from the onesidedness of forms, and their elevation into the absolute form, which determines itself as content while remaining identical with it, and is in the cognition of this content an in-and-for-itself existing necessity. This movement, which philosophy is, finds itself already accomplished, when *at the close* it lays hold of its own concept, i.e., only *looks back* on its knowledge".[185] Philosophy is the rise to the form of subjectivity of the absolute content through the cognition of that content as necessary, – and as subject, this content is free. But this content is subject, and thus free, within the mode of self-conscious absolute *discourse*: philosophic presentation.

The attainment of subjectivity, this laying hold of its concept, only occurs when the revelation and expansion of the absolute is complete, so that the newly completed whole suddenly "gels" in the self-cognition of its necessity. This is why the recognition by philosophic science of the complete manifestation of the absolute must stand "beyond" the *implicit* development, and posit a "timeless" finality for that development, since it so decisively transforms those disparate spiritual moments into an organic, self-conscious whole. The turn of scientific knowing is the stepping back into the absolute ground of the spiritual manifestation of art, religion, and pre-scientific philosophy, and we must assume that this stepping back opens out a new time-frame for the existence of absolute spirit, although Hegel does not here, or elsewhere, investigate this implication.

However the close of philosophy is by no means *simply* external to the discursive development of its content in the life of spirit. Speculative science, too, is a spiritual configuration, and as such it is a determinate, although final, moment of absolute self-externalization. We must understand "final" as signifying the sense in which the absolute is fully *present* to itself in science through the complete determination of its manifestation. But this close equally signifies the completion of the educational history of spirit, of its forms of representation and relations of intersubjectivity. It is these two aspects of presentation which Hegel seeks to reconcile, the attainment of absolute presence, and the intersubjective basis of all linguistic representation, to which we must now turn with a critical eye.

NOTES

1 *Enz.* # 574, p. 462 (313).
2 *Science de la Logique: La Doctrine de l'Essence*, tr., prés., and notes by P. – J. Labarrière and G. Jarczyk (Aubier, Ed. Montaigne, Paris, 1976), pp. IX–XXV.
3 *Logik* II, p. 3 (389).
4 *Logik* II, p. 5 (391).
5 *Logik* II, p. 9f. (396).
6 *Logik* II, p. 15f. (401).
7 *Logik* II, p. 18 (404).
8 *Logik* II, p. 21 (406).
9 *Logik* II, p. 22 (408).
10 *Logik* II, p. 357 (708).
11 It is with this larger claim that Labarrière and Jarczyk close their argument for a referential structure in the *Logik*: "Ainsi donc, il n'est point de danger de placer trop haut l'importance et la portée spéculative de 'La Doctrine de l'Essence'. En elle s'expose bien, dans son formalisme premier, 'la structure ontologique de tout ce qui est' – et bien au-delà du 'concept du concept': jusqu'au 'concept adéquat', ou encore jusqu'au 'concept complètement posé' qui, au travers et au-delà de la Subjectivité *et* de l'Objectivité de la 'Logique subjective' ressaisies dans leur fondamentale unité, porte jusqu'aux limites extrêmes du Système – expression la plus complexe mais aussi la plus exactement proportionnée à son object de la Réflexion totale, entendue comme réflexion posante, réflexion extérieure et réflexion déterminante". *Op. cit.*, p. XXIVf.
12 This is an unfortunate lack because the three syllogisms which close the system seem to give the Logic primacy in the necessary, structural mediation of the whole (# 577), and if it could be shown that this Logic itself contained a referential structure, then the larger claim for its importance would be simply a matter of inference.
13 *Enz.* # 114 R., p. 124 (165).
14 In other words the "referential structure" of the *Logik* is replaced in the system by the self-differentiating whole.
15 *Enz.* # 114 R., p. 124f. (166).
16 *Enz.* # 413f., p. 344 (III 3). Within this line of argumentation it is perhaps not an exaggeration to suggest that, if there is a referential structure or model for presentation to be found, it is rather in labour and thinghood and the linguistic object, as first described by the *Phänomenologie*, than in the *Logik*.
17 *Enz.* Vorb., # 81 R., p. 103 (116).
18 Who is this "for us"? "Us" means those subjects at the level of science, those who through transference have gone over to the presentation of the system in order to become its immanent self. In the "Us" all subjective particularity has been superseded within the discursive manifestation of absolute discourse. For "Us" is "for" absolute discourse.
19 *Enz.* # 381, p. 313 (I 25).

20 *Enz.* # 382, p. 313 (I 49).

21 *Enz.* # 383, p. 314 (I 53). The educational history of spirit understood as an absolute "manifestation" within the mode of existence presupposes that we are already at the level of science and have superseded the "appearing" of spirit as subjective cognition.

22 Absolute self-presentation understood as spiritual manifestation expresses this tention that perdures between subject and absolute through the self-recognition in an "other". B. Bourgeois remarks, "L'absolu hégélien n'est ni l'esprit absolu subjectif qui est là dans la lecture de *Encyclopédie*, ni l'esprit absolu objectif qui est là dans le Livre encyclopédique, mais il se réalise dans l'identité ultimee de la lecture de ce Livre, dans l'acte infini de la conception subjective du concept objectif, où, selon le contenu même de celui-ci, l'être vient s'accomplir en son absoluité". From his "Présentation", in the *Encyclopédie des sciences philosophiques I: La Science de la logique*, G.W.F. Hegel, trans. B. Bourgeois (J. Vrin, Paris, 1970), p. 61.

23 *Enz.* # 384, p. 314 (I 59).

24 *Ph. G.* VIII, p. 549 (479).

25 *Enz.* # 384 R., p. 314 (I 59).

26 *Enz.* # 387 R., p. 318 (I 81).

27 *Ibid.*

28 *Enz.* # 388, p. 318 (II 3).

29 *Enz.* # 389, p. 318 (II 3).

30 *Enz.* # 390, p. 320 (II 21).

31 *Enz.* # 400 R., p. 325 (II 153). The moments of natural soul are natural qualities, natural alterations, and sensation. It may be noted here that to the extent that all cognitive modes of spirit necessarily supersede the sentient soul, a residue of sensation perdures within all knowing. The element of sensation itself presupposes that the object of knowledge retains an aspect of alienation particular to the natural thing, and consequently its independence over against the knowing subject. Furthermore, this residue of sensation implies that even within the knowing characteristic of philosophy, the object of knowledge, i.e., the system, no less manifests the otherness of a natural thing.

32 *Enz.* # 391, p. 320 (II 25).

33 *Enz.* # 395, p. 322 (II 83).

34 *Enz.* # 399, p. 325 (II 147).

35 *Enz.* # 400, p. 325 (II 153).

36 *Enz.* # 401, p. 326 (II 160).

37 *Enz.* # 403, p. 328 (II 215).

38 *Enz.* # 403, p. 328 (II 215). Nowhere does Hegel offer empirical evidence or a separate discourse on the enigma of the soul's immateriality or the related problem of the soul − body dualism. Rather, these issues "dissolve" within the larger systematic structure, of which philosophic discourse is its determinate being-there. Speaking of these traditional enigma, B. Quelquejeu says, "Il faut affirmer que c'est la venue au language de cette énigma, sa mutation en discours philosophique qui *est* la dialectique typique de l'anthropologie de Hegel. C'est pourquoi il y a disparition d'un discours pariculier et séparé concernant les rapports de l'âme et du corps: c'est tout le discours conceptuel développé dans ce chapitre, qui, brossant l'épopée conceptuelle de l'âme effective, parcourt les concepts coordonnés du corps animé ou de l'âme incorporée. Moderne Oedipe de l'intelligence européenne, Hegel a résolu l'énigme en discours". *La volonté dans la philosophie de Hegel* (Ed. du Seuil, Paris, 1972), p. 103.

39 *Enz.* # 403 R., p. 329 (II 217).

40 *Enz.* # 410, p. 340 (II 391).

41 *Enz.* # 410 R., p. 342 (II 391).

42 *Enz.* # 411, p. 342 (II 409).

43 *Enz.* # 411, p. 343 (II 409). In the Remark Hegel himself "anticipates" the higher determinations of this process, where he says that this *Gestalt* is as yet an indeterminate and wholly incomplete sign for spirit, unable to represent it as a universal for-itself. "But for spirit, this

Gestalt is only its *first* appearance, while language is its most perfect expression".

44 *Enz.* # 412, p. 343 (II 425).
45 *Enz.* # 413, p. 344 (III 3).
46 *Enz.* # 415 R., p. 345 (III 11).
47 *Enz.* # 414, p. 344 (III 9).
48 *Enz.* # 415, p. 345 (III 11).
49 *Ph. G.* VIII, p. 558 (487).
50 *Enz.* # 415, p. 345 (III 11).
51 *Enz.* # 416, p. 346 (III 13).
52 *Enz.* # 424, p. 349 (III 37).
53 *Enz.* # 425, p. 349 (III 39).
54 The three moments of self-consciousness are desire (Begierde), recognitive self-consciousness, and universal self-consciousness.
55 *Enz.* # 431, p. 351 (III 55).
56 *Enz.* # 435, p. 353 (III 67).
57 *Enz.* # 436 R., p. 353 (III 71).
58 *Enz.* # 437 R., p. 354 (III 75).
59 *Enz.* # 439, p. 354 (III 77).
60 In the Preface Hegel says that, "This return of the concept into itself must be *presented*. This movement which constitutes what formerly the proof was supposed to accomplish, is the dialectical movement of the proposition itself. This alone is the *actual* speculative, and only its expression is a speculative presentation (Darstellung)". *Ph. G.*, p. 53 (39).
61 *Enz.* # 440, p. 355 (III 79).
62 *Enz.* # 441, p. 355f. (III 83).
63 *Enz.* # 445, p. 359 (III 103).
64 *Enz.* # 446, p. 361 (III 117). The three moments that make up theoretical spirit are intuition (Anschauung), representation (Vorstellung), and thought (Denken).
65 *Enz.* # 448, p. 362f. (III 125).
66 *Enz.* # 448, p. 363 (III 125).
67 Representation itself is broken up into the moments of recollection (Erinnerung), imagination (Einbildungskraft), and memory (Gedächtnis).
68 *Enz.* # 451, p. 363 (III 145). G.R.G. Mure draws the proper conclusion when he points out that, "In all thinking language survives to subserve thought as its indispensable expression. Without discourse thought cannot fulfil itself as thought. But this dependence of thought for the fulfillment of its own nature upon a lower, still sensuous phase of spirit precludes the perfecting of this fulfillment. Even philosophical thought is an incomplete synthesis of language with thought. It can never quite pass from meaning to truth, from reference to an object to utter self-identification with its object". *A Study of Hegel's Logic* (Clarendon Press, Oxford, 1950), p. 22.
69 *Enz.* # 452, p. 364 (III 149).
70 *Enz.* # 453, p. 364 (III 153).
71 *Enz.* # 454, p. 365 (III 155).
72 *Enz.* # 455, p. 365 (III 157).
73 *Enz.* # 457, p. 367f. (III 171).
74 *Enz.* # 457, p. 368 (III 173).
75 *Enz.* # 458, p. 368 (III 177). Jacques Derrida describes the manner in which speech becomes a "promoted presence" of the concept, a terminology which recalls the promoted presence of the absolute in habitual practice and foreshadows the absolute present at hand in the system: "Le langage de son, la parole, portant le dedans au-dehors, ne l'y abandonne pourtant pas simplement, telle une écriture. Gardant le dedans en soi même qu'elle l'émet au-dehors, elle est par excellence ce qui confère l'existence, la présence (Dasein) à la représentation intérieure, elle fait exister le concept (le signifié). Mais, du même coup, en tant qu'il intériorise

et temporalise le Dasein, donné de l'intuition sensible-spatiale, le language élève l'existence elle-même, il la relève dans sa vérité et produit ainsi une sorte de promotion de présence''. ''Le Puits et la Pyramide'', in *Marges de la philosophie* (Ed. de Minuit, Paris, 1972), p. 104.

76 *Enz.* # 462, p. 374f. (III 201).

77 *Enz.* # 463, p. 376 (III 207).

78 *Enz.* # 464, p. 377 (III 209).

79 *Enz.* # 465, p. 378 (III 219).

80 *Enz.* # 466, p. 378 (III 221).

81 *Enz.* # 469, p. 379 (III 231).

82 *Enz.* # 469 R., p. 380 (III 231).

83 *Enz.* # 470, p. 380 (III 235).

84 *Ph. G.* VIII, p. 556 (485).

85 The three moments of practical spirit are practical feeling, impulse and volition, and happiness.

86 *Enz.* # 480, p. 386 (III 263).

87 *Enz.* # 481, p. 387 (III 265).

88 *Enz.* # 482, p. 387 (III 267).

89 The appearance and advance of the idea are themes which will be discussed in the next chapter in an analysis of the ''three syllogisms''.

90 *Enz.* # 482 R., p. 387f. (III 267).

91 *Enz.* # 474 R., p. 384 (III 253).

92 In objective spirit these determinations are ''other'', but their externalization follows the pattern of the linguistic ''other'' that is already implicitly recollected in representation, and is not the alienated ''other'' characteristic of nature. Hegel's method in approaching objective spirit is determined according to this difference. Thus Gadamer is on questionable ground when he says that, ''In the scientific thought of the nineteenth century, what Hegel called objective spirit is conceived as the Other of spirit, and a unified consciousness of method is created after the model of the knowledge of nature''. *Philosophical Hermeneutics*, trans. D. Linge (University of California Press, Los Angeles, 1976), p. 115.

93 There is some sense in Adorno's charge of anti-psychologism in this transition to objective spirit, for the social universal is given clear precedence to the psychological universal, and the individual is said to be actually free only within the institutions of the state. Cf. *Enz.* # 482 R., p. 388 (III 269). But he goes on to suggest that the regional historicity of ethical life is also superseded by world spirit as a necessary moment of absolute externalization, with the implication that philosophic presentation, as the culmination of this externalization and the supersession of history, reduces history itself to theatre. Adorno remarks, ''[Hegel] calls it world spirit because of its power. Domination is absolutized and projected on Being itself, which is said to be the spirit. But history, the explication of something it is supposed to have always been, acquires the quality of the unhistoric''. *Negative Dialectics*, trans. E. Ashton (Seabury Press, New York, 1973), p. 357. It is the need of absolute presentation itself which renders spirit unhistoric, — the need to be absolutely present at hand in a systematic text.

94 *Enz.* # 483, p. 389 (241).

95 *Enz.* # 483, p. 389 (241).

96 *Enz.* # 484, p. 389 (241).

97 *Enz.* # 486, p. 390 (242).

98 *Enz.* # 489, p. 392 (244).

99 *Enz.* # 490, p. 392 (244). J. Ritter, in his discussion of this issue as it appears in the *Philosophie des Rechts*, attempts to avoid this unpleasant consequence of Hegel's thinking through the suggestion that the personality does *differentiate* itself from its property, although it is still dependent on the latter as the condition of its liberty. Ritter says that, ''sur le terrain

de la société civile moderne et de son droit en lequel tous, comme personnes, sont radicalement distincts des choses, l'extériorisation présuppose que la personne elle-même ne peut pas être extériorisée et qu'elle peut posséder son être propre, intérieur et extérieur, qui échappe à la société ... C'est pour cela que la liberté de la propriété est selon Hegel le principe qui seul confère l'existence à la liberté chrétienne: parce que la société se limite à la relation mutuelle des personnes venant des choses et de la propriété, elle rend l'individu, comme personnalité, libre de devenir sujet en tout ce qui constitue la richesse et la profondeur de l'être personnel, moralement spirituel, échappant à toute chosification". *Hegel et la revolution française suivi de Personne et propriété selon Hegel* (Beauchesne, Paris, 1970), p. 84. We must add, however, that in general, the nature of the "difference" between that self and its externalization varies according to the mode of appropriation.

100 *Enz.* # 491, p. 393 (244).

101 This discussion of property in the *Enzyklopädie* offers a striking contrast to the discussion of labour in Chapter 4 of the *Phänomenologie*. In the latter, labour was viewed as the active expression of the personality, an exteriorization in which the worker came to know himself. "Through work, however, the bondsman becomes conscious of what he truly is". *Phän.* IV, p. 148 (118). In the *Enz.* the actual forming activity is not considered necessary, the mere designation of property being thought a sufficient reflection of personality.

102 *Enz.* # 493, p. 393 (245).

103 *Enz.* # 462, p. 374 (III 201).

104 *Enz.* # 494, p. 394 (245).

105 *Enz.* # 496, p. 394 (246).

106 *Enz.* # 502, p. 396 (248).

107 *Enz.* # 502, p. 396 (248).

108 *Enz.* # 502 R., p. 297 (248).

109 *Enz.* # 503, p. 397 (249).

110 But in both cases there is, implicitly, a certain distancing of the self from its externalization. Already in property is the potential differentiation of the subject from the existence of his freedom in a thing characteristic of morality, since Hegel points out that, in property "the concrete return of me into myself in externality is the 'I', infinite self-relation, which as a person is the repulsion of me from myself ...". *Enz.* # 490, p. 392 (244).

111 *Phil. des Rechts,* # 44, p. 57 (41).

112 *Phil. des Rechts,* # 49, p. 61 (44). "What and how much I possess, therefore,, is a matter of indifference so fas as rights are concerned".

113 *Enz.* # 486 R., p. 390 (242).

114 *Enz.* # 495, p. 394 (246). "The contract, as an agreement which has a voluntary origin and deals with a casual commodity, involves at the same time the giving to this 'accidental' will a positive fixity (Gesetzsein)".

115 *Enz.* # 502, p. 396 (248). The reasonable will is objectively "for" consciousness through the particular will of the judge, who has the power to prosecute individual negations of the intrinsic right. Consequently prosecution and punishment takes the form of a negation of a negation, through which the criminal is restored to his proper relation *vis-à-vis* the universal self expressed in law. As all laws simply appear "alongside" each other, and have no implicit claim to the obedience or belief of individuals as such, that right is intrinsic which is truly universal, i.e., which is appropriated by a "public". As will be remembered from the last chapter, public discourse is the origin for the verification, or validation, of what can otherwise be described as particular or esoteric "chatter", as if, in the public, the absolute dimly appears. Thus as with law, philosophic presentation awaits the will of the absolute which is already "close to us": "We must hold to the conviction that it is the nature of truth to prevail when its time has come, and that it appears only when this time has come, and therefore never appears prematurely, nor finds a public not ripe to receive it; also we must accept that the individual needs that this should be so in order to verify what is as yet a matter for himself alone,

and to experience the conviction, which in the first place belongs only to a particular individual, as something universality held''. *Ph.G.* Vorr., p. 58 (44).

116 See above p. 32f.

117 *Enz.* # 512, p. 401 (253). In other words, the self-certain subject becomes merely the infinite form for the good, and in this identity (Identität) with the good, actualizes and develops it, whereby the standpoint of the "ought" is abandoned.

118 *Enz.* # 513, p. 402 (253).

119 *Enz.* # 514, p. 402 (254).

120 *Enz.* # 519, p. 404 (255).

121 *Enz.* # 519, p. 404 (255).

122 *Enz.* # 520, p. 404 (256). Indeed, the "family holdings" become the immediate representation of the group to which all of its members relate in an organic fashion, as their "universal" or objective self. The immediacy of this relationship is markedly so, because the members regard this representation as the object of their collective labour.

123 *Enz.* # 523, p. 405 (257).

124 *Enz.* # 533, p. 411 (262).

125 *Enz.* # 533, p. 412 (262).

126 *Enz.* # 527, p. 407 (258).

127 *Enz.* # 527 R., p. 407 (258).

128 *Enz.* # 529, p. 408 (259).

129 *Enz.* # 533, p. 413 (264).

130 *Enz.* # 537, p. 413 (264).

131 *Enz.* # 537, p. 418 (269). "The living totality — that which preserves, in other words continually produces the state in general and its constitution, is the government. The organization which natural necessity gives is the origin of the family and of the 'estates' of civil society. The government is the *universal* part of the constitution, i.e., the part which intentionally aims at preserving those parts, but at the same time gets hold of and carries out those general aims of the whole which rise above the determination of the family and of civil society".

132 *Enz.* # 539, p. 414 (265).

133 *Enz.* # 540, p. 417 (268).

134 *Enz.* # 542 R., p. 420 (271).

135 *Enz.* # 542, p. 419 (270).

136 *Enz.* # 544 R., p. 421 (272).

137 *Enz.* # 542 R., p. 240 (271).

138 *Enz.* # 543, p. 420 (271).

139 *Enz.* # 545, p. 424 (275).

140 See K.H. Ilting's "The Structure of Hegel's Philosophy of Right" in *Hegel's Political Philosophy*, ed. Z. Pelczynski (Cambridge Univ. Press, London, 1971), pp. 90–110, for an interesting discussion of this problem.

141 *Enz.* # 548, p. 426 (277).

142 *Enz.* # 549, p. 426 (277).

143 *Enz.* # 549, p. 426 (277).

144 *Enz.* # 549 R., p. 426 (277).

145 *Enz.* # 549 R., p. 428 (279).

146 *Die Vernunft in der Geschichte*, p. 164 (136). We must remark in passing that Hegel seems to tie all "historical production" to the life of the nation, and presumably this includes the particular linguistic universe of law, the arts and sciences. As we shall see later, ethical life itself finds its sanction through the appropriation of absolute spirit in revealed religion. Naturally the question pertinent to our investigation, is whether, and to what extent, philosophic presentation, too, is related to the needs of nationhood, — a question to be taken up in the next chapter.

147 *Enz.* # 549 R., p. 428 (279).

148 *Enz.* # 549 R., p. 428 (280).

149 *Enz.* # 549 R., p. 429 (280).

150 *Enz.* # 550, p. 430 (281). There is a very real sense in Hegel's description of the *Weltgeist*, in which the power of each state over its people, and over other nations, is wholly and indiscriminately sanctioned through the "progress" of spirit in history. Although this progress is apparently relative to the concept of freedom, there is the paradoxical impression that the freedom of the individual is no less sacrificed to the collective whole. Adorno rightly points out that, "It is precisely the thesis of this independence of popular spirits which Hegel uses to confer legality upon the rule of force over the individuals, in a way similar to Durkheim's later use of collective norms, and to Spengler's use of the soul of each culture. The more abundantly a universal is equipped with the insignia of the collective subject, the more completely will the subjects disappear in it". *Op. cit.*, p. 338.

151 *Die Vernunft in der Geschichte*, p. 30 (29).

152 *Ibid.*, p. 63 (55).

153 *Enz.* # 552, p. 430 (282).

154 *Enz.* # 552, p. 431 (282).

155 *Enz.* # 552 R., p. 431 (283).

156 *Enz.* # 552 R., p. 432 (283).

157 *Enz.* # 552 R., p. 432 (283).

158 *Enz.* # 552 R., p. 435 (286).

159 *Enz.* # 552 R., p. 436 (288).

160 *Enz.* # 552 R., p. 437 (289).

161 *Enz.* # 553, p. 440 (292).

162 *Enz.* # 553, p. 440 (292).

163 *Enz.* # 552 R., p. 439 (291).

164 *Enz.* # 554, p. 440 (292).

165 *Enz.* # 555, p. 440 (292).

166 *Enz.* # 562 R., p. 444 (296).

167 *Enz.* # 556, p. 441 (293).

168 *Enz.* # 557, p. 442 (293).

169 *Enz.* # 559, p. 442 (294).

170 *Enz.* # 560, p. 443 (294).

171 *Enz.* # 562, p. 444 (295).

172 *Enz.* # 563, p. 445 (297).

173 *Enz.* # 564, p. 446 (297).

174 *Enz.* # 565, p. 447 (299).

175 *Enz.* # 567, p. 447 (299).

176 Of course a full discussion of the nature of Hegel's philosophic appropriation of historical Christianity cannot be taken up within the confines of this aperçu of the *Phil. des Geistes*. However the lack of any discussion of the religious need as such, and his characterization of Christianity strictly through its forms of representation, makes plausible Lukacs' statement that Hegel "as good as never troubled himself with the religious need as such: Schleiermacher's *Speeches on Religion* he treats ironically; he consistently rejects Jacobi's search for a direct knowledge oriented toward religion; his Jena notes are full of extremely distanced ironic remarks on the role of religion in everyday life, etc.". Aspects of this antipathy to the ineffable inward are to be found elsewhere in Hegel's writings, for example in his critique of immediate knowing, but as to its origin, there seems to be little agreement. Lukacs consistently offers a socio-historical account, by and large convincing, of this phenomenon: "Just as the entire *Phenomenology* radiates a Napoleonic spirit, so this conception of religion is deeply influenced by Napoleon's attitude toward religion: recognition of its historical existence and power, in conjunction with a very far-reaching indifference toward its internal nature. For Napoleonic

France, religion was to be integrated into the new bourgeois state; for Hegel's Germany, into the philosophy which mentally corresponded to this''. *Hegel's False and His Genuine Ontology, op. cit.*, pp. 57f.

177 *Enz.* # 568, p. 448 (300).
178 *Enz.* # 569, p. 448 (300).
179 *Enz.* # 570, p. 449 (300).
180 *Enz.* # 552 R., p. 432 (283).
181 *Enz.* # 571, p. 449 (301).
182 *Enz.* # 571, p. 449 (301).
183 *Enz.* # 572, p. 450 (302).
184 *Enz.* # 573, p. 451 (302).
185 *Enz.* # 573, p. 451 (302). My emphasis.

III. PHILOSOPHIC PRESENTATION

1. SELF-KNOWLEDGE AND LANGUAGE

1.1 *Absolute mediation as return-to-self*

Our discussion thus far has centred on an immanent analysis of the *Phänomenologie*, as an appearing system, and the system itself, in order to demonstrate that the determination of their content presupposes the necessities of philosophic presentation. However such an analysis cannot elucidate the sense in which presentation is the original ground of both the system and its appearances, and how this differentiation of modes is related to the exigencies of the absolute idea. This is the task that lays before us now, — that of uncovering the identity of the *Phänomenologie* and the system in speculative presentation.

As has been argued in the first chapter, the knowing subject become absolute consciousness at the end of the *Phänomenologie* is still alienated from the presentation of its absolute determination because that content has only appeared to it under the guise of consciousness. On the other hand, the system, as the in-and-for-itself existing presentation of the absolute idea, fails to account for itself as absolute knowing. It is our contention that both systems can only be understood as a necessary suite of absolute manifestations "for" natural consciousness that externalize and recollect the absolute as knowledge. The *finality* of this knowledge is related to the time required by the absolute for its total manifestation, and the adequacy of presentation as the matrix of externalization and recollection.

Thus the problem we must seek to deal with in the following discussion is exactly how speculative presentation can offer itself as both the most significant instance of absolute self-manifestation *and* as a self-knowledge for natural consciousness existing within the language and spirit of a people. In other words, we must try to understand in what sense philosophic discourse is both a response to a need on the part of a particular people and epoch for self-knowledge, and a necessary mode of absolute self-knowledge. In what sense does the finite striving of people for self-awareness fall together with an absolute spirit which seeks to be present of its *own* volition?

It is only through speculative presentation that the knowing subject is able to appropriate its absolute determination, and hence become conscious of objectivity as its own. Presentation makes possible and carries out the recollection and interiorization of the externalization of natural consciousness, and in so doing raises that natural consciousness to absolute self-consciousness. The instigation to presentation derives from the primordial need of consciousness to grasp its essence, which in natural consciousness is merely a potential, a transition-point.

Consequently the discursive manifestation of the absolute in speculative presentation is as much a self-knowing by natural consciousness as a knowing of the absolute. The two important transitions between the modes of appearing of the absolute are based on this primordial drive to self-consciousness: natural consciousness takes up its presentation as phenomenal knowing in the *Phänomenologie*, and absolute knowing *goes over* to the content of the system of the *Enzyklopädie* as the system of its absolute determination, because of the reciprocal necessity that the subject know itself absolutely and the absolute as subjectivity. In this way, presentation accounts for its own differentiation into modes.

The presented system marks the rise to self-consciousness of the previous unconscious absolute determination of subjectivity, and we may say that it is the exhaustive appropriation of the absolute which closes off the historical manifestation of absolute spirit in art and revealed religion, to the extent that the system contains their truth.[1] Within the system itself, the dialectical relation of its configurations determines philosophic presentation as the moment of absolute individuality (Einzelnheit), the moment which is the result of the discursive manifestation of the absolute *and* its originary presupposition. Far from explicating an historical development of spiritual configurations which "culminates" in philosophic knowing, the dialectical process of presentation in the system is a conscious descent to the absolute horizons of Hegelian science. But the relation of the system to the *Phänomenologie*, and the references within the system to its historical appearing, suggest that this descent is related to historical time, and raises the question as to whether we can discern its merely subjective, autobiographical quality from its absolute, ahistorical determination.

This movement within the system, between an absolute presupposition and an absolute result that are finally the same, is determined as a succession of configurations which are not temporally or chronologically linked, but linked in terms of the relative "fullness" or depth of their grounding of all previous configurations. Therefore fullness is a function of recollection, and, through presentation, reflects the relative self-consciousness of absolute determination: each configuration recollects those antecedent to it. However, before each configuration is raised to its truth through presentation, it has its fortuitous appearing in history, and it is important that we distinguish between the historical connotation and the presentation. While the system also recollects these historical appearances, speculative presentation empties them of their chronological succession.

Through presentation Hegel has left us evidence of the absolute depth of his situation. But has the system truly accounted for the supersession of its historical appearing?[2] It would seem that only a self-conscious interpretation of the system as a presentation of the absolute subject can begin to make sense of this supersession. The *Phänomenologie* itself does not provide such an interpretation because it, too, presupposes the system as its truth.

On the other hand, speculative presentation, as the intended recollection of the externalization of the absolute subject, tends to behold the historical appearances superseded by its presentation in a teleological manner; the scientific philosopher brings history to an "end" when he invokes an in-depth analysis of the present moment. Indeed, the absolute self-consciousness of the present moment conceived as result is the implicit presupposition of the analysis. In this case the finality of the system *vis-à-vis* its historical appearances is less the result of an objective necessity working through history than the subjective intention of the philosopher to present his self-consciousness as a result. If this is so, then speculative presentation never fully supersedes the autobiographical, historical residue of natural consciousness.

As long as presentation is understood as a finite externalization of natural consciousness, and not, equally, as absolute recollection, it would seem that the historical concerns of the intended present-as-result determines the content of its dialectical representation. It is these concerns which are the unthought determination of the intended present and the necessary configurations that mediate it, for the self-consciousness of this present stands in a relation to its epochal disclosure. In order to understand the unthought concerns which determine the spiritual configurations of the system, we must understand the relation of its presentation to the natural consciousness of Hegel's day.

However, the system claims to have superseded the historical appearing of its configurations through their presentation in the dialectical format of absolute self-knowing. The finality of this presentation, *vis-à-vis* the historical appearing of the configurations, takes on a timeless presence in which absolute manifestation is exhaustively mediated and subject. But this finality owes much of its significance to the determination of absolute self-consciousness as the recollection of its "prior" externalization, and leaves totally open the meaning of this finality for an unknown future.[3]

Hegel says that the experience of natural consciousness itself points to the mediation implied by the immediate present: "A sensible consideration of the world distinguishes in the wide realm of outer and inner existence what is only appearance, transient and meaningless, from what in-itself truly deserves the name of actuality".[4] But is the act of presentation the result of a merely sensible consideration on the part of the knowing subject, or does the absolute itself, knowing itself in consciousness, appropriate and determine this presentation as the moment of its complete self-knowledge?

The spiritual configurations that mediate absolute knowing, as presented in the system, receive their existence and are contained through their union with subjective self-certainty. The system is "for" natural consciousness as long as we comprehend it as the presentation by a knowing subject, — through which, alone, the absolute achieves self-certainty. It is upon this description of the system as an appropriation by the knowing subject of its absolute determination that rests the conviction of natural consciousness that this system is a realization of its self-consciousness. Thus any introduction to the system that takes the form of an absolutely necessary cultural history which culminates in speculative science must fail to convince natural consciousness because it does not account for speculative science as essentially self-knowing presentation.[5]

But speculative presentation is also an externalization of the absolute, so that natural consciousness tends to understand the system as somehow historically final. This finality is at bottom an *appearing* for consciousness: the path of phenomenal knowing that leads to absolute knowing in the *Phänomenologie* has the aspect of chronological succession until we have grasped it as a presentation "for" consciousness. If absolute knowing has a finality at all, it is a finality related not to chronological succession, but to timelessness; it is the knowing of an exhaustively mediated present, and the suite of spiritual configurations which form this mediation are dialectically, and not chronologically, constituted.

The dialectical constitution implied by the immediate present is the key to the efficacy of speculative presentation, and accounts for Hegel's decided antagonism to the doctrine of "immediate" knowledge, for there is no true knowledge aside from the knowledge of this presented mediation. The retreat of thought from the mediated present he terms "misology", following Plato's criticism of his fellow Greeks,[6] which is not merely ignorance, but the thinking determination "to stop courageously at the surface, the fold, the skin, to adore appearance, to believe in forms, tones, words, in the whole Olympus of appearance. Those Greeks were superficial — out of profundity".[7] In contradistinction to Nietzsche's care for the play of tones, Hegel wishes to know absolutely the necessity of the thing itself.

This relationship of thought to experience, the mediation of its present objectivity, is neither wholly *a posteriori* nor *a priori*. Thinking is indebted to experience, indeed it is essentially the negation of what is immediately before us, but it is equally mediated with itself and indifferent to the descent into particulars.[8] Here we understand that the absolute determination of thought, the necessity of the mediation of the absolute with itself at a given moment, is balanced by the infinite subjectivity of thought itself which presents these determinations.

The mediation of absolute knowing presented by the system accounts for itself as philosophic cognition, but presents configurations which are dialectically antecedent to this result and are determined by this result as their presupposition. This means that the logical place of these configurations within the system is a function of the self-conscious fullness moving between presupposition and result. For example, *Das Recht* and *Die Moralität* are dialectically antecedent to *Die Sittlichkeit*, a relation which does not reflect the appearing of their historical succession.

The only formal discussion of history in the *Philosophie des Geistes* occurs in that section of objective spirit dealing with the interaction of nation-states and the *Weltgeist*, and we must assume that all historical phenomena are meant to be understood within the context of the nation-state as the over-riding hermeneutic principle. Of course much of the prior dicussion of the spiritual configurations that dialectically constitute absolute knowing obviously has its roots in historical evidence, and it is crucial that we comprehend the relation of speculative presentation to this evidence if the content of the system is to invoke the interest of natural consciousness. As it stands, the discussion concerning the historical determination of the nation-state has important implications for the national basis of philosophic presentation, which we will take up later.

For the moment, the relation of speculative presentation to historical evidence raises a number of questions. Are the appearances of configurations in history already implicitly dialectically determined, and if so, is the *Philosophie des Geistes* both a history and a logic of these spiritual configurations? To begin with, we may assert that the suite of configurations that present the mediation of the absolute subject is strictly a dialectical suite, and no direct reference is made by Hegel to their appearing in time. While it is tacitly accepted, for instance, that the "absolute as ideal" is in particular a Greek appropriation of the absolute, the historical content of this appropriation is used merely as an external access to the discussion of the place of this configuration within a dialectical process. Historical appearing is rooted in, but not identical with, the absolute ontology presented by the system.

The objective content which makes up the presented configurations is found in experience, content first presented by the empirical sciences in the shape of general determinations, kinds, and laws. The reception of these concrete materials into thought at the same time brings thought out of itself. Thought, then, owes its development to the empirical sciences, while giving this content the necessity and essential form of the freedom of thought. Hegel asserts, "The fact becomes a presentation (Darstellung) and reproduction by the originary and complete independent activity of thought".[9]

These facts-become-configurations must form a system if their mediation is to be absolute. Hegel believes that only the system is scientific because its development is in-itself, i.e., the system is a totality self-related, and the content has its justification only as a moment of the whole. Outside of this systematic form, any thinking of the mediation of the absolute subject is ungrounded presupposition and merely subjective certainty.[10] Speculative presentation is the mediation by thought of the empirical content necessary to absolute knowing, a content made necessary by the dialectical descent to its absolute presupposition. In this way, the presented content of absolute knowing exhibits the appearance of a circle which closes with itself, and has no beginning outside of the infinite subjectivity of thought itself.[11] This knowing is satisfied, and is in a sense final, when the fullness of its mediation accounts for, and is accounted by, its subjective presentation.

1.2 *Linguistic presentation and the dialectic*

The appropriation of the absolute in speculative presentation is universal because it happens as language. This universality has a direct bearing on the nature of the finality of this appropriation, because the empirical evidence which constitutes the presented mediation of the absolute subject is by and large linguistic, as is, of course, the system itself. The "truth" of both this evidence and the system is dependent on Hegel's claims for the universality and speculative power of language.

Language-as-sign described in *Der subjektive Geist* creates the promoted presence of a free subject which has superseded its natural determinations. Language-as-law in *Der objektive Geist* is instrumental to a nation-state which has superseded the accidental individuality of civil society through the organization and regulation of work and social interaction. The language of speculative presentation in *Der absolute Geist* aids the self-conscious supersession of the historical manifestations of the absolute within a conceptual re-presentation which is necessary and subject.

In all of the above, to *say* the natural, individual, or historical immediate is to mediate it. Language itself is an absolute constant, and has no history within the system. The historicity of the linguistic universe would tend to qualify the role of language as this universal element which unconsciously translates particularities into spiritual configurations. Language is rather the medium or element of spirit, inseparable from the implicit universality of thought: we think in names. It follows that to qualify in any way this universal status of language would equally qualify the supposed universality of the thoughts it expresses.

Language's translation of the meant or particular "this" into the universal "this" is an essential part of speculative presentation, and is therefore common to both the *Phänomenologie* as an appearing system, and the system itself. In the latter, Hegel reaffirms that "language is the work of thought, and so cannot express what is not universal. What I only *mean*, is *mine*, belonging to me as this particular individual; but when language expresses only the universal, then I am not able to say what I only *mean*. And the *unutterable*, feeling, sensation, is not the most excellent or most true, but the most insignificant, the most untrue".[12] As an example of the mediation of language, Hegel describes the plight of the *I* which means my single self to the exclusion of others, but says the universal self common to everyone.

Language translates, but its action remains unconscious even at the level of speculative science because it is denied a history. In the *Phänomenologie*, linguistic expression has a quasi-temporal aspect due to the fact that each mode of phenomenal knowing is reflected in its use of language, and each mode is linked to the next as a subjective time-seeing: but the particular linguistic universe of each mode is ignored. In the *Enzyklopädie* we are offered the timeless psycho-physiological constitution of the sign as one of the necessary spiritual configurations which mediate the absolute subject, but again, the determination of this configuration is a logical category abstracted from the thick immediacy of any particular language.

The rationality of language, the translation of the particular by the general, is very much an unconscious reflex, and Hegel accepts this rationality without questioning the development of language-use as the history of a particular language "game" involving a particular natural consciousness. The origination of signs and the creation of a linguistic, promoted presence as described in *Der subjektive Geist* fixes this inherent rationality of language as a necessary part of subjective psychology, and while we may accept the sign-making activity as a psychological constant, certainly it is evident that the meaning and interrelation of names is a matter of the linguistic group. And this is one of the most surprising aspects of Hegel's discussion of language: with his emphasis on the *Volksgeist* as the criterion of historical interpretation, one would think that a discussion of the national history of languages and the group determination of meanings-names would be forth-coming.

But this discussion does not occur and for very good reason. Any attempt to qualify the translation of the particular by the universal, by containing that translation within a particular linguistic group, would equally qualify the truths expressed within that group. An analysis which took into account the thick immediacy of group language that permeates each spiritual configuration of the system would have to justify the transition from group-meaning to group-meaning in the linking of configurations. If these transitions were not justified then the dialectical presentation of spiritual configurations would break-up into a series of relative descriptions which ground particular truths.

Such group-meanings do not qualify the individual configurations because their movement within the system is not linguistic but dialectical, and it is the system as the self-conscious presentation of the absolute that is the presupposition for the appearing of configurations within historical linguistic groups. Any language can reflect the universal structure of the concept, which is prior to all language, as in nature or the soul, for example. Consequently the absolute dialectical movement of configurations renders the history of languages a superfluous concern, for in language, as the element of thought, the concept is present to itself. And of course it is the universality of thought that ultimately guarantees the translations of language.

Inspite of the assurance of this last remark, there remains the doubt that this identification of names-meanings with the universality of thought is perhaps a little self-convincing. In Hegel's entire discussion of language in the system, there is no adequate explication of the way in which the universality of thought is itself dependent on the names-meanings that express it, i.e., on the thick immediacy of a particular language. The question at stake is whether concrete names-meanings associated with a particular linguistic group can at the same time be used by a conceptual thinking that actually transcends the particular and stands "outside" of that group. Can such names-meanings take on this universal determination without losing their sense for the particular linguistic group in which they originate? [13]

Philosophical language must be circumscribed by the use given it by the language group if it is in any way to be true for that group, and the transgression of this use creates the *illusion* of super-concepts. Within the system there appears to be an essential contradiction between the efficacy of language in expressing universal concepts and the containment of language by the relative spiritual manifestation of the *Volksgeist*. The system of absolute determinations itself is presented in language, and is related by language to the contemporary *Volksgeist* of natural consciousness. The understanding by this consciousness of its absolute determination is impossible without a prior linguistic comprehension of the configurations of the mediation, and if this determination of subjectivity is truly universal, then its expression as names-meanings must also transcend the determinations of the *Volksgeist*.

The problem increases in complexity when we take into consideration not only Hegel's knowledge of the linguistic origins of the configurations that make up the system, but our own knowledge of the linguistic peculiarities of his speculative presentation. These are the kind of issues that present themselves when we identify language with the universality of thought to the detriment of the thick immediacy of speech, an identification which tends to cover over the question of the relation between speech and the absolute idea in all speculative presentation. [14]

Before the objective content of the configurations is appropriated by presentation, it appears in the element of language as empirical information, external facts, or positive propositions. Speculative presentation appropriates this evidence through the mediating integration of this "past" with a timeless present, – rather than attempting to reconstruct an objectively true past. Such an objective reconstruction is impossible because all knowledge alters its immediate object through its thinking mediation: "Through thinking-over something is *altered* in the way in which the content was originally in sensation, intuition, and representation; thus it is only *by means of* an alteration that the *true* nature of objects comes before consciousness". [15]

The mediation of thought alters the linguistic evidence in such a way as to bring out its true object *vis-à-vis* its immediate determination, so that thinking-over the empirical world means essentially negating and comprehending its particular form to reveal its absolute mediation. What is most important in this comprehension is that thinking is a negative act toward its basis; the matter of perception, when it is determined as universality, does not remain in its first empirical form. Hegel says, "With the removal and *negation* of the shell, the inner worth of the perception becomes thrown into relief". [16]

The absolute idea mediates and recollects its externalization through negating absolutely its immediacy in every detail. This negating action both presupposes the original externalization of the absolute to work upon, and results in the new self-conscious immediacy of the presented system. Therefore the presentation and recollection of this externalization involves three essential moments: the action of the understanding, which displays this externalization as empirical evidence; the action of negative-reason, which reveals its true dialectical constitution; and the action of positive-reason, which knows this externalization as speculative presentation.[17]

The understanding remains with the fixed determinations and the differentiation of these from each other; each such particular abstract it treats as subsisting and being for-itself.[18] The dialectical moment is the inherent self-supersession of such finite determinations and their going-over into their opposite.[19] The speculative moment of positive-reason lays hold of the unity of determinations in their opposition, the *affirmative*, which is involved in their dissolving and their going-over. This reasonable result, while it is a thought and abstract, is equally a concrete, which is not a simple, formal unity, but a unity differentiated and determinate.[20] The dialectical interaction between thought and objectivity determines the logical movement of all spiritual content, a movement which results in, and presupposes, the total mediation of speculative presentation.

The presented system is really only the thinking mediation of absolute externalization, and suggests that the primacy of totality over phenomenality is to be grasped in phenomenality. But in so doing, the phenomenality of empirical evidence is fundamentally altered: the empirical particular of understanding is contained and superseded under the genus of "particularity", an organizational principle that posits the presupposed ground of identity for all particulars. In this way the opaque resistance of the particular is overcome through the presupposition of the identity of identity and difference.

The absolute is infinite unity, and all otherness lies within it. Indeed this sense of the original identity of the finite is the meaning of philosophical idealism: the truth of the finite is its ideality. Hegel asserts, "A philosophy which ascribed veritable, ultimate, absolute being to finite existence as such, would not deserve the name of philosophy; the principles of ancient or modern philosophies, water, or matter, or atoms are *thoughts*, universals, ideal entities, not things as they immediately present themselves to us, that is, in their sensuous individuality – not even the water of Thales".[21]

Once we present the dialectical self-movement of phenomenality as determined by the infinite unity of the absolute, then the particular is contained and superseded under the "moment" of particularity. The absolute mediation by speculative presentation raises the particular empirical evidence to necessity and subjectivity, giving the historic specific an invariance as if divinely willed. And furthermore, this mediation has the surety of self-certainty since the dialectical process is the occurrence of the absolute raised to self-consciousness.

It must be clear that absolute knowing does not apply an "external" method to empirical evidence, since speculative presentation is as much the self-knowing of its absolute content as it is an act by the knowing subject. The knowing subject mediates itself by thinking and presenting the dialectical oc-currence of the absolute, so that the absolute becomes self-conscious as sub-ject and the subject becomes self-conscious as absolute. But if thinking does not construe the absolute in speculative presentation, neither is thinking merely the occurrence of the absolute, for this does not account for the ac-tuality of the absolute as a presentation by the knowing subject. [22]

This linking of the process character of thinking with the dialectical "oc-currence" of the absolute again brings up this relation between the logical and chronological aspects of mediation. While occurrence denotes a disclosure in time, occurrence is not necessarily chronological succession, and the disclosure of spiritual configurations in the system is not chronologi-cal but dialectical. Rather, the dialectic is the absolute thinking itself as oc-currence, and it is this occurrence that gives the dialectic its discursive time-character. Occurrence is its own rhythm, consuming the time necessary to its proper fullness.

In thinking the dialectic as occurrence we go over to the absolute mediation of thought, but speculatve presentation is also a subjective thinking of this mediation. In as much as speculative thinking both supersedes and contains the understanding of natural consciousness, it can equally be suggested that the discursive character of the dialectic itself reflects a sublimated subjective time-viewing. Such a statement does not necessarily qualify the absolute character of presentation, since the time experience of natural consciousness presented as phenomenal knowing is the concept existing there, an experience superseded by absolute, self-conscious presentation. A suggestion that sub-jectivity has a primordial time-viewing that is not superseded by speculative presentation would, however, radically qualify the absolute content of the system, through its determination of the concept as a finite projection of subjectivity. [23] Among other considerations, this would make the true knowl-edge of objectivity, the thing-in-itself, impossible.

There is undoubtedly an element of truth to these two interpretations of the dialectic — as absolute occurrence in a passive subject and as the sublated time-experience of a legislating subject — but they tend to exaggerate one side

or the other of absolute knowing, i.e., absolute disclosure or subjective projection. Absolute knowing must both comprehend phenomenality and raise
that phenomenality to self-conscious totality. If the subject simply thinks the
absolute occurrence, we introduce an aspect of passivity into speculative
presentation, in which the subject is merely the open clearing for a revealing-
concealing absolute. On the other hand, if the dialectical format is the objec-
tification of a primordial time-experience, then absolute occurrence is determined by finite thinking, and the supersession of the particular by the absolute in speculative presentation is at best, impossible, and at worst, a fraud.

Speculative presentation must be thought of as both absolute and infinitely
determinate, because it is total self-knowledge being-there. Only in this way
is it an exhaustive mediation of the whole and a subjective knowing, and only
in this way are the spiritual configurations that make up this mediation self-
certain and true. The "coming on the scene" of speculative presentation is
inseparable from the "full" occurrence of absolute self-knowing, so that any
description of the dialectic as a rhythm of Being independent of its presentation fails to grasp the dialectic as the rhythm of the appropriation between
subject and absolute.

In like manner, the conception of the dialectic as objectified time-
experience views the logic in a two-dimensional, flat perspective. Its discursive quality results from the succession of the moments of universality, particularity, and individuality on the written page, as if a telescope were opened
for our scientific inspection. But the last moment of "individuality" is also
the presupposition for the first two moments, and each moment of individuality contains that previous, and the moment of philosophic science contains
them all, − and contains them not as a temporal succession, for the moments
are not time moments, but as instantaneously and timelessly present. The
discursive or temporal quality of the "movement" of the dialectical format
results rather from its existing in the element of language, itself representational and successive, as the reified evidence of appropriation. Furthermore,
speculative thinking supersedes this representational and successive form of
the proposition through the utilization of a series of sentences, which
manifest the comprehensiveness of the concept in referring back on each
other, and which dissolve the rigid progression of formal propositional presentation.

The question remains, of course, as to whether the representationalism of
language, and the abrupt division of the text into "moments" of the dialectic, actually is able to convey the concrete unity of speculative thinking. These
moments themselves contain analytic propositions, which receive their justification or proof wholly from their existence within the horizons of a confi-

guration that is linked dialectically to the next: "This return of the concept into itself must be *presented*; this movement which constitutes what formerly the proof was supposed to accomplish, is the dialectical movement of the proposition itself. This alone is the *actual* speculative, and only the expression of this movement is a speculative presentation (Darstellung)".[24]

Is the dualism between a dialectical chain of moments and the content consisting of a series of analytic propositions really superseded in speculative presentation? We may say that the series of propositions manifest the content of the concept, its inner dimension of multiplicity, but the proposition itself is analytical and not dialectical. This means that the movement of the concept is always merely implicit within the element of language, and that conceptual content never finds its precise expression in a single proposition, so that the textual divisions representing the moments of the dialectic must appear somewhat arbitrary. The number, kind, and connection of sentences within each moment seems entirely relative and the result of arbitrary discretion, and we can never be certain that we have the "correct" impression of conceptual content as expressed in the text, since a whimsical turn of phrase will often do more for our understanding (or for our bewilderment) than pages of plodding analysis.

Although according to Hegel we think in names, speculative thinking must be satisfied with an approximate expression of its conceptual unity, since this unity is always immanent in, but not identical with, language. Language is the element or medium of the dialectic, for it has no dialectical moments of its own. But it is precisely the promoted presence of language that gives the dialectic its discursive quality, and before we think the dialectic as objectified time-experience, we must take into consideration the implicit temporal aspect of such a promoted presence.

We cannot think the dialectic without thinking its content, whether this be the comprehension of natural and spiritual configurations or the configurations that make up a speculative logic. This is because the dialectic is the rhythm of the finite existing of absolute knowing and the absolute knowing itself, the rhythm of the self-determination and self-consciousness of speculative presentation. And the dialectical format of presentation will always be essentially "untimely" as long as it is truly the rhythm of absolute knowing certain of itself. Any attempt of approach the system as a philosophical object of interpretation cannot break into the circle of this infinite self-certainty, a self-certainty whose origin is in presentation.

The dialectical format makes manifest the moments of a self-referring and self-presenting totality, i.e., the presented determinations of absolute knowing. But if we claim that this presentation is only the finite approximation of the absolute, then the dialectic re-appears as the subjective machination of natural consciousness unable to supersede the opaque resistance of its abstract determinations, for its "speculative" totality is what guarantees philosophic presentation self-certainty and truth. Such an interpretation that posits the inadequacy of any subjective knowing of the absolute is left with two timely conclusions: the fragmentary result of all subjective thinking and the self-concealment of the absolute.

2. THOUGHTS AND SITUATIONS

2.1 *Absolute need and truth*

If we tentatively accept the efficacious supersession of natural consciousness by philosophic presentation, i.e., that philosophic presentation is potentially "for" natural consciousness, we do not, on the other hand, know how philosophic presentation *appears* to this consciousness as its true self on the level of consciousness. The hypothesis we wish to put forth is that philosophic presentation appears as an exhaustive and salutary response to a need that becomes self-apparent to natural consciousness. However it seems that this need which precedes philosophic presentation occurs only at a particular moment in the progress of spirit, and is always related to the demands of a particular people, such that we must speak of philosophic presentation as essentially a regional response.

To begin with, what is this need which brings about this appropriation of the absolute, and in what sense is the system a "true" response to this need? Before we can make sense of the absolute determinations of the system as it lies before us, we must understand how the system attempts to account for its appearance. It must be shown that the moment of philosophic presentation as the "resolve that wills pure thought",[25] is a beginning neither arbitrary nor subjective, but determined by the fullness of a comprehended epochal need.

We have already discussed the manner in which the appearance of the *Phänomenologie* responded to the need of natural consciousness for self-knowledge. But Hegel makes other suggestions to the effect that this response is the typical response of philosophy in general to the needs of any particular epoch. The source of this need is always the sense of division and difference in spiritual life. As early as his first published critical essays, Hegel asserts, "If the power of unification (Vereinigung) disappears from man's life, and opposites have lost their living relation and interaction and are gaining independence, the need for philosophy arises".[26]

The response of philosophic presentation is a response to the need engendered by thought itself, when thought falls into the divisions created by the understanding. "The insight that the nature of thought itself is dialectical, that as understanding (Verstand) it must fall into contradiction, the negative of itself, forms one of the principle sides of logic".[27] When thought is unable to overcome these contradictions created by its own movement, thought retreats from reason, becoming the hatred of reason in misology.

The reflection-thinking of the understanding, as the leading characteristic of the natural consciousness and the critical philosophy of Hegel's own day, is the contemporary form of this inherent contradiction in thought. "Reflection is chiefly the movement out beyond the isolated determinateness, positing its relativity in relation, while preserving its isolated value. In contrast the dialectic is the *immanent* movement out, wherein the onesidedness and limitation of the determinations of the understanding presents itself, as what it is, namely, as their negation".[28] The three "presentations (Stellungen) of thought to objectivity" which constitute a brief phenomenological introduction (i.e., a curtailed logic of phenomenal knowing) to the system of the *Enzyklopädie*, are designed to show the present state of affairs in philosophy as one of unresolved contradiction resulting from the singleminded use of the understanding in the attempt by philosophy to know objectivity, particularly the absolute objects of cognition.[29]

In paragraph # 25 Hegel alludes specifically to the current predicament of the understanding before going on to outline the "presentations of thought to objectivity" in paragraphs # 26–78. In this paragraph he says, "The expression 'objective thoughts' indicates the truth, which ought to be the absolute *object*, not merely the *goal*, of philosophy. But it generally suggests at once an opposition, the determination and validity of which is the interest of the philosophical standpoints of the present time, around which turns the question of the *truth* and knowledge of these latter. If thought-determinations are afflicted with fixed contradictions, i.e., if they are only of a *finite* nature, they are incompatible with the truth, the absolute in-and-for-itself, and the truth cannot enter into thought. Thought which produces only *finite* determinations, and in such moves itself, is called *understanding* (in the narrow sense of the word)".[30] Additional evidence to suggest that the following series of *Stellungen* constitutes a phenomenology of the contemporary natural consciousness (presented as phenomenal knowing) comes from the remark following paragraph # 25 in which Hegel speaks of the *Phänomenologie* and compares it to what is to follow: both are only historical and argumentative in their knowing. "But they ought particularly to contribute to the insight that the questions in representational thinking on the nature of *knowledge, faith* and so on, of a *concrete* kind, in fact lead back to *simple* thought-determinations, which have their true execution first in logic".[31]

The *Stellungen* are a kind of preparation or introduction to the system at the level of contemporary understanding, much as the *Phänomenologie* was in a more comprehensive fashion. The difference, of course, is that the *Stellungen* deal with philosophical positions exclusively and not figures of consciousness, but there is the sense that these positions represent the essence of current natural consciousness. And although there is no distinction between the exposition of the position and its criticism from the standpoint of science, there is a kind of dialectic working between the *Stellungen* based on the concept of need.

The first position is that of the metaphysical system, which is without consciousness of the contradiction in thought. It believes that reflection is the means of knowing the truth, and of bringing objects before consciousness as they truly are. This metaphysic represents the same belief to be found in natural consciousness: "All beginning philosophy, all science, even the daily activity of consciousness, lives in this faith".[32]

Empiricism came on the scene as a response to a need created by metaphysical thinking. "The need (i) partly of a *concrete* content as against the abstract theory of the understanding, which is unable for-itself to advance from its universalities to particularity and determination, (ii) partly of a *fixed hold* as against the possibility of *proving anything* in the field and by the method of finite determination".[33] Critical philosophy, like empiricism, takes its departure from experience, but responds to the lack in empiricism of the ability to explain the fact that universality and necessity are equally essential determinations of experience.[34] However, Hegel characterizes critical philosophy as an attempted synthesis of empiricism (its modes of observation) and metaphysic (independent self-apprehending thought) which falls into self-contradictory dualism, its sole effect being the revival of the absolute inwardness of thought.[35]

As well as the contradiction within the program of critical philosophy itself, there is the wider, current conflict between critical philosophy and immediate knowing, the third *Stellung*. In critical philosophy, thought is subjective, and its ultimate determination is abstract universality, formal identity; in this way thought is opposed to truth, as concrete universality in-itself. In this highest determination of thought, which is reason, the categories are not taken into account. Immediate knowing arises as the reverse mirror-image of critical philosophy, as the other half on an original, absolute identity. "The opposing standpoint is thought as the activity of laying hold of only the particular, and in this way is unable to explain or lay hold of the truth".[36]

Indeed immediate knowing, as the last and highest *Stellung*, itself conceals the manner in which the spiritual division manifested by the conflicting positions can be overcome: it maintains that immediate knowing alone, to the exclusion of mediation, can have a true content. In this exclusiveness is a relapse into the metaphysical understanding, into its "either-or", which in fact is a relapse into the relations of external mediation based on the fixedness of the finite, i.e., on one-sided determinations.[37] Thus immediate knowing falsely believes it has gone beyond such external mediation when it lies at the centre of its doctrine as a hidden contradiction.

In Hegel's view, it is the perception of the mediation of the immediate that leads to the true and absolute comprehension of the immediate, and the overcoming of contradiction in spiritual life. The doctrine of immediate knowing contains this truth through the preservation of an absolute antithesis between immediacy and mediation which cannot help but return upon itself in an original identity, – immediate knowing itself creates the need for mediation. Furthermore, it is important to note that Hegel immediately links the truth of mediation to the efficacy of educational history: "It is general experience that essentially *up-bringing*, development (also *Platonic recollection*) is requisite if what is contained in consciousness is to be brought before it (– Christian baptism, although a sacrament, itself contains the further obligation of a Christian up-bringing); i.e., that religion, ethical life (Sittlichkeit), however much they are *faith, immediate knowing*, are merely postulated through *mediation*, which means development, up-bringing, education (Bildung)".[38]

The result of our investigation of the three *Stellungen*, the uncovering of mediation as the truth of immediate knowing, thus determines the course of the presentation to follow, and seems to act as its implicit presupposition. Hegel's presentation of the positions brings out their inherent contradictions, showing the need for a more comprehensive accounting. But this "bringing out" of the contradictions itself follows a direction known by Hegel and unknown by the natural consciousness reading the text until the very end. This direction is provided by the insight into the absolute mediation of all the *Stellungen* as their truth, and as has been emphasized, the natural consciousness which follows the mediation implicit in the presentation of the *Stellungen* itself becomes educated to the level of science. The *Stellungen* thus act as a preparation, in the sense that they educate natural consciousness to the self-consciousness of the thought-determinations of current standpoints through the total mediation of their presuppositions and claims.

Hegel believes that such a preparation, which mediates all presupposition, is preferable to absolute scepticism. Scepticism, as a negative science carried out through all forms of cognition, would offer itself as an introduction where the nothingness of such presuppositions would be demonstrated. But this would be a superfluous path, since the dialectic of negative-reason itself is an essential moment of affirmative science. In addition, scepticism appropriates the finite forms of the empirical and the unscientific as it finds them, as they are given. "The insistence on an accomplished scepticism is the same as the insistence that science ought to be preceded by *all-encompassing* doubt, i.e., total all-encompassing *presuppositionlessness*. This is properly accomplished through the resolve that *wills pure thinking*, through the freedom, which, abstracting from everything and its pure abstraction, lays hold of the simplicity of thought".[39]

There are two points to be taken into consideration here: first, Hegel does not believe scepticism forms a proper introduction to science because its negativity is merely directed toward the finite forms of empirical cognition, and because science already contains negativity in the dialectic of speculative presentation, which uses this negativity in an affirmative manner. In the section which follows the *Stellungen*, the "more precise concept and division of logic", scepticism is further characterized as the dialectic applied by the *understanding* to particular philosophies, with "mere negation" as its result.[40] This is in contrast to the affirmative result obtained in the use of the dialectic by negative *reason*, which forms the basis for speculative or positive reason.

Secondly, the insistence on the "resolve" that wills pure thinking as the proper beginning of science comes at the end of the presentation of the *Stellungen*, and must be considered as an integral part of that presentation. The freedom of thought which characterizes this resolve is the result of the presentation as well as its ultimate presupposition, and shares a similar role to the "appearing" of absolute knowing at the end of the *Phänomenologie*. The resolve arises from (i) the insight into the contradictions of contemporary, spiritual life and the *need* to overcome these contradictions, and (ii) the efficacy of the mediation of immediate thought-determinations, which educates natural consciousness to the self-consciousness of all presuppositions, and hence liberates it from these presuppositions to pure thinking.

The problematic essence of the resolve lies in its "willfulness". First, we must assume that natural consciousness will opt of its own accord to follow Hegel in the presentation of the *Stellungen*, that it will decide to leave the unconscious character of its previous existence behind. Second, there is no reason to believe that once natural consciousness has followed through the presentation of the *Stellungen* and has achieved the self-consciousness of its situation, that it will feel obligated to push on into the study of the system of absolute determinations itself. Both transition-points are based on the depth of the need of natural consciousness to know itself absolutely. We must now, then, turn our attention to the absolute ground of this need, and its role as the true presupposition to the system.

2.2 *The origin of response*

Hegel understands the need for philosophy in terms of epochal movements: when division and contradiction enter the spiritual life of a people, the need for philosophy arises, so that need and response form necessarily determinate configurations in spirit's self-education. Presentation as the final response of philosophy accounts for its determinate need through the appearing of the *Phänomenologie* and the *Stellungen*, but there are other attempts in the system itself to situate its presentation within wider historical horizons.

In this connection, Hegel distinguishes in the system between three kinds of history and alludes to a fourth, which we will discuss later. The three kinds of history are the history of philosophy, world history, and the history of absolute spirit. In the introduction to the system, Hegel presents his science as the highest point and result of the history of philosophy: "In its proper form, the *external history* of the genesis and development of philosophy becomes represented as the *history of this science*".[41] The necessity of this result is possible because the *Werkmeister* of the history of philosophy is "the one living spirit, whose nature is to think, to bring before its consciousness what it is, and in becoming this object, equally to overcome it in a higher stage of its being".[42] The different appearances of philosophies therefore form only one philosophy at different levels of development, and the latest philosophy in time is the result of all previous philosophies. As this result, it must contain the principles of those previous, and is consequently the most evolved, richest, and concrete.[43]

Thus speculative science is related to the history of philosophy in two fundamental ways: (i) it is a result, and comes at the end of a determinate spiritual epoch; (ii) it contains the principles of previous philosophies raised from their contingent appearances, and repeats them in a systematic form, i.e., in their truth. Emphasizing this second point Hegel says, "This same development of thought, which is presented in the history of philosophy, is presented in the philosophy itself, but freed from its historical externality, in the *pure element of thinking*. The free and true thought is in-itself *concrete*, and so it is *idea*, and in its total universality it is *the* idea or *the* absolute. The science of this idea is essentially *system*, since the true is *concrete* only as the appropriation of its genesis and unity, i.e., as *totality*, and only through the differentiation and determination of its distinctions can there be the necessity of these distinctions and the freedom of the whole''.[44]

Speculative presentation is situated by the history of philosophy because the system looks back and comprehends its principles, raising that history to subjectivity, and the realization of this subjectivity defines the closed horizons of an epoch which has achieved self-consciousness. But there is a nuance to this apparent historical finality which must be brought out if we are to understand its true dimensions. Not only speculative science, but philosophy in general, all philosophy, looks back on its genesis and includes previous principles. This is why, according to Hegel, the *latest* philosophy, and not only speculative science, is the most concrete and true at any point in history. And it is also why all philosophy in general takes on the character of finality: we might say that philosophic viewing is by nature teleological.

This discussion of the place assigned to the system within the history of philosophy, as the realization of that history, determines philosophy in general as a necessary moment within the self-education of spirit. But it in no way elucidates the manner in which philosophy as such is an appearance in history, nor is there talk of the relation of this appearance to a spiritual need. The history of philosophy is appropriated as given, as a series of responses severed from their immediate cultural determinations, so that we do not see the full depth of spirit's self-education, but only a string of isolated moments like gleaming mountain tops separated by vast impenetable valleys. To this extent, the history of philosophy does not situate the moment of speculative presentation within the plenitude of spirit's determinacy, and in no way is the study of the appearance of this history alone an adequate preparation for science, nor is it the grounds for the recognition of the absolute as spirit.

The section entitled *Weltgeschichte* forms the last part of Hegel's systematic explication of the state, and is the only formal discussion of history in the *Enzyklopädie*. As was pointed out in the last chapter, the nation-state is the determinate mode in which spirit is "historical". Only the nation-state has a history properly speaking (in distinction from mere individuals or stateless communities), and in the dialectical interaction of nation-states which constitutes world history, spiritual substance finds its liberation and goal.[45] But spirit only lays hold of its self-consciousness in stripping away the contingent aspect of this historicity, and in laying hold of the absolute determination of its particular ethical life (Sittlichkeit).[46]

This stepping back from the immediate political situation into its absolute ground determines *Weltgeschichte* as an external access to the ontological structure and movement of spirit itself. This structure and movement is revealed in the appropriation of art, religion, and philosophy, an appropriation which somehow determines the nature of *Sittlichkeit* itself. Appropriation in this sense is a two-way movement in which consciousness appropriates the absolute determinations of its situation, becoming fully self-conscious, and in which the absolute appropriates consciousness as the revelation of itself, becoming fully self-conscious.

It would seem, then, that absolute history, the history of art, religion, and philosophy, would together situate the moment of speculative presentation within the ontological structure of the absolute. But is this really the case? As we have seen in our brief discussion of the history of philosophy, the separate history of each mode would not account for its appearance as a response to a cultural need. Only taken together, as three moments within a particular culture, can we begin to understand their dialectical interaction as the rise to self-knowledge of subjectivity in general. It is in this sense that Hegel speaks of the later development of philosophy than religion in a nation, citing the response of Greek philosophy to the particularity and divisiveness of a degenerating Greek religion and art: "But Greek philosophy could only present itself in opposition to Greek religion, and the unity of thought and the substantiality of idea could take up only a hostile relation to the polytheism of the imagination, the bright and frivolous playfulness of its poesy. The *form* in its infinite truth, the *subjectivity* of spirit, broke forth first only as subjective free *thinking*, not yet identical with *substantiality* itself, this latter was not yet appropriated as absolute spirit".[47]

The particular idea of a national culture finds its developed determination in this dialectical movement between the absolute modes of art, religion, and philosophy. Thus religion can appear purified only first through the pure, for-itself existing thought, i.e., through philosophy. But this relationship between the modes is determined by the particular idea of the national culture, so that in the case of Greek culture, the substantial immanent form of Greek religion attacked by philosophy was its poetic imagination.[48] Consequently we may say that, parallelling the movement between the modes within a national culture, there is also a movement between the particular ideas of cultures revealed in history. This trans-historical movement containing these epochs reaches the self-consciousness of its necessary integrity with the realization that "only in the principle of spirit does the absolute possibility and necessity exist of state power, religion, and the principles of philosophy falling together in one".[49]

The unity of cultural need and the response of philosophy is guaranteed in the postulation that the absolute is spirit. The absolute knows itself, seizes itself, through its discursive self-education as spirit, a movement we have come to know as dialectical. Thus the need and the response are understood by Hegel as determinate dialectical moments within the educational history of spirit itself. If this is so, then it would seem that the proper preparation for the final response of philosophy given by the system would be an educational history of spirit up to the moment of its greatest need, followed by an explication of the system as the necessary and exhaustive response.

This fourth kind of history, the possibility of which is only hinted at in the *Enzyklopädie*, would delineate the movement of culture in its totality, including the ensemble of its political, artistic, religious, and philosophic aspects. Hegel describes such an educational history of spirit, a *Bildungsgeschichte*, as properly the task of a philosophy of religion, which would relate a particular determination of the absolute to the nature of its "cultus", – in short, how "the nature of the ethical life (Sittlichkeit) of a people, the principle of its law, its actual freedom and constitution, its art and science, accords with the principle which constitutes the substance of a religion. That all these moments of the actuality of a people constitute one systematic totality, that one spirit creates and imagines them, this insight depends on the wider, grounding insight that the history of religion falls together with world history (Weltgeschichte)".[50]

An educational history of spirit, in systematically relating its moments, would seem to provide the only possible historical "introduction" to the moment of speculative presentation. It would do so in delineating the overwhelming current need for the system as a necessary result of spiritual development. But is not the delineation of this need precisely what the *Phänomenologie* has set out to do?

The need for philosophy only "appears" as need at the level of natural consciousness, since the moment of philosophy described at the level of speculative science in an educational history of spirit is simply dialectically necessary. Consequently, only the *Phänomenologie* can be an introduction or preparation to the system because it appears in history as both the need for philosophy and its response. Such an appearing guides natural consciousness to the knowledge that need and response exist in an original dialectical unity, a unity explicated by the presentation of the absolute as spirit. An educational history of spirit, or a philosophy of religion, must be totally "for us" at the level of science, and presupposes both the *Phänomenologie* and the fully mediated presentation of the absolute subject given in the system. Only the three moments of "natural consciousness", "*Phänomenologie*", and "system", fully exhaust the movement of absolute self-consciousness, a self-consciousness necessary to any history of absolute appropriation. Indeed, the relationship of these three moments, its syllogistic nature, − in contrast to *Bildungsgeschichte* − provides the only possible grounds for the need and response of philosophy.

2.3 *Externalization and recollection*

Before we focus on the relation between the *Phänomenologie* and the system, and the three syllogisms at the end of the *Enzyklopädie*, we will examine the need and response of philosophy within the mode of its appearing. The understanding of how philosophy is "for" natural consciousness may begin to explain how speculative presentation is possible and necessary, and to what extent this presentation can be considered final within the determinate horizons of philosophy itself.

Philosophy, as philosophy, raises the finite form of absolute content in art and religion to subjectivity through the cognition of the differentiated content as necessary, and this necessary as free.[51] Philosophic cognition is the elevation of this content to absolute form, meaning that the absolute becomes self-conscious of its essential integrity. "This movement, which philosophy is, finds itself already accomplished, when at the close it lays hold of its own concept, i.e., only looks back on its knowledge".[52]

Why is philosophy a looking back, and how is this looking back related to "the close"? In one sense we already have the answer to this question when we say that philosophic cognition raises absolute content to its proper form, such that the absolute cognizes itself as subject. The achievement of subjectivity both closes off the epochal appearing of the absolute as appearance, and knows its differentiated content as necessary and free.

As we have emphasized, no science of the educational history of spirit can prepare the response of philosophy, but that response is nonetheless dependent on previous spiritual development for its content, and it is this which makes philosophy a "looking-back". Furthermore, this dependence determines philosophy as a *regional* response: the spiritual development and cultural need which situates the moment of appropriation expresses the expansion and decline of the nation-state, the basic unit of history according to Hegel. It follows that the finality of philosophic response is always a regional finality, which leaves the future of philosophy open, while at the same time not relativizing its achievements.

The dependence on regional, cultural history explains why Hegel believes philosophy is simply its own time apprehended in thoughts, and why it is absurd to think that philosophy can transcend its contemporary world.[53] But the determination of philosophy as response distinguishes philosophy in an important way from the prevailing natural consciousness, which the "thoughtful" character of philosophy does not at first fully disclose. An example of this relation taken from the *Vorrede* to the *Philosophie des Rechts* accurately describes the aspect of response: "In the course of this book, I have remarked that even Plato's *Republic*, which passes proverbially as an *empty ideal*, is in essence nothing but an interpretation of the nature of Greek ethical life (Sittlichkeit). Plato was conscious that there was breaking into that life in his own time a deeper principle which could appear in it immediately only as a longing still unsatisfied, and so only as something corruptive. To combat it, he needs must have sought aid from that very longing itself. But this aid had to come from on High and all that Plato could do was to seek it in the first place in a particular *external* form of that same Greek ethical life. By that means he thought to master this corruptive invader, and thereby he did fatal injury to the deeper impulse which underlay it, namely free infinite personality".[54]

This passage makes several important points about the nature of philosophic response: it is dependent, as an interpretation of immediate ethical life, on *previous* spiritual development; it is a regional, culturally determined response to *Greek* ethical life, and not an empty ideal; the response was prompted by a sense of *division* and corruption in spiritual life; the response should have been based on the *same longing* that lay at the centre of the corruption, i.e., free infinite personality; the response failed because it remained within the same *mode* of the expressed need, i.e., the external mode of ethical life, instead of investigating the nature of the appropriation of the absolute evident in this life. It seems that the true response, which, in any case, could only have come from "on High", should have been the Christian doctrine of the subjective moral "ought", that combines free personality with divine universality.

In regarding this passage as a description of the typical traits of philosophic response in general, it is surpising to note that, by and large, they accord with the intention of the *Phänomenologie*. This latter is a looking-back on previous spiritual configurations, and is a response to the divisions within modern European spiritual life that is based on the longing for self-consciousness already implicit in natural consciousness. As to its success, we can say this much: the origin of the need is in natural consciousness, but the mode of response distinguishes between the external appearance of consciousness and its truth "for us" at the level of science, thus avoiding the mistake of the *Republic*. Indeed it is this distinction of modes, as expressed in the last three syllogisms of the *Enzyklopädie*, that provides for the concordance of response to need through the presupposition of their original identity.

The distinction of modes suggests that the response of philosophic presentation must not be a simply ideal reconciliation, posited by the reflective understanding, of its divided reality. However, the presentation of the philosophic response will always be in a sense "ideal", as the inevitable result of the need inherent in division. For example, the path of phenomenal knowing is a path presented by the phenomenologist in response to perceived divisions within contemporary natural consciousness. [55] In his own draft (1830) of *Vernunft in der Geschichte*, Hegel states that only philosophic response as "thinking reason", in contrast to reflective understanding and its abstract representations, can capture the concrete unity of spiritual life: "Philosophy, too, must make its appearance as soon as political life is established. For that which confers the property of culture upon any given content is, as already mentioned, the form proper to thought itself; whereas philosophy is merely the consciousness of this form, the thinking of thinking, so that the material which it requires for its own peculiar edifice is already prepared for it through the general process of culture. And in the development of the state itself, periods must occur in which the spirit of nobler natures is forced to flee from the present into ideal regions, and to find in them that reconciliation with itself which it can no longer enjoy in an internally divided reality; for the reflective understanding attacks all those sacred and profound elements which were artlessly introduced into the religion, laws, and customs of nations, and debases and dilutes them into abstract and godless generalities. Thought is then impelled to become thinking reason, and to pursue and accomplish in its own element the undoing of that destruction which had previously overtaken it". [56]

We find re-emphasized once again in this passage the important relation between philosophic response and the spiritual life of the surrounding nation, which provides it the material "for its own peculiar edifice". But the most striking sentence is certainly the last, in which thinking reason, within its own element, can "undo" the destruction that had previously overtaken it. Is Hegel speaking of the destruction wrought by the reflective understanding in its abstract renderings of concrete spiritual life, or is the destruction spoken of the internally divided reality itself, a culture reaching the stiffness and decay of old age? If it is the divided reality itself which is superseded in the reconciliation of thinking reason, then it would seem that the response of philosophy's grey in grey does indeed go farther than a mere understanding of its cultural heritage, − although, centainly, not as far as a wholesale rejuvenation of that heritage.

We begin to perceive the nature of philosophic response once we move beyond its depiction as a reflective understanding merely looking back on its cultural antecedents, to its characterization as an active, mediating recollection (Erinnerung) of the *Volksgeist*. Recollection as it appears "for us" in the *Phänomenologie* already presupposes the discursive manifestation of absolute determination presented by the system, where recollection is under its necessary aspect in subjective spirit. Here, as a psychological function, recollection is the gathering together of the immediate finding of intuition into one moment, the abstract identical direction of spirit: "The active *recollection*, the moment of own-ness (Seinigen), but as the yet *formal* self-determination of intelligence".[57] Recollection removes the intuition from its contingent situation and is a preparation for its representation in an image or sign.

We must assume that recollection is restricted to this role as a psychological function because the system is not an appearing at the level of natural consciousness as in the *Phänomenologie*, and consequently does not have the outward form of a "response" to an apparent historical need. The system is the presupposed identity of both need and response, and as this identity, it is the timeless self-consciousness of absolute determination, in which recollection is presented as a dialectical moment devoid of all "historical" significance. The essential meaning of recollection as presented in the system finds its appearing for consciousness in the *Phänomenologie* as a recollecting of spiritual immediacy, whose significance and structure is for us at the level of science. Its mode reflects the essentially hybrid nature of the *Phänomenologie* itself, as a recollection of the historical material of past natural consciousness', and as the scientific presentation of this material in the movement of phenomenal knowing towards absolute knowing.

The integral structure of recollection remains the same in its truth and in its appearance. It recollects a spiritual immediacy, sheds its contingent aspects, and re-integrates the moments of that immediacy within a higher spiritual unity, thus preparing the original immediacy for its presentation by self-conscious spirit. Indeed the activity of recollection provides us with an insight into the character of self-consciousness itself. As has already been indicated, recollection is not the mere reproduction of the past immediacy in all its minute detail, but has a dialectical movement which negates that immediacy and recombines it with a mediation of a determinate whole, — so that self-consciousness is not the simple, random rememberance of its immediate determinations, but is the mediation of that immediacy by an absolute subject. Such a mediation is fundamental to, and is itself the manifestation of, spiritual own-ness (Seinigen).

The response of philosophy is the manifestation of the *Seinigen* of the *Volksgeist* to the extent that philosophy re-presents the essential spiritual unity of a now decaying nationhood, allowing spirit to become self-conscious of its previously implicit unity. The importance of the transforming quality of recollection is underlined in a striking passage from the *Phänomenologie* in which Hegel describes the death of Greek culture from the standpoint of Roman law or right: "So Fate does not restore their world to us along with the works of antique art, it gives not the spring and summer of the ethical life (Sittlichkeit) in which they blossomed and ripened, but only the veiled recollection (Erinnerung) of that actual world".[58]

The response to the spiritual life of Greece is fundamentally different from that life itself, for we no longer participate in its divine worship, but are restricted to the external activity of placing and organizing the outward existence of its products. We do this not in order to enter into their very life, but only to possess them in our imagination, and it would seem from this that all knowledge of past culture is severely limited to superficial externals. The result of this position would be that all philosophy is inevitably locked within the particular experience of finite subjectivity as long as it cannot properly ascertain the true needs manifested by a decaying culture and provide an adequate response.

Of course Hegel goes on to argue that, although we certainly cannot rejuvenate a culture, we can know it in a fundamental way. "But just as the girl who offers us the plucked fruits is more than the nature that directly provides them − the nature diversified into their conditions and elements, the tree, air, light, and so on − because she sums all this up in a higher mode, in the gleam of her self-conscious eye and in the gesture with which she offers them, so, too, the spirit of the Fate that presents us with these works of art is more than the ethical life and the actual world of that nation, for it is the *inwardizing* (Er-Innerung) in us of the spirit which in them was still (only) *outwardly* manifested; it is the spirit of the tragic Fate which gathers all those individual gods and attributes of the (divine) substance into one pantheon, into the spirit that is itself conscious of itself as spirit".[59] Through recollection, the spiritual manifestation of the absolute previously externalized in ethical life is "inwardized" as self-conscious absolute subjectivity.

Erinnerung, as the essence of philosophic response, is both a recollecting of spirit and an inwardizing by spirit which is simultaneous to its achievement of self-certain *Seinigen*. The movement of spirit from its immediacy in ethical life to the exhaustive mediation of that life as existence raised into representation, and the expansion of this existence into a world which finally appropriates itself as a universality which is at the same time a pure certainty of itself,

– this movement completes the circle of the forms of the externalization (Entäußerungen) of absolute substance.[60] Philosophic presentation and recollection, as the final *Entäußerung*, looks back on its substantial content as its own. The self-consciousness of this mediation makes explicit the original identity of the external "productions".

An investigation into the systematic ground relating the need of natural consciousness and the appearance of philosophic response will be undertaken later, but a few remarks can now be made about the adequacy of the *Phänomenologie* as an apparent philosophic response. Our review of Hegel's thinking on the "appearing" of philosophy has uncovered one consistent result, and that is the relationship of philosophy to a particular *Volksgeist*. Philosophy is that *Volksgeist* rising to self-consciousness, making philosophy a regional response to a local situation. But the *Phänomenologie* seems to transcend national boundaries and cultures, in an attempt to outline the overwhelming need in Occidental culture as a whole, and to point out its necessary satisfaction in the system: this seems to contradict the regional finality assigned to philosophy in general, and again raises the question as to whether Hegel did not indeed think of the system as somehow finally and exhaustively true.

The crisis of modern natural consciousness is explicated in the first few paragraphs of the chapter entitled "Das absolute Wissen" at the end of the *Phänomenologie*. The division in spiritual life is that between the consciousness of absolute content in revealed religion and the self-certain form of moral self-consciousness: "The unification of the two sides has not yet been exhibited; it is this that closes the series of shapes of spirit, for in it spirit attains to a knowledge of itself not only as it is *in-itself* or as possessing an absolute *content*, nor only as it is *for-itself* as a form devoid of content, or as the aspect of self-consciousness, but as it is *in-and-for-itself*".[61] The necessity of this reconciliation has been the object of the presentation of phenomenal knowing previous to the depiction of the crisis, so that modern natural consciousness will become self-conscious of its explicit division and the need for its supersession.

The historical material appropriated by this presentation transcends the contemporary *Volksgeist*, but the crisis of this latter finds its roots in this common Occidental heritage. This heritage is therefore not presented for-itself, i.e., no attempt is made at historical "objectivity", rather it is presented for modern natural consciousness and as part of the response to its crisis. Thus the past is mediated from the standpoint of a present problem, – that of self-consciousness, a problem unknown to the Greeks. We may say, then, that even though historical material is introduced in an inferential manner, the need of contemporary natural consciousness and the philosophic response it necessitates is a matter of the particular *Volksgeist* of Hegel's day, making his reading of history, and his proposed solution, only "regionally" final.

This is the conclusion we must reach as long as we consider the moment of absolute knowing within the mode of its appearing as response, i.e., for natural consciousness. But Hegel says, "the unification (Vereinigung) that is still lacking is the simple unity of the concept".[62] The actuality of speculative presentation, grounding its appearance as a response to a given need, or the reconciliation of two principles of consciousness, is simply necessary according to the concept. This timeless actuality, which is the appropriation of the absolute as manifested discursively in the system, is the result which makes the appearing of the *Phänomenologie* possible. And the necessity of the system depends to a large extent on the adequacy of the supersession and comprehension of its prior appearance not only as the *Phänomenologie*, but as natural consciousness. The nature of this adequacy must now be examined from the standpoint of the system itself.

3. THE ACT OF PRESENTATION

3.1 *Speculation and praxis*

In this chapter we have been looking at how the absolute idea as system is *for* the knowing subject under its two superseded moments as natural consciousness and appearing science. These two appearances find their original ground in a system existing for the knowing subject as speculative presentation.

But before we begin our investigation of presentation, let us briefly review the broad outlines of the exigencies of absolute appearing. As has been tentatively suggested in the first chapter, the two appearances of the absolute idea from the standpoint of spirit are natural consciousness and the *Phänomenologie*, the result and presupposition of which is the system itself. The system *should* supersede and include its appearances: but the system presents the categories of the absolute as an externalization alien to the knowing subject, much as the absolute of revealed religion is alienated from consciousness.[63] What is missing is the subjective form of absolute knowing, in which the system of absolute content accounts for its own presentation by the knowing subject. Such a reconciliation finds its realization in the concept of scientific presentation.

This interpretation suggests that the transition between the *Phänomenologie* and the *Enzyklopädie* should not be understood "chronologically", i.e., as a transition from the chapter on *Das absolute Wissen* to the first part of the logic, but "dialectically": the appearance of absolute determination in natural consciousness and phenomenal knowing is recollected by the system of philosophy described at the end of the *Enzyklopädie*, such that the moment of philosophic presentation contains both the absolute appearances and system. In other words, the truth and satisfaction of absolute knowing is the act of speculative *presentation*, the principle which is the philosophic result and necessary presupposition of the system as it exists for absolute knowing. Any interpretation which simply proceeds to the determinations of the logic as the true content of absolute knowing fails to comprehend how this content is only "for" the subject through speculative presentation.

Presentation exists immediately before us as language. This language is for natural consciousness, and uses words and idioms drawn from the natural language of the particular *Volksgeist*; for example, in Hegel's case, the presentation makes philosophy speak German. As remarked in the *Wissenschaft der Logik*, the philosophy of a nation is closely related to the thick immediacy of the surrounding linguistic universe: "Philosophy has the right to select from the language of common life which is made for the world of representations, such expressions as *seem to approximate* to the determinations of the concept. There cannot be any question of *demonstrating* for a word selected from the language of common life that in common life, too, one associates with it the same concept for which philosophy employs it; for common life has no concepts, but only representations, and to recognize the concept in what is else a mere representation is philosophy itself".[64] Through the grammar of a people, one can recognize the expression of spirit as such, that is, logic.[65]

With this ability of philosophy to use the common expressions of its particular *Volksgeist* in the explication of its concepts, "philosophy, therefore, generally needs no special terminology".[66] This would at first seem to limit the meaning of all speculation to the regional expressions and concerns of local dialect, and as we have emphasized, the nation is indeed the form of the determinate historical manifestation of spirit.[67] But philosophy transforms the particular expressions of common life by raising the spiritual categories implicit in them to self-consciousness through their determination according to the concept. It is this determination which gives the linguistic universe its philosophic value, not any mysterious "power" of language itself.

The speculative sentence includes and supersedes natural language through the overt recognition of the implicit role of thought in determining its meaning, and we may say that the natural sentence becomes speculative through the way we think it. In the *Phänomenologie*, appearing science as a philosophic response to the need of natural consciousness finds its counterpart in the use of language. "The need to represent the absolute as *subject* has found expression in the propositions: *God* is the eternal, the moral world-order, love, and so on".[68] The problem with such propositions is that the true is only posited *immediately* as subject, and not presented as the movement of reflecting itself into itself. As it stands, "God" is an empty sound which is given meaning and content only through the predicate, making its role somewhat superfluous to the action of the sentence.

But Hegel insists that it is just this word which indicates that what is posited is not a universal in general, − that it is something reflected into itself, a subject. This signification is only *anticipated* at the present moment, because the subject is assumed as a fixed point to which predicates are affixed as their support. Actually the predicates are affixed by a movement belonging to the knower of this subject, and which is not regarded as belonging to the fixed point itself; yet it is only through this movement that the content could be represented as subject. Consequently, once this point has been presupposed, the nature of this movement can only be looked upon as external. "Hence, the mere anticipation that the absolute is subject is not only *not* the actuality of this concept, but it even makes the actuality impossible; for the anticipation posits the subject as an inert point, whereas the actuality is self-movement".[69]

The subject-predicate sentence of natural language fails to apprehend the concept of subjectivity as self-movement because it cannot account for the movement of reflection on the part of the knowing subject. For all such ratiocinative thinking, the self is a subject to which the content is related as accident and predicate. Speculative thinking, on the other hand, comprehends the concept as the object's own self, and not as a passive subject inertly supporting the accidents: the self-moving concept takes its determinations back into itself. "In this movement the passive subject itself perishes; it enters into the differences and the content, and constitutes the determinations, i.e., the differentiated content and its movement, instead of remaining inertly over against it".[70] The subject ceases to go beyond its content and the content is bound together under the self, so that the content is no longer a predicate of the subject, but is the substance, the concept of what is under discussion.

The speculative sentence does not change the structure of the proposition itself, but transforms the relation of consciousness to the sentence. In natural language, the subject is made the ground, as the objective, fixed self, from which the movement to the multiplicity of determinations proceeds. Actually, what happens is that the subject is replaced by the knowing "I" itself, which links the predicates with the subject holding them. In the speculative sentence, the role of this knowing "I" is considerably altered: since, now, the first subject enters into the determinations themselves and is their soul, the knowing "I" cannot function as the determining agent in the movement of predication. Instead, the knowing "I" is "still occupied with the self of the content, having to remain associated with it, instead of being for-itself".[71]

Hegel says that in this speculative consideration of the sentence, thinking loses the firm objective basis it had in the subject, so that in the predicate it is thrown back on the subject, — and thereby thinking does not return into itself, but into the subject of the content. This means that the former determining power of the reflecting self is *externalized* in the sentence itself, so that the sentence is a self-determining substance. In as much as this substance is"under discussion", it is, of course, still related to thinking; however the self is no longer the arbitrator of determinations, arguing back and forth whether to attach this or that predicate, for it is simply the existential ground of the determinations already found in the sentence.

The "presentation" of the substance of thinking in the speculative sentence externalizes the determinations of the concept, while recollecting them under the moment of subjectivity. It is this presentation which demands a change in our understanding of the subject — predicate proposition and in our attitude towards knowing. Hegel asserts that, "This return of the concept into itself must be *presented*. This movement which constitutes what formerly the proof was supposed to accomplish, is the dialectical movement of the proposition itself. This alone is the *actual* speculative, and only the expression of this movement is a speculative presentation (Darstellung)".[72] In the externalization of the substance of thinking in the presentation of the speculative sentence, we are able to witness and recollect the dialectical movement of the proposition itself: presentation is the existential return of the esence into itself, in which the true is subject.

Through speculative presentation, the proposition is only this dialectical movement, this course that generates itself, going forth from, and returning to, itself. And only in this way can thinking express that the absolute is subject, as the authentic response to the anticipation of ratiocinative exposition we described earlier. Speculative presentation, as the proper mode of thinking reason, thus equally "appears" as a philosophic response in the *Phänomenologie*.

The externalization of the substance of thinking in speculative presentation allows the recollection of the dialectical movement of the concept. But the single sentence alone, because of its propositional structure, cannot express this dialectical movement; it is the speculative thinking of this proposition that makes it a speculative sentence. Thus the natural sentence is only superseded by the speculative within a context of sentences which presents the dialectical substance of thinking.[73] Hegel says, "In keeping with our insight into the nature of speculation, the presentation (Darstellung) should preserve the dialectical form, and should admit nothing except in so far as it is comprehended, and is the concept".[74]

Again we come back to the fact that the externalization of the substance of thinking in the presentation alters the relation of thinking to the determinate being of language. The knowing subject is no longer the determining agent as in ratiocinative thinking, i.e., it is no longer the exterior reflection movement of the proposition. In speculative presentation, this knowing is not an activity that deals with the content as something alien, or a reflection into itself away from the content. Hegel maintains that, on the contrary, since knowing sees the content return into its own inwardness, its activity is totally absorbed in the content, for knowing is the immanent self of the content; yet it has at the same time returned into itself, for it is pure self-identity in otherness.[75] The determinations of thinking are externalized in presentation, so that the knowing subject is no longer the determining agent, but the "immanent self" of this content.

In this externalization, the knowing subject recollects its determinations and raises them to self-conscious subjectivity, because all the while it is pure self-identity in otherness. The "otherness" of presentation is the existential return of the essence into itself, a return that is intimately bound up with the "act" of presentation; this act is true to the extent that is expresses its content in a dialectical movement. Speculative presentation, then, is the existing of the dialectical movement of the concept through the *act* of the externalization of knowing in its other: the immanent self is the *existing* of this dialectical movement in its presentation, as knowing in its total externalization.

When the knowing subject becomes simply the immanent self of the presented substance of thinking, the knowing subject has returned to a sense-certainty in which it knows absolutely that its other is itself. The immanent self is merely the residue of the pure existing of the knowing subject, which contains in subjectivity the total externalization of its determinations. But why does this externalization of thinking take on the form of a dialectical presentation?

Hegel says time is the concept itself that *is there*, and which presents itself to consciousness as an empty intuition. When the knowing subject grasps its objectivity as itself, then it sets aside its time-form and is a comprehending intuiting.[76] The presentation of the content of this intuiting, as in the system, follows a dialectical format because the dialectic is the externalization of the time-experience of natural consciousness: both manifest the rhythm of the concept. The presentation of absolute knowing is particularly timeless because the knowing subject has externalized its time experience and is only a comprehending intuiting.

Furthermore, absolute knowing, as a recollecting of the externalization of the universal self, is the knowing of this externalization as the self's own act, and in its presentation, act and knowing coincide. "Thus what in religion was *content* or a form for representing an *other*, is here the *self's* own *act*; − for this concept is, as we see, the knowledge of the self's act within itself as all essentiality and all existence, the knowledge of this subject as substance, and of the substance as this knowledge of its act".[77] Absolute knowing is unthinkable aside from "doing", because it is the knowledge of the actions of its self.

Following this line of thought, absolute knowing is consumately realized as speculative presentation. Here the act of presenting falls together with the knowing of itself in its externalization. The substance of actions and the looking-back of knowledge are welded into one self-recollection which raises the hitherto opaque, alienated objectivity of the self into transparent, self-conscious subjectivity. It is important to emphasize that knowing is *not* a passive "receiving", but the active presentation of the substance of its actions which is itself an act. On the other hand, this act of presentation is far from being arbitrary, since it externalizes the universal dialectical form of the substance of thinking; − the externalization of the concept already in natural consciousness guarantees the truth of speculative presentation. Science necessarily comprehends, therefore, both the actuality of the dialectical movement of the concept in presentation, and its appearance in consciousness.[78]

In summary, we may say that presentation is related to the knowing subject in two fundamental ways. The presenting of the rhythm of the concept is equally its existing, its presence, to which the continuity of the immanent self bears witness. The realization of this presentation in the system consequently does not diminish the fact that its being-there is related to the original being-there of the presenting subject. It is true that this original being-there of the presenting subject is superseded in the absolute universality of the system but the nature of this supersession, or that the system is a supersession at all of the knowing subject, is not accounted for in Hegel's presentation of the system.

Secondly, the concept and act of presentation alone can account for the transition between the *Phänomenologie* and the system, and as we have indicated, Hegel was clearly aware of its importance for the former. Such a transition is possible not through a transition-text, but in the comprehension of the continuity and fundamental unity of the underlying principles of presentation in both works. Speculative presentation is a kind of *praxis* that overcomes the alienation between the empty form of absolute knowing as described at the end of the *Phänomenologie*, and the discursive determination of the absolute that is the content of the system.[79]

This element of praxis is extremely vital. There is no absolute knowing, nor the residue of its content, without the act of presentation. Presentation transforms the knowing subject by emptying out the unconscious determinations of natural consciousness, so that subjectivity may know and recollect these determinations in their externality, − becoming self-conscious of these determinations as its own and thus knowing itself absolutely. What is forgotten, and lies beneath the surface of the system everywhere, is that its externalization devolves from this vital, active source of "being-presented": in other words, what the system has forgotten, is that it is itself a presentation, and necessarily supersedes the facticity of natural consciousness.

3.2 *Time and the dialectic*

Speculative presentation supersedes the facticity of natural consciousness through its active externalization of the universal substance of thinking. The substance of thinking for Hegel is thinking itself, thinking as the discursive manifestation of the absolute presented in the system. This is why the system is an encyclopedia of philosophical sciences of general appeal, a student handbook, which requires only the resolve that wills pure thinking.

Facticity, the contingent life-world of the knowing subject, is superseded through speculative presentation by the empty, intuitive comprehending of the immanent self. As we have indicated, this supersession is evident on a primordial level in the transformation of the time-experience of natural consciousness. An understanding of the relation between the time-experience and the dialectical form of presentation would go a long way to providing an "absolute" ground for the system and its two appearances, i.e., as natural consciousness and appearing science.

Time is the outer intuited pure self, which is not yet grasped by the self.[80] In other words, time is the experience of objectivity which does not yet grasp that objectivity as the self's own externalization. The changes in this objectivity, actually determined by the concept, are merely "withstood" by the intuiting self as temporal, so that temporality has its origin in the alternation of the objective spatial field. But in order to experience this alternation, a fixed point, a "now", must be posited, which supersedes the alienation of objectivity and consciousness. This timeless "now" is the presentation of absolute knowing, a presentation which supersedes the time-experience while making that experience possible as the apparent difference of its original "I" = "I". "But this "I" = "I" is the movement which reflects itself into itself; for since this identity, being absolute negativity, is absolute difference, the self-identity of the "I" stands over against this pure difference which, as pure and at the same time objective to the self-knowing self, has to be expressed as *time*".[81] Thus the time-experience of phenomenal knowing as it is presented in the *Phänomenologie* is dependent on the original identity of consciousness and objectivity achieved by the presentation of phenomenal knowing at the level of science. Such a presentation itself is only possible as the appearance of science, − an appearance for natural consciousness which presupposes the knowing of the absolute determinations presented in the system. If we can untangle these "recursive" dialectical presuppositions, then it would seem that the time-experience of natural consciousness presented as phenomenal knowing ultimately presupposes the original identity of the self-presenting absolute idea as delineated in the last three syllogisms of the system.

The time-experience is determined by the rhythm of the concept, a rhythm which becomes known in the externalization of the substance of thinking in the dialectical form of speculative presentation. But if the dialectical form of presentation does contain, and is the presupposition for, time elements, then what does this say about the time-experience of consciousness itself according to Hegel? As we have indicated, time is the experience of the alternation of objectivity, an experience which does not know this alternation as a determination of the self. Consequently, time originates in the beholding of what is present at hand, in the "whatness" of objectivity as opposed to the experience of "thatness", that objectivity "is". The alternation in "whatness" expresses the identity of thought and extension as time.

If time is experienced as changes in objectivity or extension, then time "occurs" through the thinking of objectivity as a series of "now-points". As we have seen, the translation of the meant "here" and "now" into language consistently results in an ideal "here" and "now" which resists the contingent particularity of the intended objectivity of consciousness. As the experience of the successive differences of now-points, time is intuited becoming, because the differences are understood as external, and external to themselves, and the succession does not get thought but simply presents itself as a series of self-enclosed "nows". Such a determination of time defines the "now" as simply present, and present ideally.[82]

This comprehension of time as a series of discrete, ideally present moments is necessary of we are to posit time as the rhythm of the concept that is "there". The annulment of time in the speculative presentation of objectivity as the truth of the concept is superseded in the dialectical rhythm of text which mirrors the discrete, ideal moments of time itself. Such a parallel makes it possible for the discursive determinations of the absolute presented in the dialectical format to "appear" first in consciousness, and accounts for the particularly timeless quality of speculative presentation.

The leading question of this posited relation between time and speculative presentation is whether the contingent, factual content of time is given justice. Hegel determines the now-point as simple presence, but does not this determination disregard coming-to-be and ceasing-to-be, categories which emphasize the existing of objectivity as opposed to its essential "whatness"? The decay and flux of the time-experience of natural consciousness, the ineffable quality of time, is given no room in the structuring of time as a succession of distinct moments which prefigure the dialectical ordering of configurations in the system. An accounting of the system as a presentation by the knowing subject would make these deficiencies in the supersession of the time-experience explicit.

However this relation between the time-experience of natural consciousness and the dialectical format of speculative presentation does tend to underline the identity which "holds together" the knowing subject and the externalization of absolute determination posited in the system. The knowing subject is the immanent self of the system, in which knower and known are reconciled in the act of presentation. But does not this identity only hold for the knowing subject which actually does the presenting, an identity which is the result of a willful act? [83] If speculative presentation is the necessary mode of knowing the absolute determinations, then it would seem that the content of the system must remain to some extent an alien externality for those of us who merely perceive it, at least until we can supersede the system, as part of absolute externalization, in a presentation equally *our own*.

As long as we do not supersede the system in such a presentation, then our perception of the system does not guarantee that we know it as our own truth. This is what may be tentatively termed the Hegelian fallacy, that to perceive an externalization is necessarily to recollect and know it as our own at the level of science. Does genuine truth lie in pure beholding, or are there other ways in which the absolute can know itself, one of which may be suggested by the salutary *act* of presentation?

Hegel's determination of time as the "appearing" of the concept in consciousness seems to have precluded any such alienation of the knowing subject from the content of absolute determinations as it is presented in the system. But the relationship of the knowing subject to this content is more than lifeless identity: an element of interest, and perhaps belief, is central to all manifestations of absolute spirit as part of its particular "cultus".

3.3 *Begriffsmystik*

The efficacy of speculative presentation "appears" as the conviction by the knowing subject that the absolute determinations of the system are its own. This aspect of conviction indicates that the identity of knowing and the absolute idea is not a simple unity, but an identity returning and ever returned into itself: if it is the one and universal substance, it is so as spirit, the judgment of itself into a self and a knowing, for which it is as substance.[84] If the presentation of the absolute idea by the knowing self constitutes a single moment of absolute self-mediation, the aspects of knowing and substance retain a certain difference in identity, a difference manifested in the relation of belief.

Hegel remarks in this connection that belief (Glaube) and knowing (Wissen) are not opposed to each other, but that belief is a particular form of knowing. Absolute knowing, realized in the act of presentation, derives its implicit unity and the self-certainty of its objective content from the concomitant movement of belief. Hegel says, "The subjective consciousness of absolute spirit is essentially in-itself a process, the immediate and subtantial unity of which is the *belief* in the witness of the spirit as the *certainty* of objective truth".[85] This process, which is the mode of absolute manifestation, is for consciousness as the dialectical format of speculative presentation, and the guarantee that the beholding of this content by consciousness is true transforms this beholding into belief. Otherwise, the representation of the absolute content would remain simply exterior and alien to the knowing subject in the manner of the pictorially represented absolute of revealed religion.

Belief is the appearing of the immediate unity of a speculative presentation "for" consciousness. Belief is the beholding of the relatedness of the differentiated determinations, which in presentation, as the definitive cultus of the absolute, is the act of devotion. But this description of belief still emphasizes the difference between consciousness and its absolute content: belief understood as active devotion, on the contrary, reveals the reconciling character of the *process* of presentation which supersedes this contrast until it becomes spiritual liberation. Such a liberation, which is in actuality the total mediation of the absolute subject, raises this first certainty of its concrete determinations (i.e., the system) and its reconciliation (Versöhnung) to truth.[86]

Belief is liberating because it dissolves the contrast between the knowing subject and the substance of its absolute determination. But belief, and its liberating effect, is only realized in the act of presentation; it is merely the appearance of a reconciliation already determined by presentation as result, a presentation necessitated by the self-manifestation of the absolute idea. That the essential ground of speculative presentation lies in the essence of the idea is demonstrated by the three syllogisms that delineate its appearing "for" consciousness.

We have already discussed the derivative relationship between the content of these syllogisms (575, 576, 577) and the representational events of revealed religion, but what concerns us here are the indications they provide for the structural unity of the presentation of the absolute idea. That presentation is in need of such an absolute ground follows from our discussion thus far: first, speculative presentation is an externalization by the knowing subject of his absolute determination. Second, the subject knows this externalization in its totality as true through a pure beholding, the appearance of which is belief. However the aspect of belief reveals the tendency of presentation to break up into two moments, i.e., the knowing subject, and the content of his determinations presented in the system.[87] This tendency is tentatively held in check through the salutary effect of the act of presentation as devotion.

The absolute self-certainty of speculative presentation is ultimately due to the fact that it is not simply a subjective or arbitrary undertaking, but is equally an act of the absolute idea, – and it is clearly the reconciliation of these particular and universal determinations that contributes to its salutary effect. This "double" appropriation which constitutes the single moment of absolute witness is guaranteed through the original identity of its subjective and substantial elements, an identity which is now for-itself in speculative presentation. The supersession of the contrast between these elements is possible and necessary because the concept of the philosophizing subject is the self-thinking idea, self-knowing truth.

We can only comprehend the system as the self-thinking idea as long as we comprehend it as both (i) a philosophic presentation, and hence a part of the educational history of spirit, and (ii) itself a determinate mode of absolute self-presentation. Consequently, the three syllogisms which conclude the *Enzyklopädie* terminate the determinate modes of absolute externalization as such, i.e., as logic, nature, and spirit, *and* the self-appropriation of the absolute as spirit, as is explicated in the philosophy of spirit.[88] The knowledge of this self-appropriation therefore includes the full range of absolute presentation: "the logical, with the signification that it is universality *certified* in concrete content as in its actuality".[89] And so the completion of the system, understood as the appropriation of absolute self-presentation, is now seen to be a return to its beginning – the logic – but as a result, as spiritual.

Comprehended as the result of spirit, and thereby as wholly mediated by nature and spirit, the logic has raised itself from the immediacy of its beginning, from its appearance (Erscheinung), to its pure principle and element.[90] Thus it is the purpose of the three syllogisms which follow this "conclusion" to demonstrate the manner in which the appearance of the idea has been raised to its proper element through the appropriation of its determinations implicit in existence. In the last chapter of the larger *Logik* Hegel offers a simular methodological discussion centering on the transition from logic to nature and spirit, and comments that nature and spirit are in general different modes of presenting the idea's *existence*,[91] – so that with the appropriation of the logic of presentation within these modes, the philosophic presentation of the logic (itself an existential mode of the absolute) coincides with the idea's ultimate self-externalization and self-knowledge. This development of the absolute from out of its immediacy through its existential modes as nature and spirit to its self-knowledge as a spiritual principle means that the immediacy was in fact an appearance, a lack or need, and essentially a transition point within the absolute's full realization. Hegel says, "Hence it can be said that every beginning must be made with the *absolute*, just as all advance is merely the presentation (Darstellung) of it, in so far as its *existing in-itself* is the concept. But because the absolute is at first only *in it-self* it equally is *not* the absolute nor the posited concept, and also not the idea; for in these latter, the being in-itself is only an abstract, onesided moment. The advance is thus not a kind of superfluity; this it would be if that with which the beginning is made were in truth already the absolute; the advance consists rather in the universal determining itself and being for-itself the universal, that is, equally an individual and a subject. Only in its completion is it the absolute".[92]

The absolute must be presented if it is to exist for-itself. It must be presented as nature and spirit, the highest moment of which is philosophic presentation, – where the absolute fully knows itself and is fully for-itself. Prior to this recollecting and knowing which coincides with absolute self-presentation, the immediate existences of the idea are still appearances which display a lack or need and so are on-the-way within the return of the idea to itself as spiritual. The first two of the three syllogisms which complete the system are characterized by Hegel as appearances, and are determined by the judgment of the idea into its moments as the in-itself objective existence of the idea and the for-itself subjective activity of the idea, which when mediated by the logical idea form the absolute syllogism: but as appearances, the preceding two syllogisms are partial mediations and on-the-way because not fully self-knowing, i.e., the logic is not absolutely present, it is simply reflected in its existences.

Hegel says that syllogism # 575 is the appearance which grounds further development, with logic as the starting-point, nature as the middle, and spirit coupled with them. This is the immediate presentation of the idea in existence as objective, existing idea: the logical becomes nature, and nature becomes spirit. Nature is the mode of existence which mediates, standing between spirit and its essence, but in so doing it does not divide itself into the extremes of finite abstraction, for nature is a presented mode of the logical, and as such is essentially a transition-point, a negative moment, or the idea *in-itself*. Consequently, the spiritual subject that is reinstated by the movement of nature[93] knows the logical idea which is its essence only as the objective existence of the idea: this "in-itself" is the subject's natural world. The mediation of the concept appears in this natural world as transition, and the science of this transition has the external form of the course of necessity.[94]

In this appearance, the idea is presented in nature, and knows itself only as an "other" and as external, natural transition. We might say that the idea's pure logical form and its spiritual recollection of itself are still, in a sense, divided or alienated by the intercession of nature as a determinate negative moment. Spiritual knowledge of the idea as both organic and inorganic nature is an unmediated direct appropriation of the existing world, and the mode of spiritual knowledge not unlike the immediate knowing of natural consciousness which is implicitly scientific. Again at the end of the larger *Logik* where he speaks of the presentation of the idea in nature, Hegel says that, "In so far as this externality is only the abstract immediacy of being and is apprehended by consciousness, it is as mere objectivity and external life; but in the idea it remains in-and-for-itself the totality of the concept and science in the relation of divine cognition to nature".[95] The immediate consciousness of an external nature characteristic of spirit in the first syllogism is equally divine or absolute cognition to the extent that it cognizes, even if only in a finite mode, the logical in nature.

The self-presentation of the absolute within the mode of nature establishes or reinstates the spiritual subject as existing. This first appearance of the idea in its objective immediacy is superseded by the second syllogism, # 576, which sets forth the advance of absolute self-knowledge as spirit. The second syllogism supersedes the first in that it presupposes the natural objective existence of the idea and the positing of the spiritual subject in its immediacy: but in this second syllogism, spirit mediates the process, presupposing nature and coupling the logical with it, so that the absolute presents itself as the for-itself subjective activity of the idea over against its presupposed natural world. Hegel says that it is the syllogism of spiritual reflection in the idea; science appears as a subjective cognition, of which freedom is the aim and itself the way to bring it about.[96]

When Hegel is speaking of the second syllogism as the standpoint of spirit, it is clear he does not intend to identify it with any text or part of the presented system anymore than he intended to do so in the first syllogism, for these two syllogisms do not seek to represent the manipulation or appearance of scientific texts as external objects. Rather, they set out the manner in which the method or presentation of speculative science itself originates in the advance of the absolute as a self-presentation in its logical, natural, and spiritual modes. When the self-presentation of the absolute as spirit consciously coincides with the subjective presentation of science, then the logical immediate becomes a spiritual result, and subjective presentation is equally and fully absolute presentation because it is the presentation of a reason which is truly self-knowing.

Therefore the second syllogism, which delineates the subjective activity of the idea primarily as cognition, and hence as subjective presentation by which all cognition is possible, is not a veiled reference to the *Phänomenologie* as such. The evidnce for this assertion does not derive from an historical study of the concern or lack of it for this earlier work at the moment of the formulation of the syllogisms,[97] but from an understanding of the intention of these syllogisms which relate logic, nature, and spirit to the necessities of absolute presentation. In any case, that spirit which is for-itself and has freedom for its aim cannot easily be confounded with the path of phenomenal knowing which is the "way of despair".[98]

If we look at the Introduction to the *Philosophie des Geistes* in the system we see that the revelation of the idea as spirit is free, positing nature as its world, and as reflection equally presupposes the world as independent nature. Ultimately, this revealing in the concept is the creation of the world as its being, in which it procures the affirmation and truth of its freedom.[99] Surely it is this relation to nature and its supersession which is indicated by the relation of the second syllogism to the first, − spirit finding a world as its presupposition, the generation of a world as its own product, and the freeing of spirit from this world and in it.[100] And the generation and freeing of spirit certainly reaches its culmination in the philosophic presentation of the logic as the completion of spirit's educational history *and* the self-presentation of the absolute in general. It is this philosophic presentation which terminates the appearance of the idea in spirit and raises it to self-knowing reason, a development which Hegel seems to sketch at the end of the larger *Logik*: "But in this next resolve of the pure idea to determine itself as external idea, it thereby only posits itself as the mediation out of which the concept elevates itself as free, out of externality to an existence withdrawn into itself, that completes itself through its liberation in the *science of spirit* and that finds the highest concept of itself in the logical science as the self-comprehending pure concept". [101]

From out of the spiritual mediation of the second syllogism the absolute ascends to perfect self-comprehension in the third and containing syllogism through the spiritual presentation of the logic, where at last subjective and absolute presentation are explicitly the same in the self-certifying system. In the analysis of consciousness in the system, Hegel remarks in several places that Kant's philosophy displays the determinations of perceptive consciousness, [102] and so we must assume that it is only quite recently that consciousness has made the transition to spirit for-itself which culminates in the presentation of the *Logik* and the system of self-knowing reason.

The *philosophie des Geistes* is the presentation of that educational history as it is absolutely in-and-for-itself, and there is consequently no reason to categorically refuse an historical role to the *Phänomenologie* at the level of the logical idea's *appearance* in spirit: in the above citation from the *Logik*, is not the "science of spirit" by which the concept is liberated to itself prior to its presentation as a logical science nothing else than the *Phänomenologie*? At the time of writing, the latter was still considered to be the first part of the system of science, and, indeed, was followed by the science of logic. [103] Furthermore, the Introduction to the *Logik* seems to echo the liberating function of the *Phänomenologie* alluded to above, where Hegel says that, "The concept of pure science and its deduction is therefore presupposed in the present work in so far as the *Phänomenologie des Geistes* is nothing other than the deduction of it. Absolute knowing is the truth of every mode of consciousness because, as the course of the *Phänomenologie* showed, it is only in absolute knowing that the separation of the *object* from the *certainty* of itself is completely eliminated, and truth becomes equated with this certainty and this certainty with truth. This pure science presupposes liberation from the opposition of consciousness. [104]

The historical contingency adhering to the appearance of the *Phänomenologie* within the educational history of spirit is superseded in the logically self-conscious presentation of that history as it is presented by the *Philosophie des Geistes*, where the transition from the standpoint of consciousness to that of spirit is shown to be simply dialectically necessary at the level of self-knowing reason. The reflection of the logical idea in spirit which is characteristic of the spiritual mediation in the second syllogism implicitly contains the *Phänomenologie* as one of its moments, but it is only the syllogism as a whole which provides the *Phänomenologie* with its absolute determination within the on-going modes of the idea's self-presentation. In other words, the *Phänomenologie* cannot be identified with the second syllogism as such, although this syllogism presupposes the transition from consciousness to spirit effected by the *Phänomenologie* within the educational history of spirit in its fortuitous appearing.

The third and containing syllogism # 577 displays the identity of what at first was the logical idea in-itself, with the idea of philosophy, so that we can now speak of the logical as a result, as spiritual, through its philosophic presentation. And it is through this presentation, which coincides with absolute self-presentation, that the modes of this absolute presentation have been exhausted and raised to self-consciousness in the system, i.e., the system is the absolute fully in-and-for-itself. Of course the absolute in its apparent immediacy was always implicitly this result, for we learn that the idea, which mediates this syllogism, divides itself into the subjective activity of the idea characteristic of spirit, and the in-itself, objective, existing idea of nature, and thus determines both of these appearances of the idea in its existential modes as the manifestations of self-knowing reason. [105] But nature and spirit are only manifestly mediated by the logical idea in the presentation of the system, so that this third syllogism can be considered as explicating the absolute truth of the system itself as the highest mode of absolute self-presentation.

It is only in this final presentation, as indicated by the movement of the three syllogisms, that we behold the reconciliation of the nature of the thing, the self-moving and self-developing concept, and the movement of the activity of cognition. Again, this presentation, as grounded by the three syllogisms, completes not only the self-presentation of the absolute, − it equally completes the process of presentation by spirit outlined in the *Philosophie des Geistes*. What we do learn above all from the syllogisms is that the reflection of the idea in the concrete modes of nature and spirit "in themselves" and as appearances display a lack and a *need* for their self-completion by the philosophic presentation of the system, i.e., the educational history of spirit needs the *Enzyklopädie* as its proper fulfillment.

The insistence that the act of speculative presentation explicitly brings together the implicit identity of cognition and the concept raises certain questions, however. Speculative presentation marks the recollection and return of the absolute to itself, and as such is the close of that spiritual development which is still a reflection in the idea and an appearance. By "close" we mean that the philosophic presentation of the system brings to an end prior divisions in spiritual life, divisions which manifest a need for their supersession in a higher self-comprehending totality. Perhaps the most important question in this transition from the educational history of spirit in its fortuitous happening to its self-appropriation in the system, is whether this sense of a close is prior to, and thus instigates, the philosophic response, or whether, on the contrary, it is the philosophic presentation itself which brings about the perception of an epochal close?

In a Remark to paragraph # 573 Hegel asserts that, "The close of philosophy is not the place, even in an exoteric account, to waste a word on what 'to conceptualize' means".[106] When we look at paragraph # 573 itself, we see that the close is the end of the movement of philosophy, where it lays hold of its own concept and is only a looking-back on its knowedge, so that the system is a close to the extent that it successfully supersedes the mere reflection of the logical in spirit.[107] But philosophy perceives itself as this close only in relation to the felt need manifest in the current divisions within spiritual life: philosophy comprehends these needs and supersedes them through the absolute determination of its comprehension. Therefore out of the close arises the belief in the original identity of the absolute determinations of spiritual life, and the devotion to their presentation by the system. We have already remarked that the relation of cognition to the self-moving concept in presentation is one of belief, but what is suggestive in this assertion by Hegel is that the mystical devotion to the absolute efficacy of conceptual thinking its related to a reality divided against itself.

Furthermore, it is the conviction of the truth of this cognition, as presented in the system, that provides the connection between natural consciousness, the *Phänomenologie*, and the system itself. This connection is determined by the relative fullness of the cognition of the absolute idea, and if for one moment we question the belief in our exhaustive presentation of the concept, then this connection dissolves and we are left with interesting philosophic hypotheses that only partially and approximately present an essentially ineffable idea. The finality of speculative presentatiion in this case would derive less from the absolute self-certainty of its determinations and more from its comprehension as the epochal disclosure of a self-concealing truth.

The collapse of belief in the unfolding of the absolute idea by speculative presentation leaves the knowing subject in an irreconciliable state of irony. This occurs, according to Hegel, when the result, spirit existing for-itself, is appropriated in a merely formal, contentless sense, so that spirit is not equally known as existing in-itself and objectively self-unfolding. Irony is the attitude of self-consciousness which is only a formal infinite subjectivity, and which knows itself in-itself as absolute. Irony nullifies all objective import, and arbitrarily and willfully gives its content its determination. Arguing against this alternative, Hegel says, "Only when the pure infinite form for the existing of self-manifestation throws off the onesidedness of subjectivity, the vanity of thought, is it free thought, which has its infinite determination at the same time as its absolute in and for itself existing content, and has that content as an object in which it is also free".[108]

The certainty that the system is in fact the system of absolute determinations depends very much on the notion that the system itself, and the *Phänomenologie*, is determined by the self-presentation of the absolute in modes as described by the three closing syllogisms. However proof as to the veracity of these three syllogisms, i.e., that all reality is implicitly and, now, explicitly, mediated by the concept, is not adduced through placing the syllogisms within a context of covering statements. What formerly the proof was supposed to accomplish is now accomplished concretely through the *act* of speculative presentation itself, such that speculative science is the witness to the total and dialectical mediation of reality by the concept. Indeed, it is the total and dialectical nature of this presentation that guarantees that this witness is also true.

We turn and return again to the speculative system because it responds to the need for self-knowedge in man; and the system offers itself as such a knowedge because it exhaustively mediates and cognizes all nature and spirit, the modes within which the absolute *exists*. If we remain unconvinced by the total and exhaustive nature of this mediation, then the relation between self-knowedge and the absolute must be put into question once again. If we remain unconvinced, then the following propositions return as key presuppositions: "To know what God as spirit is – to apprehend this accurately and distinctly in thoughts – requires careful and thorough speculation. It includes, in its forefront, the propositions: God is God only so far as he knows himself; his self-knowedge is, further, a self-consciousness in man and man's knowedge *of* God, which proceeds to man's self-knowedge *in* God".[109]

NOTES

1 This relation between the self-certain system and the historical appearing of non-philosophic life poses one of the more difficult problems in our understanding of the "finality" of speculative presentation.

2 It is this question, originally posed by Kierkegaard, which is at the heart of the critique of Hegel by Merleau-Ponty in *Sens et Non-Sens*: "Le Hegel de la fin a tout compris, sauf sa propre situation historique; il a tenu compte de tout, sauf de sa propre existence, et la synthèse qu'il nous offre n'est pas une vraie synthèse, justement parce qu'elle affecte d'ignorer qu'elle est le fait d'un certain individu et d'un certain temps (p. 111)". (Les Editions Nagel, Paris, 1966).

3 G.R.G. Mure remarks, quite appropriately, that "The reflective historian interprets the accumulated record of the past, but anachronistically. The philosopher interprets the past as a process sublated in result, and so as a present which is in a sense timeless, but not as a present in which the future, too, is sublated". *The Philosophy of Hegel* (Oxford University Press, London, 1965), p. 183.

4 *Enz.* Einl. # 6, p. 38 (8).

5 It is for this reason that the various lectures on the history of philosophy, religion, etc., can never act as an introduction to the system, since they presuppose the absolute self-knowledge presented by the system.

6 *Enz.* Einl. # 11, p. 44 (16).

7 F. Nietzsche, *The Gay Science*, trans. W. Kaufmann, (Vintage Books, New York, 1974), Preface p. 38. Nietzsche seems to have liked the same Greeks which Plato and Hegel condemned, and of course he considered these two to be incorrigible theologians of the first order. The citation also illuminates the contrast between Hegel's phenomenology and Nietzsche's phenomenalism.

8 *Enz.* Einl. # 12 R., p. 45 (17).

9 *Enz.* Einl. # 12 R., p. 46 (18).

10 *Enz.* Einl. # 14, p. 47 (19).

11 *Enz.* Einl. # 17, p. 50 (22).

12 *Enz.* Vorb. # 20 R., p. 56 (31).

13 Wittgenstein's *Philosophical Investigations* states the problem of a universal determination of language in a most precise manner: "We are under the illusion that what is peculiar, profound, essential, in our investigation, resides in its trying to grasp the incomparable essence of language. That is, the order existing between the concepts of proposition, word, proof, truth, experience, and so on. This order is a *super*-order between — so to speak — *super*-concepts. Whereas, of course, if the words 'language', 'experience', 'world', have a use, it must be as humble a one as that of the words 'table' 'lamp','door' ''. Trans. Anscombe (Basil Blackwell, Oxford, 1958), p. 44.

14 As we saw in the previous chapter, the mode of representation is developed in the *Phil. des Geistes* not only as an externalization of subjectivity, but equally as the product of con-

crete, intersubjective relations, such as in the contract or the constitution, where the state marks the determinate "horizon" of these relations. The question we are asking, is to what extent absolute self-presentation can, and does, supersede the thick immediacy of these particular, linguistic *regions*?

15 *Enz.* Vorb. # 22, p. 57 (34).

16 *Enz.* Vorb. # 50 R., p. 75 (81).

17 *Enz.* Vorb. # 79, p. 102 (113).

18 *Enz.* Vorb. # 80, p. 102 (113).

19 *Enz.* Vorb. # 81, p. 102 (115).

20 *Enz.* Vorb. # 82, p. 103 (119).

21 *Wiss. d. Logik* I, p. 145 (155).

22 Heidegger's various interpretations of the dialectic inevitably tend toward this exaggeration of the passivity of the subject: "The process-character of thinking is determined by the dialectic of Being. For Hegel, the matter of thinking is: Being, as thinking itself; and thinking comes to itself only in the process of its speculative development, this running through stages of the variously developed, and hence of necessity previously undeveloped, forms". *Identity and Difference*, trans. Stambaugh, (Harper & Row, New York, 1969), p. 45.

23 Such an assumption is at the root of Adorno's criticism of Hegel's dialectical logic in the following: "An element of truth might even be squeezed out of Hegel's theory of time, provided one will not let logic produce time by itself, as he does; to be perceived in logic, instead, are coagulated time relations, as indicated variously, if cryptically in *Critique of Pure Reason*, in the chapter on schematism in particular. Preserved likewise in the discursive *Logic* – unmistakeably in its conclusions – are time elements that were detemporalized as subjective thinking objectivized them into pure legality; without such detemporalization, on the other hand, time would not have been objectivized at all". *Op. cit.*, p. 333.

24 *Ph.G.* Vorr. p. 53 (39).

25 *Enz.* Vorb. # 78 R., p. 102 (112).

26 *Differenz etc.*, p. 14 (91).

27 *Enz.* Einl. # 11 R., p. 44 (15).

28 *Enz.* Vorb. # 81 R., p. 103 (116).

29 *Enz.* Vorb. # 10, p. 43 (14).

30 *Enz.* Vorb. # 25, p. 58 (45).

31 *Enz.* Vorb. # 25 R., p. 59 (46).

32 *Enz.* Vorb. # 26, p. 59 (47).

33 *Enz.* Vorb. # 37, p. 64 (60).

34 *Enz.* Vorb. # 40, p. 67 (65).

35 *Enz.* Vorb. # 60 R., p. 85 (93).

36 *Enz.* Vorb. # 61, p. 86 (95).

37 *Enz.* Vorb. # 65, p. 91 (101).

38 *Enz.* Vorb. # 67, p. 93 (102).

39 *Enz.* Vorb. # 78 R., p. 101 (111).

40 *Enz.* Vorb. # 81 R., p. 103 (116).

41 *Enz.* Einl. # 13, p. 46 (18).

42 *Enz.* Einl. # 13, p. 47 (18).

43 *Enz.* Einl. # 13, p. 47 (18).

44 *Enz.* Einl. # 14, p. 47 (19).

45 *Enz.* # 548f., p. 426 (277).

46 *Enz.* # 552, p. 430 (282).

47 *Enz.* # 552 R., p. 437 (289).

48 *Enz.* # 552 R., p. 437 (290).

49 *Enz.* # 552 R., p. 437 (290).

50 *Enz.* # 562 R., p. 444 (296).

51 *Enz.* # 572, p. 450 (302).
52 *Enz.* # 573, p. 451 (302).
53 *Phil. des Rechts*, Vorr., p. 16 (11).
54 *Phil. des Rechts*, Vorr., p. 14 (10).
55 *Phil. des Rechts*, Vorr., p. 17 (13). "The teaching of the concept, which is also history's necessary lesson, is that it is only when actuality is mature that the ideal first appears over against the real and that the ideal apprehends this same world in its substance and builds it up for itself into the shape of an intellectual realm. When philosophy paints its grey in grey, then has a shape of life grown old. By philosophy's grey in grey it cannot be rejuvenated but only cognized".
56 *Vernunft in der Geschichte*, p. 173f. (143).
57 *Enz.* # 448, p. 362 (III 123).
58 *Ph.G.* VII, p. 524 (455).
59 *Ph.G.* VII, p. 524 (456).
60 *Ph.G.* VII, p. 524 (456).
61 *Ph.G.* VIII, p. 553 (483).
62 *Ph.G.* VIII, p. 553 (483).
63 The *Phänomenologie*, as an appearance of the system in consciousness, is the rise to self-consciousness of this alienation, and the ladder between the externalization of the absolute implicit in consciousness and the self-conscious recollection of this externalization in the system.
64 *Wiss. der Logik* II, p. 357 (708).
65 *Wiss. der Logik* I, p. 39 (57).
66 *wiss. der Logik* I, p. 10 (32).
67 Gadamer takes up this extreme position when he says that it is the real power of the German language, and not any schematic conceptual apparatus, which breathes life into Hegel's philosophy. It follows that all attempts to translate his thought are utterly futile: "The speculative power lying in the connotations of the German words and in the range of meaning extending from them in so many directions is so completely unable to penetrate the cloak of the foreign language". *Hegel's Dialectic*, trans. Smith (Yale University Press, New Haven, Conn., 1976), p. 112.
68 *Ph.G.* Vorr., p. 22 (12).
69 *Ph.G.* Vorr., p. 23 (13).
70 *Ph.G.* Vorr., p. 49 (37).
71 *Ph.G.* Vorr., p. 50 (38).
72 *Ph.G.* Vorr., p. 53 (39).
73 Gauvin thinks an analysis of terms and their changing significance throughout the text would best bring out this speculative truth, i.e., through treating the words as "phénomènes du sens de l'oeuvre". This follows the insight that, "la signification des mots est définie par la corrélation entre les structures de l'oeuvre et ses récurrences selon ces structures". From "Le sens et son phénoméne", *Hegel-Studien*, Band 3 (Bonn, 1965), p. 273.
74 *Ph.G.* Vorr., p. 54 (41). W. Marx suggests that thinking proves its power against the customary sentence by forcing it to accept the speculative content, so that some of the functions normally expected of language "get lost". *Reason and World* (Nijhoff, The Hague, 1971), pp. 31f. If this is so, then the externalization of thinking in language becomes an alienation (Entfremdung), in which thought does not fully recognize itself in its other. But surely the relation of thought to language is dialectical, so that instead of positing the absolute "servitude" of language, we would do better to think of the supersession of natural language by the speculative sentence.
75 *Ph.G.* Vorr., p. 46 (33).
76 *Ph.G.* VIII, p. 558 (487).
77 *Ph.G.* VIII, p. 556 (485).

78 *Ph.G.* VIII, p. 563 (491). "Science contains within itself this necessity of externalizing the form of the concept, and it contains the passage of the concept into *consciousness*".

79 Lukacs, following Karl Marx, believes that philosophy as absolute knowing cancels all externalization (Entäußerung), which, he suggests, is a contradiction since all philosophy is itself an externalization. But Lukacs confuses externalization with alienation: Hegel does not want to cancel externalization, rather he wants absolute knowing to know its objectivity as its own, and certainly presentation is the epitome of this externalizing and knowing. *The Young Hegel, op. cit.*, p. 551.

80 *Ph.G.* VIII, p. 558 (487).

81 *Ph.G.* VIII, p. 560 (489).

82 For Heidegger, such a construction of the now-point means that the now "remains levelled off and covered up, so that it can be intuited as something present-at-hand, though present-at-hand only 'ideally' ". *Being and Time*, trans. Macquarrie and Robinson (Harper & Row, New York, 1962), pp. 480f.

83 Hegel's certainty of this identity tends toward a system which the thinker has not merely in mind, and presents partially each time, but is certain of itself as the essential structure of what is actual. Cf. Heidegger in *The End of Philosophy*, trans. Stambaugh (Harper & Row, New York, 1973), p. 48.

84 *Enz.* # 554, p. 440 (292).

85 *Enz.* # 555, p. 440 (292).

86 *Enz.* # 555, p. 440 (292).

87 An emphasis on the true "act" of presentation, as opposed to its textual residue, would dissolve the dilemma of alienation vs. belief.

88 Although B. Bourgeois astutely describes the three syllogisms as a series of mediation modes, there is no discussion of the important relation between absolute self-presentation and the philosophic presentation by spirit. He does say that the syllogisms "n'indiquent pas la possibilité ou la nécessité d'autres élaborations du contenu du savoir absolu, mais ils expriment les trois modes selon lesquels le savoir absolu – qui est le savoir de lui-même comme de la *Logique* par laquelle l'*esprit* conçoit la *nature*, comme de la logique (c'est-à-dire de la nature se comprenant logiquement dans l'esprit) en tant qu'auto-fondation de l'être – appréhende son propre processus fondateur, sa propre médiation absolue". *Op. cit.*, p. 51.

89 *Enz.* # 574, p. 462 (313).

90 *Enz.* # 574, p. 462 (313).

91 *Wiss. der Logik* II, p. 484 (824).

92 *Wiss. der Logik* II, p. 489f. (829).

93 *Ph.G.* VIII, p. 563 (492).

94 *Enz.* # 575, p. 462 (314).

95 *Wiss. der Logik* II, p. 505 (843).

96 *Enz.* # 576, p. 462 (314).

97 It is this kind of reasoning which lies behind Pöggeler's denial of any relationship between the syllogisms and the *Phän.*: "Dans l'*Encyclopédie* Hegel prend trop nettement ses distances à l'égard de la *Phénoménologie* pour avoir pu penser à elle lorsqu'il a exposé dans les derniers paragraphes de l'*Encyclopédie*, le syllogisme primitif. De plus la *Phénoménologie*, en vertu de sa propre détermination, ne peut pas fournir ce qui est exigé dans le syllogisme primitif: elle ne peut pas rassembler les parties du système, parce que dans la *Phénoménologie* les parties du système ne se présentent pas selon leur vérité". *Op. cit.*, pp. 231f. Nonetheless the appearance in the second syllogism does suggest some kind of relation to the appearing science, which we must clarify.

98 In what is perhaps the best analysis of the syllogisms to date, H.F. Fulda points out that, "Als Weg der Erfahrung des Bewußtseins und der Überwindung desselben – also in inhaltlicher Bedeutung genommen – stellt die *Phänomenologie* kein subjektives Erkennen dar, dessen Zweck die Freiheit sein könnte, sondern einen "Weg der Verzweiflung". Die Bestim-

mung, sich die Freiheit zum Zweck zu setzen, kommt erst dem Geist als solchem, nicht dem Bewußtsein zu''. *Das Problem einer Einleitung in Hegel's Wissenschaft der Logik*, V (Klostermann, Frankfurt a.M., 1965), p. 286.

99 *Enz.* # 384, p. 314 (I 57).
100 *Enz.* # 386, p. 315 (I 71).
101 *Wiss. der Logik* II, p. 506 (843).
102 *Enz.* # 420 R., p. 347 (III 27). (Cf. *Enz.* # 415 R., p. 345 (III 11) and the introductory *Stellungen*.)
103 *Wiss. der Logik* I, p. 7 (28f.).
104 *Wiss. der Logik* I, p. 30 (49).
105 *Enz.* # 577, p. 463 (314).
106 *Enz.* # 573, p. 459 (311).
107 *Enz.* # 573, p. 451 (302).
108 *Enz.* # 571 R., p. 450 (301).
109 *Enz.* # 564 R., p. 447 (298).

IV. CONCLUSION: THE EMPTY SEPULCHRE

In the preceding we have attempted to explicate the manner in which spculative or philosophic presentation is a subjective act arising out of the absolute need for self-knowedge by spirit. Of course this act is by no means arbitrary or simply willful, for it occurs at a determinate moment within the educational history of spirit and is situated by that absolute which is already close to us. It is the meaning which we attach to this occurring and situating which has occupied much of the foregoing discussion, and it cannot be denied that even in this conclusion our discussion persists in raising more questions than can be answered.

Rather than making a summary of the facts, then, perhaps we would be better to highlight some of the difficulties in understanding Hegel's concept of philosophy, since a hard and fast "conclusion" would tend to blur the process character of the speculation peculiar to our own presentation. The central difficulty, and perhaps the deepest paradox, is that Hegel asks us to accept speculative science both as a regional self-knowledge that looks back on the spiritual history of a particular people *and* as a self-manifestation of the absolute which somehow brings time to an end. It is natural that common sense immediately looks askance at the second aspect of this suggestion, for it seems inconceivable that any reasonable philosopher would lay such a claim on the inscrutable grace of destiny, with the implication that those living on the other side of this water-shed are languishing on the directionless shoals of post-history.

But as has been at least implicit in our reading, Hegel is in no need of extended apologia on this score, for he sought to abolish neither philosophy nor temporality as such. As the highest standpoint, a certain philosophy may *close* a particular spiritual realm and offer for contemporary natural consciousness the essential structure of the actual, – and yet it must be remembered that this structure is actual according to the terms of reference established by this *present* spiritual realm. Hegel simply believed that such a transition from one realm or epoch to another was taking place in his own day, one of the manifestations of which was the different manner in which we came to experience history, and that his philosophy was important because it brought to full self-consciousness the significance of one aging spiritual edifice *vis-à-vis* the new horizons that were opening before it. As is pointed out in the Preface to the *Phänomenologie*, "Besides, it is not difficult to see that ours is a birthtime and a transition to a new era. Spirit has broken with the being-there and representation of the prevailing world, and is of a mind to submerge it in the past and in the labour of its own transformation".[1]

It would seem, then, that philosophy is to be more than a looking back and comprehension of past glories, for it is equally a new opening on the future. This does not mean that philosophy predicts the future, for it cannot overleap its age, but it can provide the structures of thought by which this new world can be understood and which may provide a tentative basis for the realization of its peculiar principle. Again, Hegel asserts that this world "comes on the scene for the first time in its immediacy or its concept. Just as little as a building is finished when its foundation has been laid, so little is the achieved concept of the whole the whole itself".[2] Therefore the appearance of philosophy is at once the presentation of the universal ground for that to come and the preserved wealth of previous existence still present to consciousness in recollection, – and thus both a reminiscence and a free anticipation.

In as much as philosophy appears only in its immediate concept it remains the esoteric possession of a few individuals, with the result that if it is to be truly a *spiritual* recollection and anticipation then it must offer contemporary natural consciousness as such an exoteric "ladder" to the current standpoint. Of course the failure of philosophy to provide this accessibility would diminish greatly the historic significance of its epochal close and preparatory ground-work. The danger for philosophic science itself is that in its early stages it is vulnerable to criticism, a criticism which can lead to irreconcilable divisions within scientific culture such as that between the critical philosophy and immediate knowing of German Idealism. While these divisions are sometimes characterized by Hegel as the symptoms of cultural senility, it is clear at least in the *Phänomenologie* that they are at the same time the birth-pangs of a new spiritual order: that philosophy is "true" which can mediate these divisions with the *completed* educational history of spirit, and offer this new order its recollected existence as it stands arrayed in an exoteric presentation and as it is determined by the concept alone.

If this recollecting and offering is to have general appeal, then it must come on the scene for a particular natural consciousness and it must speak the language of this consciousness' current concerns. Once natural consciousness has been raised to the level of science, it is in a position to take account of its educational history as it is presented in and for itself, and become the "immanent self" of its absolute determination as present at hand in a systematic text. And this is really the central question, — as to whether the essential structure of the actual truly abides within the promoted presence of language, and how this structure is for the self through a pure beholding?

It is certainly not our intention at this point to recount our previous interpretation of Hegel's thinking about language, but there is one paradox arising from this discussion worth restating. Language has its universality because it maintains a certain independence from the knowing subject and acts as an objective matrix for social interaction. However this same independence of language is the result of its supersession of the natural thing, and even though language is that transparent element in which the self most justly recognizes itself in externality, as with the opaque resistance of the natural thing there persists within language a degree of alienation of spirit from itself. Indeed it is this alienation which guarantees language its salutary independence.

The determinations of the concept therefore "appear" within language, for in the scheme of things Hegel would be hard pressed to posit a simple identity between the actual and the textual. What is missing is the infinite interest of thought, whereby the reconciliation of the subject-object fulfilled in the system is present to existence and actual through our thinking of it. But because in language there perdures the opaque resistance of the thing, this appropriation in thought, this going over to the system, must always contain a substantial element of alienation and, consequently, of belief. It is this necessity of belief, as opposed to the certainty of self-evident truth, which dogs those of that spiritual future prepared and anticipated by Hegel; it seems impossible that, within the either/or of a devoted appropriation, poisonous irony not enter into the recollection of our beginnings.

Yet, after all, are we not asking too much of Hegel, is not this sense of irony the result of unrealistic expectations? The presented system is the essential structure of the actual and timeless within the terms of its reference, i.e., within the terms of the educational history of spirit it recollects, but this actuality and timelessness must change its meaning within that new world whose horizons speculative science was only at first dimly aware. True, this science contains within itself the necessity of externalizing the form of the pure concept, of presenting the system of absolute determinations, as it no less contains the going-over of this concept into consciousness through the thinking appropriation we have described. But at the end of the *Phänomenologie* Hegel also tells us that the close of speculative science is contemporaneous with spirit's self-release in the form of "free contingent happening", whereby spirit once again seeks to raise itself to maturity from the substantial immediacy or "beginning" provided by science.[3] In this way the turning point or movement between one spiritual realm and the next is marked by and *exists* as a philosophic presentation which both recollects and anticipates, even though this "anticipation" is compared with that of the acorn *vis-à-vis* the fully grown oak.[4]

This indicates that although Hegel believes he has set out in the system the concept of the spiritual whole that is to come, this concept yet apears in its immediacy, with the result that it is impossible for us to precisely determine the manner in which this immediacy will be mediated with the free contingent happening of the new world. Perhaps the most that can be said is that speculative science provides us the conceptual structures by which we are able to understand the reality of freedom in our present existence, or the sense in which this freedom is a function of the insight into objectivity as the subject's own. In the system a reconciliation between the finite self and a manifest absolute is accomplished: it remains for us to "go over" to the concept of this reconciliation and to realize it within all existence, making it fully actual and giving it a determinate "cultus".

There is some evidence to suggest that the later Hegel did indeed shy away from the implicit aspects of anticipation lurking everywhere within the *Phänomenologie*, but this shift in position is by no means an about-face. In the Preface to the first edition of the *Logik* Hegel continues to affirm the backward *and* forward looking nature of philosophy, with his comment that "logic shows no traces so far of the new spirit which has arisen in the sciences no less than in the world of actuality. However, once the substantial form of the spirit has inwardly reconstituted itself, all attempts to preserve the forms of an earlier culture are utterly in vain; like withered leaves they are pushed off by the new buds already growing at their roots. Even in the philosophic sphere this ignoring of the general change is beginning gradually to come to an end".[5] The "new ideas" which are making themselves felt everywhere in society and thought are both the result and inwardizing of a previous spiritual realm *and* the first elaboration of a new principle.

It is in the *Enzyklopädie* and the *Philosophie des Rechts* that the characterization of philosophy as strictly a thinking recollection of past spiritual glories gains increasing weight, and now with nary a mention of the "new world" which was once upon us. In that section of the system dealing with philosophy (as the terminal configuration of the whole and its absolute presupposition), Hegel tells us in a straightforward manner that, "This movement, which philosophy is, finds itself already accomplished, when at the close it lays hold of its own concept − i.e., only *looks back* on its knowledge".[6] The *Philosophie des Rechts* is even more emphatic in its picturesque descriptions of philosophy as symptomatic of cultural old age, an "ideal" which arrives on the scene only with the falling of dusk. Hegel repeatedly admonishes us that philosophy is at most the apprehension of the present and actual, not the erection of a beyond.[7] Certainly, at least on the surface of it, this characterization of philosophy is very different from that thinking we find in the *Phänomenologie*, which was prepared to claim that the concept of a spiritual whole appears *before* the whole itself![8]

However there continues to cling to these later texts an air of ambiguity which provides evidence for the suggestion that they represent a development of the earlier position rather than a wholesale negation of it. To begin with, this description of a scientific recollection which looks back on a *completed* spiritual realm is no less strongly put in the *Phänomenologie* itself, as we have repeatedly pointed out in previous discussions. But in addition, at the end of the system Hegel talks about the manner in which science is verified within the spiritually concrete and actual, i.e., that the eternal in and for itself existing idea eternally sets itself to work, engenders and enjoys itself as absolute spirit,[9] − which brings to mind those last pages of the *Phänomenologie* where Hegel describes the opening of speculative science toward the free contingent happening of spirit that seeks afresh to raise itself to maturity. One would assume that the close of philosophy is simply one moment within this never-ending play of spirit itself, that the moment of absolute recollection is at the same time the release of spirit to a new struggle and development through which the depth of the idea is progressively revealed.

As to the unrelenting condemnation of philosophy as anticipation in the Preface to the *Philosophie des Rechts*, perhaps this can be explained by the implicitly polemical nature of its exposition. Hegel was intent on clearly distinguishing his own science of right from what he considered to be the mere fancies of prescriptive political philosophies that appealed only to the heart, citing the unfortunate Herr Fries as "the ringleader of these hosts of superficiality".[10] But the anticipation of a new spiritual realm such as we find in the *Phänomenologie* is far from the prescriptive "ought" Hegel was seeking to condemn in his later works: speculative science describes the conceptual structures of actual freedom, an actuality which provides the basis for and is *mediated with* the free contingent happening of spirit to come. Even as late as 1830 in his own draft for the lectures on the philosophy of history, Hegel was still able to claim, as he had done many years earlier, that the concept of freedom as set out most perfectly by speculative science *precedes* the actual whole of its full realization. "The spirit's consciousness of its freedom (which is the precondition of the reality of this freedom) has been defined as spiritual reason in its determinate form, hence as the destiny of the spiritual world, and ... as the ultimate end to the world in general''.[11]

This full self-consciousness of actual freedom which is the goal of one spiritual realm equally signals the emergence of a new spiritual principle and provides the immediate conceptual structures through which this freedom and a new world develops. Philosophic presentation as the being-*there* of both the close and the anticipation is mediated with the past and open to the contingent future, just as the future, too, is mediated with this presentation as the future's significant and signifying past. What we have here is not an imaginary description of the way things "ought" to be, but the description of an actuality which in some sense must determine or mediate that which is to come if the idea of spirit is to have any meaning at all.

How then, precisely, are we to understand this indwelling of the absolute system in the natural consciousness of our *own* day? In what sense is this systematic text, representing the logical reconciliation of subject and object, mediated with the free, contingent happening of spirit in the present? In that section of the *Enzyklopädie* dealing with philosophy, Hegel suggests that philosophy not only cognizes and supersedes the necessity of the content of preceding absolute representations, meaning representation within the domain of art and religion: he also suggests that philosophy supersedes the necessity of their two *forms* as well.[12] Thus we are invited to consider philosophy as that science which properly includes and supersedes both the manner in which the absolute is represented in art and religion as well as the manner in which that absolute previously brought about its own indwelling in self-consciousness.

The central problem with the representational technique of art is that it seeks to embody the absolute in a sensuous externality, or, as Hegel says, in the form of immediacy, so that the absolute only appears as the beautiful. The absolute only appears because it is represented by a natural thing and the implicit spirituality of the absolute is still determined by its natural element or existence, so that the "thingness" of nature qualifies what it contains.[13] Now we have argued earlier that this is a problem, or at least a potential problem, that carries over into the realm of philosophic presentation itself; philosophy no less than art labours on the natural world, in this case on language, in order to behold its universal self in externality. Indeed, it is the natural determination of the object that provides language the necessary independence for it to act as the existing matrix for the labour of thought and intersubjective recognition. The difficulty with this superseded, and yet included, independence of the natural thing in philosophic presentation is that we are left with the notion that the absolute still merely appears within philosophy, that the textual is not identical with the actual.

Hegel takes account of this problem within artistic representation by pointing out that the unity of nature and spirit attained within the domain of art is only an immediate unity, and not a spiritual unity as such. The latter is one in which the natural would be posited simply as ideal and superseded, so that the spiritual content would only be in self-relation. [14] That spirit within the mode of representation enters into pure self-relation means that nature is exhaustively mediated by spirit and that the alienation of the absolute in the natural world is successfully overcome, and this is only possible if we presuppose and state at the beginning, as Hegel does, that spirit is in fact the absolute *prius* of nature, of which it is the truth. [15] Nonetheless it is by no means clear, given the potential spiritual transparency of nature, exactly how the necessary independence of the linguistic object is to be preserved.

Because the absolute only appears in an artistic representation and because the unity of nature and spirit achieved by this representation is only an immediate unity, two important results follow. First, the subject, due to the fact that he appropriates the absolute solely through intuition, has his liberty only under the guise of a manner of life or custom, without the infinite self-reflection and the subjective inwardness of conscience. Second, the immediacy of the absolute-as-ideal within artistic representation entails the notion that the absolute is something made by the artist and that "the artist is the master of God". [16] It follows, of course, that if we suggest that in philosophic presentation, too, the natural element is not successfully put by and superseded then we must be prepared to confront the implications of this fact for the achievement of self-determining freedom and for the purported absolute and universal basis of speculative science.

These difficulties are at least partially remedied within the representational mode of religion, the fundamental concept of which may be summed up as that of "revelation". Revelation implies that absolute spirit is for spirit, or for free intelligence, such that the absolute is no longer appropriated through the sensuous immediate as in art, but stands in a mediate relation to free intelligence through revelation and the subjective movement of belief. While it is true that the absolute is represented in religion by a successive series of pictorial images and events, this finite representation is superseded by the belief in one spirit and in the devotion of worship, and it is precisely this subjective inwardness and the subjective movement of faith that overcomes the immediate intuition of art and is the basis for the infinite freedom of thought. [17]

The absolute of religion reveals itself to men and brings about its own indwelling in self-consciousness through the Son, or the divine man, who represents and is a sign for the universal substance. However, as the object of belief, the divine man is not simply the sheer incursion of an alien universal into the finite world but is this substance as actualized out of its abstraction into an individual self-consciousness and existing within the world of time. Thus the divine man of religion signals the implicit reconciliation of nature and spirit, or rather the spiritual supersession of nature, and, as this objective totality, is a pathway and the presupposition for the finite immediacy of the individual subject. It must be added that what the divine man signifies as yet within the realm of representational imagery (the spiritual supersession of nature), the speculative system equally presents and makes actual according to the precise determination of the concept. In both the religious sign and the philosophic text we are faced with the problem of understanding how their immediate appearing for consciousness is superseded by an appropriation and actualization within spirit.

It would seem that within absolute religion the divine man at first simply appears as an "other" for the individual subject, but then, through the witness of spirit, he has in this divine man the intuition of his own implicit, existing truth. While the witness of this truth leads the individual subject at first to characterize himself as nought and evil because of his immediate nature, later, with this example of his truth and by means of belief in the unity of universal and individual essentiality, this same subject is also the movement to throw off his immediate natural determinateness and self-will. It is through this throwing-off or loss of self that the subject closes with his example and implicit truth in the pain of negativity, and knows himself as reconciled with the essence. Conversely, the essence, through this mediation, brings about its own indwelling in self-consciousness and is the actual presence of universal spirit existing for-itself. [18]

Surely there is no doubt that this process by which the truth of the divine man is appropriated by natural consciousness is a process reminiscent of the appearance and appropriation of speculative science presented by the *Phänomenologie*. While it may be unwise to draw an exact parallel between the self-presentation of the absolute in religion and in philosophy due to the different modes of presentation involved, there are nonetheless certain similarities in the manner through which the absolute brings about its own indwelling in self-consciousness. For instance, as with the appearance of the divine man, speculative science, too, simply arrives on the scene for the individual subject as an *other*, as another possible standpoint among many, and lays a claim on that subject only through offering itself up as the subject's implicit, existing truth. The truth that speculative science offers, a truth which is already implicit within and witnessed by consciousness, is the truth of self-knowedge: natural consciousness is implicitly superseded by spirit. Such a truth at first appears for consciousness as a path of phenomenal knowing and, as with the example of its truth within religion, leads the subject to negate the particularity of its immediate nature, — which is why this path is called the pathway of despair and incurs a "loss of self". Indeed it is only through this loss of self that, again, the subject is able to go over and close with its implicit truth, in order to become the immanent self of the presented system of absolute determinations.

The most important element in the above description of the indwelling absolute of religion is the individual subject's belief in the unity of universal and individual essentiality, since it is belief which mediates the example of this unity with the free, contingent happening of spirit. That religious belief, as with artistic intuition, is eventually superseded by a higher standpoint is implied by Hegel's statement that this mediation contracts itself in the result where spirit closes in unity with itself, not merely to the simplicity of belief and devotional feeling, but even to thought.[19] The continued unfolding within the realm of thought is the truth of philosophy, with the difference that the result of the mediation and belief characteristic of religion is now for-itself existing spirit, in which all mediation, understood here as revelation, has superseded itself. We may restate this by suggesting that while in religion the unity of universal and individual essentiality is made actual through the mediation of belief, that unity is still *given*, still an *other*. On the other hand it is in philosophy, and particularly in philosophic presentation, that the subject recognizes the continued unfolding of absolute determinations as its own and as its own act.[20]

What must be emphasized, however, in this description of the absolute made actual in philosophy, is that actuality in this case cannot be simply identified with a present text, — free thought always contains the double determination of infinite subjectivity as well as an absolute and in and for itself existing content. Indeed it is the infinite interest of thought that continues to mediate this content with contingent existence, making spirit for-itself and free. Hegel says that, "absolute spirit, while always an existing identity, is also identity returning and ever returned into itself; if it is the one and universal substance it is so as spirit, discerning itself into a self and a knowing, for which it is as substance".[21]

Thus those of us coming on the scene in that new spiritual epoch to which Hegel alludes in the *Phänomenologie* must once again mediate the implicit reconciliation of universal and individual essentiality accomplished by the system with our own free, contingent existence. This mediation occurs through the infinite interest of thought in the presented structures of absolute determination, a mediation which both determines and guarantees our freedom. The difficulty with this mediation, with this making the system actual, is that we have previously argued that the interest of thought does not fully or adequately supersede the attitudes of belief and intuition, and this is primarily due to the problem of language. If thought is to exhaustively mediate an absolute content, if spirit is thus to close with itself and become actual, then the language of a philosophic text must be a wholly transparent element for spirit, in which the concept is simply there. However, we have sought to demonstrate that the necessary independence of the linguistic object is due to a persisting residue of natural alienation, with the corollary that the text as natural thing is not wholly transparent but in an important respect opaque. Briefly put, we posit that the determinations of the concept still merely appear within speculative science.

If this alienation characteristic of the natural thing perdures within language then the immediate, sensuous aspect of language and its existence as an absolute "other" *vis-à-vis* the knowing subject is not superseded by the interest of thought, nor are the concomitant attitudes of intuition or belief. Of course the consequences for subjective liberty given this breakdown in absolute self-knowedge would be enormous: within Hegel's scheme, any lack in the understanding of the absolute determinations of subjectivity would be met by a corresponding lack of freedom. We may tentatively suggest for the moment that the self-determining subject embodying spirit for-itself would be thrown back into a time-bordered existence in which that subject no longer knew objectivity as its own, but simply suffered alternations within its spatial field.

Oddly enough, in his *Philosophie der Weltgeschichte* Hegel points to an historical event which gives us an idea what might be the consequences of substituting the sensuous appearance of the absolute for its spiritual actuality, and this is the controversy which surrounded the interpretation of the eucharist. Just as the divine man was the example of the unity of universal and individual essentiality, so the eucharist is this divine man set forth as actually present to consciousness, subject to human contemplation and ever and anon offered up. While in the Catholic mass the presentation by the eucharist of the divine man and its appropriation is rightly regarded as an actual and eternal transaction, an error is made through isolating the sensuous phase. In this mass the eucharist is adored even apart from its being partaken of by the faithful, and so the presence of the divine man is not exclusively spiritual but somehow locked-up within this natural thinghood, just as the absolute is locked-up within the sensuous, opaque element of language. [22]

Since the process of appropriating the absolute as eucharist or as a philosophic text is not one that takes place in spirit, but is conditioned by its thinghood, then the absolute takes on the character of externality and can be the exclusive possession of a class, which has as its role to determine the true. This means that, in both cases, the absolute is no longer present at hand in an exoteric manner, nor is the absolute within these modes for natural consciousness as such, or for a public; rather, the absolute as merely appearing in externality becomes subject to the esoteric interpretations of a determinate group of priests or intellectuals. [23] It follows that the public is cut off from the on-going mediation of spirit with its truth and from self-knowedge and is left simply with the duty to believe, – a situation which lends itself to the worship of relics and texts. [24] This dependence of the public on the esoteric interpretations, provided by a privileged group of spiritual custodians, of a self-concealing absolute leads to a reduction, indeed a reversal, of spiritual freedom, if we understand that freedom as absolute self-determination.

Referring to the predominantly sensuous character of the eucharist within the Catholic mass, Hegel states that, "With this perversion is connected the absolute separation of the spiritual from the secular principle generally. There are two divine kingdoms – the intellectual in the heart and cognitive faculty, and the socially ethical whose element and sphere is secular existence. It is speculative science alone that can comprehend the kingdom of God and the socially moral world as one idea, and that recognizes the fact that the course of time has witnessed a process ever tending to the realization of this unity". [25] Because the Catholic understanding of the eucharist renders its sensuous phase predominant, spiritual life becomes the possession of a special group and natural consciousness as such, since it is not directly mediated with the absolute, is left to lead its own secular life. If we extrapolate from this example and suggest that there is a sensuous determination attaching no less to speculative presentation itself, then we must posit within this science, too, the development of a specialized interpretive elite and a breakdown in the mediation between a system of absolute determinations and the free, contingent happening of spirit.

What is lost is the realizaton within actuality of philosophy's articulate idea, and what is thwarted is the water-shed transition from an existence which is time-bound and determined by a world it merely suffers, to an existence which is self-knowing and self-determining as spirit for-itself. While Hegel would certainly balk at the suggestion that he was ever trying to change the world, there is no doubt that the world on the other side of that watershed described as the "public appropriation of speculative science" would be a very different world indeed, since it would be a world released to the truth of its concept and a world in which, for the first time, absolute freedom was actual. Since absolute freedom presupposes the close of philosophy or, more precisely, presupposes the close of spirit with itself that occurs through philosophy, then any deficiency attributed to the presentation characteristic of philosophy would obstruct that close and limit the resultant self-knowedge and self-determination.[26]

The deficiency in presentation characteristic of the eucharist led medieval Christians to identify the absolute with a thing and in a very real sense prepared those successive crusades intended to recapture and possess such divine objects as the Holy Sepulchre. In a similar manner the deficiency in the language theory of speculative philosophy has led successive theorists to identify the absolute system with Hegel's timely rendering of it, as if the genius of his particular presentation has trapped within it once and for all the essential structure of the actual. Yet Hegel himself has emphasized again and again that the letter is dead without the infinite interest of thought, and it follows that, without the on-going critical interest of thought in his presented reconciliation of universal and individual essentiality, we shall find in the system a sepulchre no less empty than that which the Crusaders found in the holy land. Speaking to this medieval dilemma, Hegel says, "You must not look for the principle of your religion in the sensuous, in the grave among the dead, but in the living spirit in yourselves. We have seen how the vast idea of the union of the finite with the infinte was perverted to such a degree as that men looked for a definite embodiment of the infinite in a mere isolated outward object".[27] This insight should not be lost on speculative philosophy itself: the scholarly dissection and possession of Hegel's works must not find its completion in that textual fetishism which seeks to adore the word rather than comprehend it. Instead, this scholarship must be superseded by the critical interest of thought which takes a negative attitude toward its basis, since it is only through the infinite negation of thought that Hegel's philosophy will be mediated with the concerns of the present and made alive.

It is almost to our own chagrin that we have posited that speculative science's very language theory lends itself to the cul-de-sac of textual fetishism, where a truth is merely intuited within a sensuously immediate. It is for this reason that we must emphasize the fundamental, and salutary, importance given to the primordial, critical interest of thought within speculative science, as the key to an amelioration of the deficiencies within its own language theory. This on-going, critical interest of thought in the *presented* system will have a twofold result: first, the realization that problems in the articulation of form, special to speculative presentation, are rooted in a deficiency within its language theory; and second, the thoughtful mediation of the speculative sentence with current developments in language philosophy. Vague as these intimations for the future of speculative science may be, what they suggest is a renewed concern for the presented reconciliation of universal and individual essentiality. This is not merely archeological curiosity in a dead artifact from an historical past, since truth within speculative science is never a finished and completed thing, but that labour of the concept whereby the subject itself becomes embued with truth, surrendering its particular being in exchange for the substantial truth, making that truth its own through the mediation of thought. It is thus that spiritual freedom is won, and made actual.

NOTES

1 *Ph.G.* Vorr., p. 15 (6).

2 *Ph.G.* Vorr., p. 16 (7). Those actual configurations which become moments in the simple systematic whole of science now take shape afresh and develop in their new element.

3 *Ph.G.* VIII, p. 563 (492).

4 *Ph.G.* Vorr., p. 16 (7).

5 *Wiss. der Logik* I, Vorr., p. 4f. (26).

6 *Enz.* # 573, p. 451 (302).

7 *Phil. des Rechts*, Vorr., p. 17 (10). Just prior to the much quoted Owl of Minerva passage, Hegel again cuts off the suggestion of any opening toward the future which a misguided philosophy may seek to arrogate to itself, this time without metaphor: "One word more about giving instruction as to what the world ought to be. Philosophy in any case always comes on the scene too late to give it. As the thought of the world, it appears only when actuality is already there cut and dried after its process of formation has been completed". *Ibid.*, p. 20f. (12f.).

8 *Ph.G.* Vorr., p. 16 (7).

9 *Enz.* # 577, p. 463 (315).

10 *Phil. des Rechts*, Vorr., p. 8 (5f.).

11 *Vernunft in der Geschichte*, p. 63 (55).

12 *Enz.* # 573, p. 451 (302).

13 *Enz.* # 557, p. 441f. (293).

14 *Enz.* # 557, p. 441f. (293).

15 *Enz.* # 381, p. 313 (I 25). "In this its truth nature is vanished, and spirit has resulted as the Idea entered on possession of itself".

16 *Enz.* # 560, p. 443 (294f.).

17 *Enz.* # 565, p. 447 (299).

18 *Enz.* # 570, p. 449 (300f.).

19 *Enz.* # 571, p. 449 (301).

20 Apparently it is the universality of thought aware of itself that guarantees the absolute basis of philosophic production and supersedes that one-sided subjective determination which is a major deficiency in artistic technique.

21 *Enz.* # 554, p. 440 (292).

22 *Phil. der Weltgeschichte* IV, p. 822f. (377).

23 In the *Phänomenologie* Hegel already points to the consequences of a less than exoteric presentation. He says that, "Without such articulation [the articulation of form], science lacks universal intelligibility, and gives the appearance of being the esoteric possession [sic] of a few individuals: an esoteric possession, since it is as yet present only in its concept or in its inwardness; of a few individuals, since its undiffused manifestation makes its existence something singular. Only what is completely determined is at once exoteric, comprehensible, and capable of being learned and appropriated by all". *Ph.G.* Vorr., p. 16f. (7). What we are suggesting

here is that the lack of "complete determination" is not due merely to a lack in the articulation of form, understood as a conceptual problem. Rather this lack in the articulation of form is rooted in the residual opacity of language itself.

24 *Phil. der Weltgeschichte* IV, p. 824f. (378).

25 *Phil. der Weltgeschichte* IV, p. 827 (379f.).

26 In this light, Adorno's statement at the beginning of his *Negative Dialectics* seems strikingly apropos: "Philosophy, which once seemed obsolete, lives on because the moment to realize it was missed. The summary judgment that it had merely interpreted the world, that resignation in the face of reality had crippled it in itself, becomes a defeatism of reason after the attempt to change the world miscarried". *Op. cit.*, p. 3.

27 *Phil. der Weltgeschichte* IV, p. 849 (393).

GLOSSARY

allgemein	-	universal
aufheben, Aufhebung	-	to supersede, supersession
Begriff	-	concept
besonder	-	particular
Bestimmung	-	determination
Bildung	-	education, culture
Darstellung	-	presentation
Dingheit	-	thinghood
Dasein	-	existence, being-there
einzeln	-	individual
Entäußerung	-	externalization
Entfremdung	-	alienation
Erinnerung	-	recollection
Erscheinung	-	appearance
Geist	-	spirit
Gestaltung	-	configuration
Gewißheit	-	certainty
Idee	-	idea
Recht	-	law, right
selbständig	-	independent
Sittlichkeit	-	ethical life
unmittelbar	-	immediate
Vernunft	-	reason
Verstand	-	understanding
Vorstellung	-	representation
wirklich, Wirklichkeit	-	actual, actuality
Wissenschaft	-	science

BIBLIOGRAPHY

1. HEGEL'S TEXTS

Sämtliche Werke, Jubilee Edition, ed. Hermann Glockner. Frommann, Stuttgart, 1927–30.
Differenz des Fichte'schen und Schelling'schen Systems der Philosophie, ed. G. Lasson. Meiner Verlag, Hamburg, 1962.
The Difference between Fichte's and Schelling's System of Philosophy, trans. H.S. Harris and W. Cerf. State University of New York Press, Albany, 1977.
Phänomenologie des Geistes, ed. J. Hoffmeister. Meiner Verlag, Hamburg, 1952.
Phenomenology of Spirit, trans. A.V. Miller. Clarendon Press, Oxford, 1977.
Wissenschaft der Logik, 2 Bde., ed. G. Lasson. Meiner Verlag, Hamburg, 1932.
Hegel's of Science Logic, trans A.V. Miller. George Allen & Unwin, London, 1969.
Science de la logique: La doctrine de l'essence, trans., introd. and notes P.-J. Labarrière and G. Jarczyk. Aubier, ed. Montaigne, Paris, 1976.
Enzyklopädie der philosophischen Wissenschaften im Grundrisse (1830), ed. F. Nicolin and O. Pöggeler. Meiner Verlag, Hamburg, 1969.
Hegel's Logic, trans. W. Wallace. Clarendon Press, Oxford, 1975.
Hegel's Philosophy of Mind, trans. W. Wallace; Zusätze, trans. A.V. Miller. Clarendon Press, Oxford, 1971.
Hegel's Philosophy of Subjective Spirit, 3 vols., ed. and trans. M.J. Petry. D. Reidel Publishers, Boston, 1979.
Grundlinien der Philosophie des Rechts, ed. J. Hoffmeister. Meiner Verlag, Hamburg, 1955.
Hegel's Philosophy of Right, trans. T. Knox. Oxford University Press, London, 1967.
Die Vernunft in der Geschichte, ed. J. Hoffmeister. Meiner Verlag, Hamburg, 1955.
Lectures on the Philosophy of World History. Introduction: Reason in History, trans. H. Nisbet. Cambridge University Press, London, 1975.
Vorlesungen über die Philosophie der Weltgeschichte, Bd. II–IV, ed. G. Lasson. Meiner Verlag, Hamburg, 1923.
The Philosophy of History, trans. J. Sibree. Dover, New York, 1956.

2. BOOKS ABOUT HEGEL

Adorno, T.W., *Negative Dialectics*, trans. E. Ashton. Seabury Press, New York, 1973.
Althusser, Louis, *Lénine et la philosophie suivi de Marx et Lénine devant Hegel*. Maspero, Paris, 1975.
Bloch, Ernst, *A Philosophy of the Future*, trans. J. Cumming. Herder & Herder, New York, 1970.
Bloch, Ernst, *Subjekt-Objekt*. Suhrkamp, Frankfurt a. M., 1962.

Cook, D.J., *Language in the Philosophy of Hegel*. Mouton, The Hague, 1973.

Fackenheim, E.L., *The Religious Dimension in Hegel's Thought*. Beacon Press, Boston, 1967.

Findlay, J.N., *Hegel: A Re-examination*. George Allen & Unwin, London, 1958.

Fulda, H.F., *Das Problem einer Einleitung in Hegels Wissenschaft der Logik*. V. Klostermann, Frankfurt a. M., 1965.

Gadamer, H.G., *Hegel's Dialectic*, trans. P.C. Smith. Yale University Press, New Haven, Conn., 1976.

Gadamer, H.G., *Philosophical Hermeneutics*, trans. D. Linge. University of California Press, Los Angeles, 1976.

Greene, Murray, *Hegel on the Soul*. M. Nijhoff, The Hague, 1972.

Haering, Th., *Hegel: Sein Wollen und sein Werk*, 2 vols. Leipzig-Berlin, 1929/1938.

Harris, H.S., *Hegel's Development: Toward the Sunlight*. Oxford University Press, Oxford, 1972.

Heidegger, Martin, *Hegel's Concept of Experience*, trans. J. Gray. Harper & Row, New York, 1970.

Heidegger, Martin, *Identity and Difference*, trans. J. Stambaugh. Harper & Row, New York, 1969.

Heidegger, Martin, *The End of Philosophy*, trans. J. Stambaugh. Harper & Row, New York, 1973.

Hyppolite, Jean, *Genèse et structure de la Phénoménologie de l'Esprit de Hegel*. Aubier, Ed. Montaigne, Paris, 1946.

Hyppolite, Jean, *Logique et existence* P.U.F., Paris, 1953.

Kaufmann, Walter, *Hegel: Reinterpretation, Texts, and Comentary*, 2 vols. Anchor Books, New York, 1965.

Kelly, George A., *Idealism, Politics and History*. Cambridge University Press, London, 1969.

Kojève, A., *Essai d'une histoire raisonnée de la philosophie paienne*, Tome I. Gallimard, Paris, 1968.

Kojève, A., *Introduction à la lecture de Hegel*. Ed. Gallimard, Paris, 1947.

Kroner, Richard, *Von Kant bis Hegel*, 2 Bde. J.C.B. Mohr. Tübingen, 1921/1924. (Nachdruck Tübingen, 1961).

Labarrière, P.-J., *Structure et mouvement dialectique dans la phénoménologie de l'Esprit de Hegel*. Aubier, Ed. Montaigne, Paris, 1968.

Labarrière, P.-J., *Introduction à une lecture de la Phénoménologie de l'esprit*. Aubier, Ed. Montaigne, Paris, 1979.

Litt, Theodor, *Hegel: Essai d'un renouvellement critique*, trad. P. Muller. Ed. Denoël, Paris, 1973.

Löwith, Karl, *From Hegel to Nietzsche*, trans. D. Green. Holt, Rinehart & Winston, New York, 1964.

Lukacs, Georg, *Hegel's False and His Genuine Ontology*, trans. D. Fernbach. Merlin Press, London, 1978.

Lukacs, Georg, *The Young Hegel*, trans. R. Livingstone. MIT Press, Cambridge, 1975.

Marcuse, H., *L'ontologie de Hegel et la theéorie de l'historicité*, trans. Raulet and Baatsch. Ed. de Minuit, Paris, 1972.

Marcuse, H., *Reason and Revolution*. Beacon Press, Boston 1960.

Marcuse, H., *Studies in Critical Philosophy*, trans. J. de Bres. Beacon Press, Boston, 1972.

Marx, Werner, *Hegel's Phenomenology of Spirit*, trans. P. Heath. Harper & Row, New York, 1975.

Marx, Werner, *Reason and World*. M. Nijhoff, The Hague, 1971.

Merleau-Ponty, M., *Sens et Non-sens*. Ed. Nagel, Paris, 1966.

Mure, G.R.G., *A Study of Hegel's Logic*. Clarendon Press, Oxford, 1950,

Mure, G.R.G., *The Philosophy of Hegel*. Oxford University, Press, London, 1965.

Puntel, L.B., *Darstellung, Methode und Struktur*. Hegel-Studien, Beiheft 10. Bonn, 1973.

Quelquejeu, B., *La volonté dans la philosophie de Hegel*. Ed. du Seuil. Paris, 1972.
Ritter, Joachim, *Hegel et la révolution française suivi de Personne et propriété selon Hegel*. Beauchesne, Paris, 1970.
Robinson, Jonathan, *Duty and Hypocrisy in Hegel's Phenomenology of Mind: An Essay in the Real and Ideal*. University of Toronto Press, Toronto, 1977.
Rosen, S., *G.W.F. Hegel: An Introduction to the Science of Wisdom*. Yale University Press, New Haven, Conn., 1974.
Rotenstreich, N., *From Substance to Subject*. M. Nijhoff, The Hague, 1974.
Rousset, Bernard, *G.W.F. Hegel: Le savoir absolu*. Aubier, Ed. Montaigne, Paris, 1977.
Royce, Josiah, *Lectures on Modern Idealism*. Yale University Press, London, 1919.
Stace, W.T., *The Philosophy of Hegel*. Macmillan, London, 1924.
Taminiaux, Jacques, *La nostalgie de la Grèce à l'aube de l'idéalisme allemand*. M. Nijhoff, La Haye, 1967.
Taylor, Charles, *Hegel*. Cambridge University Press, New York, 1975.
Wahl, Jean, *La logique de Hegel comme phénoménologie*. Les cours de Sorbonne, Paris, 1959.

3. ARTICLES ABOUT HEGEL

Bourgeois, B., "Présentation", in *Encyclopédie des sciences philosophiques I: La Science de la logique*, pp. 7–112 (G.W.F. Hegel, trans. B. Bourgeois). J. Vrin, Paris, 1970.
Bubner, Rüdiger, "La philosophie et ses apparences (Système et phénoménologie)", in *Hegel*, pp. 65–81 (Actes du IIIe Congrès International pour l'étude de la philosophie de Hegel). Faculté des Lettres et Sciences humaines de Lille, Lille, 1970.
Derrida, Jacques, "Le Puits et la Pyramide", in J. Derrida, *Marges de la philosophie*, pp. 79–127. Editions de Minuit, Paris, 1972.
D'Hondt, Jacques, "Genèse et structure de l'unité de l'Esprit objectif", in *Hegel*, pp. 99–112.(Actes du IIIe Congrès International pour l'étude de la philosophie de Hegel). Faculté des Lettres et Sciences humaines de Lille, Lille, 1970.
Dupré, Louis, "Hegel's Concept of Alienation and Marx's Reinterpretation of it", in *Hegel-Studien*, Band 7, pp. 217–236. Bonn, 1972.
Gauvin, Josef, "Le sens et son phénomène", in *Hegel-Studien*, Band 3, pp. 263–275. Bonn, 1965.
Geraets, T.F., "Les trois lectures philosophiques de l'Encyclopédie ou la réalisation du concept de la philosophie chez Hegel", in *Hegel-Studien*, Band 10, pp. 231–254. Bonn, 1975.
Habermas, Jürgen, "Labour and Interaction: Remarks on Hegel's Jena 'Philosophy of Mind'", in J. Habermas (trans. J. Viertel), *Theory and Practice*, pp. 142–170. Beacon Press, Boston, 1973.
Ilting, K.H., "The Structure of Hegel's Philosophy of Right", in Z. Pelczynski (Ed.), *Hegel's Political Philosophy*, pp. 90–110. Cambridge University Press, London, 1971.
Kisiel, T., "Hegel and Hermeneutics", in F. Weiss (Ed.), *Beyond Epistemology*, pp. 197–220. M. Nijhoff, The Hague, 1974.
Koyré, A., "Hegel à Iéna", in *Etudes d'histoire de la pensée philosophique*, pp. 135–173. Armand Colin, Paris, 1961.
Labarrière, P.J., "La phénoménologie de l'Esprit comme discours systématique: Histoire, Religion et Science", in *Hegel-Studien*, Band 9, pp. 131–153. Bonn, 1974.
Mueller, G.E., "The Interdependence of the *Phenomenology, Logic,* and *Encyclopedia*", in W. Steinkraus (Ed.), *New Studies in Hegel's Philosophy*, pp. 18–33. Holt Rinehart & Winston, New York, 1971.
Mure, G.R.G., "Hegel: How, and How Far, is Philosophy Possible?", in F. Weiss (Ed.), *Beyond Epistemology*, pp. 1–29. M. Nijhoff, The Hague, 1974.

Pöggeler, O., "Qu'est-ce que la phénoménologie de l'Esprit"?, *Archives de Philosophie*, avril-juin (1966), pp. 189–236.

Sallis, John, "Hegel's Concept of Presentation", in *Hegel-Studien*, Band 12, pp. 129–156. Bonn, 1977.

Surber, J.B., "Hegel's Speculative Sentence", in *Hegel-Studien*, Band 10, pp. 211–230. Bonn, 1975.

4. OTHER BOOKS

Heidegger, Martin, *Being and Time*, trans. J. Macquarrie and E. Robinson. Harper & Row, New York, 1962.

Marx, Karl, *Writings of the Young Marx on Philosophy and Society*, ed. L. Easton and K. Guddat. Anchor Books, New York, 1967.

Nietzsche, Friedrich, *The Gay Science*, trans. W. Kaufmann. Vintage Books, New York, 1974.

Schelling, F.W.J., *On University Studies*, trans. E. Morgan. Ohio University Press, Athens, 1966.

Schiller, Friedrich, *On the Aesthetic Education of Man*, trans. R. Snell. Ungar, New York, 1965.

Wittgenstein, Ludwig, *Philosophical Investigations*, trans. G.E.M. Anscombe. Basil Blackwell, Oxford, 1972.

INDEX